LIFE BEGINS AT SEVENTY

LIFE BEGINS AT SEVENTY

The Story of Blue Pearl

Frederick Harsant

Book Guild Publishing
Sussex, England

First published in Great Britain in 2008 by
The Book Guild Ltd
Pavilion View
19 New Road
Brighton
BN1 1UF

Typesetting in Times by
Keyboard Services, Luton, Bedfordshire

Printed and bound in Great Britain by
CPI Antony Rowe

A catalogue record for this book is available from
The British Library

ISBN 978 1 84624 233 5

To my wife, Joan who encouraged me so much to write this story, who meticulously read and checked the several versions of the work as it developed and who contributed so much with her diaries.

Contents

Acknowledgements

I am grateful to Oyster Marine Ltd for allowing me to use a copy of the Oyster Mariner plan in Appendix III, taken from an early brochure. Oyster Marine gave me much help in the early stages of completing *Blue Pearl*.

Thanks to Imray Laurie Norris and Wilson, the publishers, and Rod Heikell, the author, for permission to use maps and a quotation from *Greek Waters Pilot*. I used ten of their excellent Pilots on our cruise.

And to my daughter, Jill, for allowing me to quote from her letters and faxes.

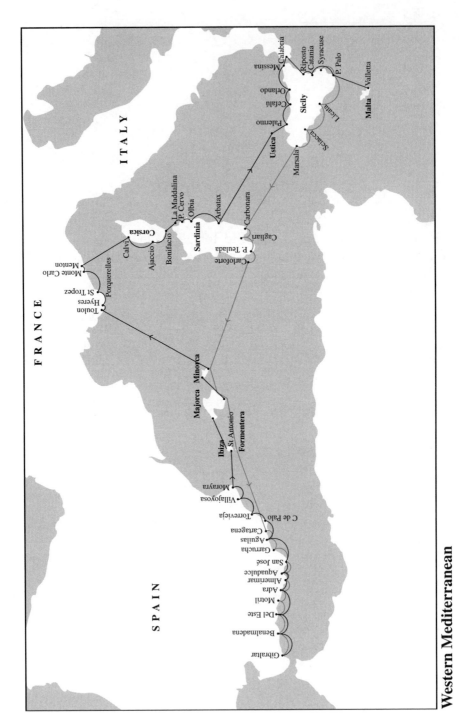

Western Mediterranean

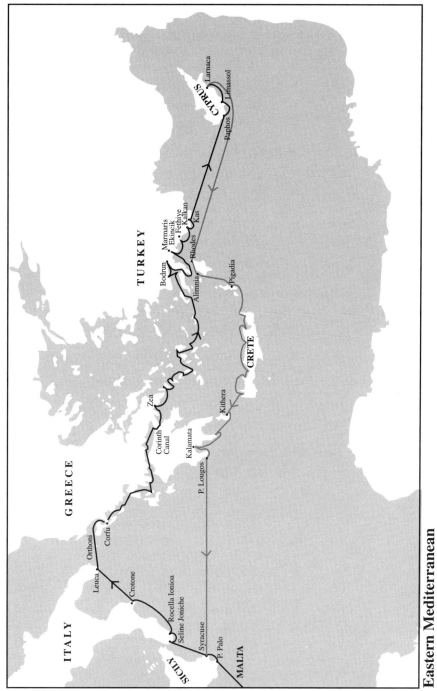

Eastern Mediterranean

1

Leigh on Sea

The story begins in October 1980 when *Blue Pearl* was collected from Oyster's and delivered to Benfleet Yacht Club, a huge, empty shell of a boat, thirty-five feet long and twelve feet in the beam, with just three core bulkheads to maintain the shape. My wife, Joan, and I were living in Leigh-on-Sea, only two miles away, and it was easy for us to get to the boat at weekends. Benfleet was the club where Sir Robin Knox-Johnson fitted out *Souhaili* and where *Aziz*, sailed by Nicolette Coward, the first woman to sail alone across the Atlantic, was laid up almost next to us. I felt that we were in good company.

With no windows and no hatches (the hatches were stowed inside), the boat was open to the weather and my first task was to make it watertight. I still had more than a year to go before my retirement as Principal of Palmer's Sixth Form College and the time I could give to the boat was limited to weekends. Joan and I soon fell into a rhythm of down to the boat early on Saturday morning, a long day working, home at dusk to the household chores and a cooked meal and repeating the routine on Sunday.

The hull and deck had been joined by a series of nuts and bolts that protruded upwards through the deck along the edges of the boat. These would tear a canvas cover, so first I constructed the toe-rail by laminating together strips of teak to match the curve of the boat, into which I could bury the bolt ends. Now, at last, we could put a canvas cover over the boat and pump out the gallons of water inside.

Wet and windy weather followed at most weekends and I left *Blue Pearl* under wraps whilst I dealt with the end of term College work and set up a boat room at home and a workshop where I

1

could work in comfort. Poor weather continued throughout the spring term of 1981 and most of my Easter holiday was taken up with College commitments.

Joan and I had to prepare our last boat, *Pendragon*, for sale, so the remainder of the holiday and the weekends in May 1981 were occupied with cleaning and servicing *Pendragon*. I used this time to acquire a complete set of drawings for *Blue Pearl*, to measure for and estimate the wood I required and to order fifty sheets of teak-faced plywood and hundreds of feet of teak timber in various sizes. I also purchased several thousand stainless steel screws, nuts and bolts, and self-tappers. Later, as I became more heavily involved, I took on a once-a-week evening course at a technical college to qualify in the use of industrial machinery. I was then able to select rough teak in lengths of twelve feet by eleven inches wide and two and a half inches thick and cut it, plane it, thickness it and, where necessary, rebate it in my own time in the College workshop. Throughout this time I received help from my Head of Technology, John Sach.

By June *Pendragon* was ready and up for sale. Now we were able to work at weekends on *Blue Pearl*. These were good days, with long sunny spells and Joan and I sharing the work. First we cut up mahogany planks into two-inch strips for the cabin floors which we then bonded to the hull with glass fibre and covered with temporary, cheap plywood soles, so that at last we were able to walk on a flat surface instead of crawling round the curved sides of the boat.

By July we were cutting out the quarter-inch teak-faced plywood to line each side of the bulkheads, three sheets to a side. These were pressed into position by long, slightly bent stretchers, buttressed against the opposite bulkhead. The bulkheads were now one and a quarter inches thick and it was time to cut out the doors, each about five feet high with semi-circular tops and bottoms. I had equipped myself with heavy-duty portable electric tools, including two drills, a jigsaw, circular saw, planer, grinderette and router, and these now came into full use and saved me many hours of back-breaking manual work. At last we were able to get to all parts of the boat without climbing up and down through the hatches. Eighteen of my sheets of plywood had been used and I was acquiring a growing pile of remnants.

Now that the serious work on the boat was under way, two

2

important needs had to be met. When you start work on an empty hull there are virtually no angles, uprights or horizontals to work to. Everything must be done by means of a spirit level, so the boat must be perfectly level fore and aft and athwartships. To achieve this I used the lubber line that had been marked all round the hull by the boat builders. I stretched a clear plastic tube under the boat with both ends upright, filled this with water and tilted the boat until the water level on both sides exactly matched the lubber line. I used a similar technique along the length of the boat.

The second necessary feature was access to the boat. I would be working on it for many months, possibly even years. I had already experienced difficulties climbing up a ladder with an armful of equipment. Now I constructed a strong stairway up the side of the boat with a platform at the top from which I could step into the cockpit. This was to prove invaluable and saved much time and effort over the years.

Two entries from Joan's diary show how our lives were spent:

28th July. After housework and two loads of washing we both went to the boat at 10 a.m. I cut out shaped pieces of glass fibre while F cut lengths of mahogany for the floors in a compartment originally intended as a sail locker and now to be developed as a workshop for long-distance cruising. We started glassing at 12.00, I mixing pots of resin, F inside the boat glassing in the floors. Stopped for lunch at 1.00 and finished at 7.00. Home at 8.15, where I cooked a meal and we watched a Hyde Park fireworks display on T.V. Bed at 11 p.m.
29th July. Our thirty-seventh wedding anniversary. We stayed and watched the royal wedding – marvellous pageantry – great, excited crowds. Sunshine all day. After lunch we went to the boat and finished glassing in the floors. Home by 5.30. I prepared a lovely dinner, grapefruit, fresh salmon, new potatoes and cauliflower, followed by pineapple and ice-cream and washed down with a German hock.

The diary frequently reveals that no matter how hard we worked on the boat our meals were never neglected, the household chores were always completed and somehow we achieved sufficient sleep. It was a hard life but a very happy one! August was a good month, hot and dry, and we installed many of the outside fittings, including

3

windows, stemhead roller, chainplates, pulpit, pushpit and stanchion bases. At the end of the month *Pendragon* was sold and no longer required our attention. Work on fitting continued at weekends throughout September and October, often in spite of wet, cold and blustery weather. Each fitting had its own problems. The chainplates were bolted through the deck to stainless steel knees, which had to be glassed into position. All the deck fittings were reinforced by wooden plates glassed in underneath the deck, and all of them took time. Sometimes we were forced to delay our work because the weather was too cold or wet for glassing. Nevertheless, by the end of term we had completed the deck fittings and fitted some drains and stopcocks and the three hatches, which could now be locked to provide enough security for me to leave tools and timber in the boat overnight. We were glad to put the boat to bed under its wraps, remove all valuable tools and depart to our daughter's house in Cornwall for a welcome Christmas break.

My intention was to retire within a year or two and move to a town on the south coast where there was a good harbour for a deep-keeled yacht. We decided to use the cold winter months to start redecorating our house in Leigh ready for selling. However, by mid-February the snow had cleared, we had finished redecorating the kitchen and were back at work on the boat, glassing in new bulkheads in the main and stern cabins, and facing them with teak ply.

The diary for Sunday 28th February 1982 reveals:

To boat at 8.45. Cut out door to anchor locker and fitted it. Measured stretchers. Started gluing at 1.45. Set up and glued two forward facings. Very tricky work in such a small space. Home at 5.0 p.m.

And the following Sunday:

Very pleasant day. Both to boat at 8.0 a.m. Fitted three bulkheads with teak facings and cut stretchers. Glued the first before and the other two after lunch. Finished at 6.20. Both very tired, but pleased with the day's work!
Saturday 12th March. To boat 9.0 a.m., F with violent headache. Cut out door and fitted it. Did dummy run and finally glued facing

4

on galley side of stern cabin. Packed up at 5.0 p.m. F straight to bed and stayed there for the evening.

Minor ailments could not be allowed to interfere with the day's work!

By the end of the Easter holiday we had put in place all the remaining bulkheads and faced them with teak ply. We also completed the floors to the stern cabin.

During May, when the weather was dry, we worked on the glass-fibre shelf in the anchor locker and when it rained, on fitting the glass-fibre heads, or bathroom (left loose in the main cabin by the boat builder), and lining the outside of it with teak ply.

In June we were woodworking again, when wet at home on the doors and when dry in the boat on the architraves. With the help of John Sach I had steam-bent one-eighth inch thick strips of teak and laminated them to form half-inch thick corners for the doors and architraves. Now I was able to finish the trim along the edges, dovetailing the corners into the half-inch thick side and top pieces. The effect was fascinating, giving the appearance of the grain in the wood flowing round the corners of the doors and architraves.

A note in the diary for Saturday 17th July records that David Ayers had an open day on his Holman and Pye thirty-two-foot sloop that he had built from a bare hull. It was being launched the following Saturday. He and Phillip Lovejoy, completing a Colvic thirty-four, Chris Elliot with his Snowgoose catamaran, ourselves with the Oyster, and a young couple with a huge one-off fifty-footer, which they had built themselves, formed the nucleus of our boat builders' group. We encouraged each other, sought each other's advice and occasionally helped out or lent tools. In the middle of our group of boats was an electricity post with several points and nearby were toilets with a water tap and a hot and cold water system, which we found useful for cleaning up. Although we did not overdo the social life, we all found it supportive, especially when things went wrong.

At the end of July Joan and I decided to have a holiday and, picking up our granddaughter Julia, we set off for Falmouth where we chartered a Westerley Centaur, which we sailed to the Scilly Islands. The cruise brought back our love of the sea and strengthened our determination to finish *Blue Pearl*.

On the way home we stopped off in Dartmouth to look at properties for sale. We had short-listed five seaside towns for possible retirement, the main requirement being a deep-water harbour and mooring. Dartmouth was our first choice. We had first visited the town several years earlier when cruising *Pendragon* up the Channel on the French side and back on the English side. Now we inspected several properties and decided to make an offer for a flat on the riverbank, which, after some haggling, was accepted. We would use it as a holiday home until I retired.

Back in Leigh we were soon working hard on the boat. We completed the installation of the heads, and then began work on the engine room. Joan's brother-in-law, Jack Cox, a knowledgeable engineer, visited us during the holidays and helped me to install the exhaust system.

When term started I had the usual full timetable of events, often lasting late into the evening, but I reserved the weekends for the boat. Joan and I completed the oily locker, the engine room and the life-raft locker.

Early in September we had bad news from Dartmouth. On the day that our contracts were to be exchanged our solicitor telephoned me to say that we had been gazumped. We decided to go to Dartmouth at half-term and look for another property. The agents took us to see many houses and flats, but none came up to our expectations. We passed one grand-looking building on the corner of Mount Boone and I remarked that I would like to live there. It was the Dartmouth Vicarage, a fourteen-roomed house, standing in half an acre and surrounded by a twelve foot high seventeenth-century wall, with marvellous south views over the estuary and out to sea and north to the Naval College and along the Dart.

On our way home we stopped at Brixham and were shown about twenty properties, none of which appealed. At three o'clock, tired and disheartened, we were sitting in a café eating a late lunch when the proprietress noticed our agent's brochures. She suggested that we should look at *The Western Morning News* and lent us a copy. There Joan noticed an advertisement of the sale by auction of the Dartmouth Vicarage. Without telling me, she telephoned the agents and found that the price expected was within our range. She went down to the auction in February, bid for the house and it was ours – fourteen rooms and half an acre, when we were only looking for a flat or bungalow with a small garden!

Work on the boat continued at weekends throughout the autumn term, whatever the weather:

Monday 28th November. To boat at 8.30. Temperature below forty degrees. Heated the stern cabin, then glassed four large pieces before lunch. After lunch glassed the other four, so achieving what we had set out to do. Home at 5.00.

And at home:

Sunday 12th December. F's birthday. He had socks from his sister-in-law, two pairs of brown socks from his sister, a long blue pair, and socks from me, two pairs of brown mixture. He worked on the new kitchen worktop all day – looks very nice. Quiet evening.

1982 finished with a long day at the boat, followed by a New Year's Eve party at a friend's house.

In 1983 I continued at weekends working on trim to door and cupboard openings. At the same time John Duce, a local marine engineer, began work on the engine. I am not an engineer and I had asked Oysters to install the Perkins 4108 before delivery. Now that the engine room was completed and the exhaust system installed, John was able to complete the engine electrics and the fuel system.

In February 1983 disaster struck. I slipped a disc near my collar bone which trapped a nerve so that I was unable to use my right arm. I was in severe pain and the prescribed painkiller had little effect. This was the time when Joan went to Dartmouth and bought the Vicarage. I was also suffering from a slipped disc at the base of my spine and was unable to travel. I was unable to attend College and had my secretary come to me daily to deal with College matters and to pass on my instructions to the staff.

By the beginning of March I had shown no improvement. I was still in pain and could not use my arm. On the fourth I began daily attendance at the physiotherapy department of Southend Hospital and had massage, heat treatment and a cervical collar that I was to wear for six months. A week later I was put on traction. Severe pain continued throughout the week and was not helped by the need to attend College for governors' meetings, staff appointments and the Old Palmerians' dinner.

I had my last traction on 28th March and started back at College, driven by a member of staff, still wearing the collar but with the pain diminishing. I attended the end-of-term leaving dinner given to my Vice-Principal, and the next day, 31st March, Joan recorded:

Suddenly F did not need any drugs. Time went on – twelve – twenty – twenty four hours since he had taken them. Still needed the collar though.

I was now relying on hot baths at home and, of course, the collar. I started the summer term still driven by staff, still wearing the collar and having to resume physiotherapy three times a week with hot baths and heat treatment at home. I was now working on the plans for the new kitchen at the Vicarage in Dartmouth and dealing with the conversion of the property into two dwellings, a maisonette for us and a downstairs flat, which we would sell.

On Tuesday 3rd May I resumed driving and on 13th May I was discharged from hospital and told to return to physical work gradually. Joan left to spend three weeks in Cornwall, looking after our granddaughter while her parents were on holiday in Greece, and I was left to cope on my own. This was good for me and gave me a chance to rehabilitate myself. I drove myself to College, cooked, did the household chores, mowed the lawn and planted dahlias, still suffering some pain, but helped by hot baths and heat treatment each night. On one occasion, at a Chief Education Officer's meeting, the pain was so intense that I had to get up from my chair and stretch my back against the wall to ease it.

Through June and July I continued to attend College, worked in the garden, went for walks, visited Dartmouth and attended the National Schools Regatta, of which I was Chairman.

At last I felt well enough to visit the boat, repair its cover, collect winches at Burnham and start work again, completing shelves in the cabin, which I had abandoned seven months before.

Sunday 7th August. Long day at boat. 9.00 started on fitting the first bunk in the fore cabin. Very tricky. Much trial and planing. Made the inset for the sliding door into the main cabin. No time to start the second bunk. Left at 5.15. F very tired – went to bed immediately after meal.

At last we were back on course. I spent every day of the rest of the summer holiday at the boat, sometimes up to eight o'clock in the evening, with Joan helping on most days, working on the bunks and their lockers in the fore cabin and on the chain locker in the forepeak.

Thursday 18th August was one of 'those' days:

Dreadful day at the boat. I fell heavily on the base of my spine in the stern cabin. Then F cut a hole for the drainage pipe in the wrong place. Glassing didn't go right. And finally F knocked over a jar of cleaner which ran into the bilges. Home at 8.20.

However, on Saturday 20th:

Long day at boat. Finished the glassing on both ends of two drainage pipes and all round the shelf in the anchor locker. Repaired the hole and painted over it and round the ends of the pipes with gel coat, finishing on the outside with blue, and covering it with a polythene square taped on with Sellotape to exclude air and allow the gel coat to harden. Left at 8.15.

We fitted long shelves over the berths in the fore cabin, and on Thursday 25th set off to Dartmouth for four days. We mowed the large lawn at the Vicarage, had a meeting with the architect, who seemed to be having trouble with Building Regulations, and made a contract with one of the electricians who had tendered for re-wiring the house as two properties.

Term started on 1st September, and we were back to weekend working. Philip and Joan launched their Colvic on the fifth. My back had given me trouble again, this time at the base of the spine, and I started a series of six sessions with a chiropractitioner. I was back to hot baths, heat treatment and early bed.

September was a difficult month. I had numerous evening engagements at College. Our architect in Dartmouth was giving us problems; he seemed unable to get his plans for the modifications passed by the Building Regulations Inspector. Our daughter, Jill, and her husband, Bart, were unable to start work on the Vicarage. We took delivery of a cockpit hood, but, when I fitted it, the metal rail snapped as I bent it round the coaming. And my back was giving me great pain.

9

On Sunday 25th, after we had worked all day on the boat, we returned home to a telephone call from our daughter. She had checked with Building Regulations – the plans had not even been submitted. The architect had told her that a set of plans had been left for them at the Vicarage. Jill and Bart had driven from Cornwall to Dartmouth to find that the detailed drawings were inadequate. In the following week Jill was informed by Building Regulations that the plans had eventually been submitted but not passed. She was in contact with RIBA, with our solicitor and finally with the architect. She had two pages of faults and pointed out that his plan to remove the existing staircase would cost an extra £20,000. By Friday 7th October I had had enough. I telephoned my solicitor in Dartmouth, who agreed that the architect had failed us, and he dictated over the telephone a letter for me to write, dispensing with his services.

On 18th October I had a last meeting with the chiropractitioner, who told me she could do nothing for me. The pain continued.

Jill, who had once worked in a council planning office, now took over the planning application. She discovered from the Planning Officer that the main objection to the architect's plans had been his new staircase, which offered a fire hazard to our maisonette. We decided to go back to our original idea of retaining the lovely old staircase, and over the telephone discussed, modified and agreed new layouts. Jill had ten days to submit the new plans before planning consent was out of time. She achieved this with a day to spare. Now she was in business, and her husband, Bart, and his team took up residence in Dartmouth to begin the serious work of reconstruction.

Meanwhile we had glued, screwed, and glassed all the remaining pieces of *Blue Pearl*'s fore cabin and taken delivery of our steering gear. Whitlocks, who were supplying it, had sent a man to design rod steering with a special drive unit to link to the Autohelm self-steering. Fitting this was beyond me, so again I engaged John Duce and acted as his assistant.

Jeckylls of Burnham, who had made our spray hood, now made a cockpit cover for us and at last we could dispense with the overall canvas cover. It became much easier to open up the boat, and put it to bed at the end of the day. Moreover, I soon invented a system where, by combining the cockpit cover with the spray hood, I had a sort of tent over the cockpit which kept the rain out but allowed air into the boat. In wet weather working inside the boat was now much more comfortable.

At the start of December I worked on the battery boxes – a double one under the wardrobe astern of the engine room and a single one for the engine in the workshop next to the engine room – and the elbows of the steering gear installation. We then tidied the boat and left it for a ten-day Christmas holiday with our daughter, Jill, in Cornwall. We took this opportunity to inspect kitchens, windows and bathroom equipment for the Vicarage and to discuss and, where necessary, to modify the plans.

January 1984 was a difficult and expensive month. It began with John, our engineer, spending a full seven days on finishing his work, and an unexpected but necessary large bill. He had been a careful and precise engineer and we were well satisfied with his work. At Dartmouth we confirmed our choice of Mobalpa oak kitchens for the two flats at a cost of £6320, and Iroko double-glazed windows costing £13,000 plus glass and fittings. The worst news was from our daughter – sadly she and her husband had decided to divorce. They were the managing partners of the building firm contracted to renovate the Vicarage, so what would happen to our house now?

Between long-distance telephone calls we managed, at weekends, to continue at the boat, finishing the outstanding work in the stern cabin and working on the holding tank, which I was making out of glass fibre. At the end of the month we had confirmation of Jill's divorce. I sent her the monthly cheque of £5000 for the stage payment and wondered if it would be returned. To add to our misery we were each sent a summons by Southend County Court to pay the balance of the architect's fee, which our solicitor was disputing as the work had not been completed. On 14th February we had a telephone call from Jill. Although the divorce was going through, her husband was at Dartmouth continuing with the work and we must choose bathroom suites.

Throughout February we worked to complete the holding tank, to install a winch and a bilge pump on the port side of the cockpit and to make a glass-fibre container for the instrument panel and glass it into the side of the cockpit.

Joan was now besieged with telephone calls from the Chairman of the College Governors, from the staff, from the students and from the Old Palmerians, all wanting to know what I would like for leaving presents. I had made my decision to retire at the end of the spring term and already my successor had been appointed. With Joan's help they chose a splendid Seiko watch, an excellent sextant, a signal lamp and a brass Sestrel clock, all of which would be put to good use on our cruise. The Governors had also paid for a large portrait of me to hang in the College library with those of other Principals and Heads, going back to the beginning of the eighteenth century.

It was too wet and cold to continue working in the cockpit so we turned our attention to constructing the wardrobe in the stern cabin. We had built the base earlier with a battery box beneath it. Now we built the sides and faced the bulkhead above and on either side of it with matching quarter-inch teak-faced ply. When ordering this three years earlier I had insisted on sheets of matching ply, meaning that where two sheets abutted, the grain could be matched, like wallpaper. This provided a continuous grain across the width of the boat and had the effect of losing the join.

Throughout March I attended a number of dinners and other functions to mark my retirement, with the staff, the Old Students, local Heads, county Heads (I was chairman of their association) and the Schools Sailing Committee, of which I was chairman. Term finished with a memorable evening when my wife and I were guests of honour at a staff dinner.

This was my last College function. I would soon enter that strange world where you are no longer governed by the clock, where you are free to laze or work as you wish and where you work harder than at any other time of your life. Fortunately, the problems of my back were just a memory. In the last weeks of term I spent the weekends on finishing off the work in the stern cabin and on the exhaust system. On Saturday 14th April, John Duce came to the boat, checked the last fittings, put in some diesel fuel, filled up a huge container with water for cooling, and turned the starter key. The engine rumbled into life and ran sweetly until the cooling water was used up.

Now it was time to turn to the pressing problems at Dartmouth. In the past month Bart had sacked two of his men and work on the house had deteriorated dramatically. We were needed on site. We cleared up in the boat and removed our tools, tidied up the garden and the house and left early on Tuesday 17th April.

We arrived at the Vicarage at 2.15, after what should have been the men's lunch hour. They did not return to work until 3.15. I had a straight talk with Bart and gave him an ultimatum, either manage the building site properly or go. He took a day to consider and decided to stay.

We had a meeting with our solicitor who told us that if the case with the architect went to court we might incur expenses of up to £2000. He persuaded us to attempt a settlement. We also had a meeting with our plumber, agreed his plans for central heating and chose our bathroom suites.

A stressful holiday finished at the end of April and we were happy to return to Leigh – to more problems, this time of our own making and therefore capable of solution. It was time to consider putting our Leigh house up for sale and I felt that there was still a considerable amount of decoration to be done. We renewed a garden fence and repaired a wall, cut out and replaced rotted wood in windows and replaced the television aerial that had blown down and was suspended from the gutter. This work was interrupted by a telephone call from Dartmouth – Bart wanted to withdraw from the site. I told him that I would meet him there in two days' time and continued with the work at Leigh.

I finished the three windows and on Tuesday 8th May caught a train to Dartmouth where I found that Bart had collected his tools and withdrawn from the site. The house was in an appalling, even frightening, state. The south wall had been taken down to ground level and the roof was being held up by large jacks, called acrows. I spoke to Rob, the carpenter, a man of considerable site management experience, and he agreed to take over the management of the Vicarage. The next day I left for home, feeling much happier.

I had received further requests for money in addition to the £5000 per month I was paying for the work at Dartmouth – £7500 for plastering, £1979 for the electrical re-wiring and £8000 for plumbing. The bridging loan was mounting and the interest on it was becoming a worry, so it was imperative that we sold our home. Once again I abandoned *Blue Pearl* to spend all our time redecorating the Leigh-on-Sea house. In seven weeks Joan and I re-built the balcony and papered and painted four rooms, the hall and the landing.

On 5th June we put our house in the hands of an agent On the seventh we set off for Dartmouth to check on the work there. We borrowed a Honda mower and cut the waist-high grass, and helped the plumber by lagging the pipes that would be under the ground floor. We were pleased with the progress, discussed with Rob the work still to be done and left after five days.

We continued working on the Leigh house for a week or so, and during this period had several prospective buyers. On Tuesday 25th June we returned to the boat to install a sacrificial anode and link it to the engine and stopcocks.

Each day was fully occupied, on the boat, on the house, showing buyers around, dealing with queries from Dartmouth, making decisions. Negotiations for the divorce were proceeding slowly and with difficulty, and we had constantly to give Jill our support. She, in her turn, shared her life between sorting out her own domestic issues and giving her attention to our Dartmouth house.

Joan showed several buyers over our Leigh-on-Sea house, and on Monday 16th July we had a call from our agent in Dartmouth about a possible buyer for the downstairs flat at the Vicarage. We decided to meet him at the Vicarage and take the opportunity to see our daughter. The flat was nowhere near ready and the buyer made a ridiculously low offer, which I rejected out of hand. Jill had prepared a draft divorce agreement with Bart and I arranged to meet him and discuss it. I secured his signed agreement.

The Building Inspector had insisted that we cover the lovely moulded doors of the upstairs maisonette with asbestos or some other fire-proof material. Jill had discovered a fire-retardant paint, Nullifire, and we went to the council offices to secure approval for it. We also sought approval to remove a large beech tree that stood in the middle of where we wanted to build our drive and garage. We were successful in both of these missions. In the evening we worked on a flow chart for the remaining work at the Vicarage.

We returned to Leigh on Saturday 21st and on Sunday I worked on the flow chart, making copies for Jill and Rob. On Monday we worked in the boat until 10.0 p.m. and on Tuesday till 8.0 p.m., constructing a bench for the workshop, and on Friday we fitted it together.

Sunday 29th July 1984 was our ruby wedding anniversary and for this we had a large family gathering to feast on the food that Joan had prepared on the Saturday – roast beef and chicken, boiled ham, quiches, salads, gateaux and trifles. The weather was fine and we were able to spread out into the garden.

I continued working long days at the boat, constructing cupboards and tool racks behind the bench and eventually, with Joan's help, glassing it all in. When not at the boat Joan spent her time caring for our home and showing buyers around. Our agents in Dartmouth also reported interest in the Vicarage flat and had taken two clients to view.

On 7th August we had an offer for the house, which we accepted, only to find that our prospective buyer had first to sell his own home. On this day we learned that Bart had withdrawn his acceptance of the divorce agreement and it would now go to court. On the ninth I had a letter from our Dartmouth solicitor: the architect would settle for £600, the cost of the work he had carried out plus his costs, the offer to be withdrawn if not accepted within fourteen days.

Three more buyers came to view our house – Joan showed them around while I worked on the boat, finishing the workshop. One young couple were particularly interested. On the 22nd the first couple informed us that they had had a survey done which showed that the house needed re-wiring, with one or two other minor faults. As we had had the house re-wired only three years before by a professional electrician, I asked to see the survey report. The buyer wanted the price reduced by £3000. I offered a reduction of £500 to cover the known blemishes in a window and refused to go lower – I was sure the buyer was 'trying it on'. On 31st August the young couple made a good offer. We were still under offer from the previous purchaser, so I gave them first refusal. The first buyer kept us waiting till 10th September when he withdrew. I contacted the young couple, who came the next day, and we shook hands on the deal. This proceeded rapidly and without a hitch, and we had one worry off our minds.

Meanwhile I worked continuously on the boat, with Joan helping when she could be spared from the house, using 'Perfection', a hard, polyurethane paint, to paint all the bulkheads, cupboards, shelves and doors in the workshop, as well as all the pieces in the oily locker – three coats, a long, painstaking job.

The purchasers of our house wished to take possession on 7th October and events were now rushing to a work-crowded conclusion – clearing out the house and depositing loads of unwanted rubbish in the local tip, packing valuables into packing cases, mowing the lawn and tidying the garden. I made a visit to my old college to make one last use of the machinery to cut up, plane and rebate teak for decking, and again to the boat to fasten the decking onto the cockpit seats and finish all the unfinished jobs. We found time to make a round of our suppliers and to purchase £500 of wall lights for our new house.

We had telephone calls from Dartmouth to say that the plasterers were delayed a week and the plumber could not finish our work on time. On Thursday 4th October we were at the boat early, cleaning and vacuuming and making it ready for Dauntless Marine to take it to Totnes on their low loader. I still worked on *Blue Pearl* next day, clearing and cleaning, dismantling my stairs and loading them alongside the boat together with spare lengths of teak.

At the weekend we drove to Dartmouth ready to receive the boat at Totnes on Monday 8th. The boat seemed huge, and Dauntless had needed police outriders through the narrow Devon lanes. Simon Elyat, Managing Director of Totnes Marine, took over the unloading and we were glad to leave the shoring up in his capable hands. We went on to the Vicarage at Dartmouth, where the plasterers had finished our living room and were about to start on our bedroom. We had a meeting with our solicitor to discuss the business with our architect and the lease of the flat we were selling.

We returned to Leigh on Tuesday 7th to pack china into packing cases and to fill over twenty cartons with books. We sold some unwanted furniture, made more trips to the tip, took jumble to the scouts' headquarters, packed more cartons with sheets, towels and pillow-cases, and made more visits to the tip. We collected our dinghy and trolley and tied them onto our roof rack.

Finally, on 18th October, the removal van arrived. The men were worried by the large load and told us that some would be left till later when they were making another delivery in our area. We had been up since 4.0 a.m., clearing and packing. When the men left we did a final clean up of the house and left at 10.0 p.m.

After a nightmarish drive through the rain-drenched night to Dartmouth, we arrived in the early hours of the morning. The rain continued to pour down and through it all the removal men worked with patience and humour.

The carpenters were in the lounge half of the living room. Our bedroom and the dining half of the living room were finished. We asked the men to store our furniture in the dining area, leaving the bay window to live in. The kitchen was unfinished and uninhabitable; we had no kitchen sink or running water there; we lived in the bay window, ten feet by four feet, and we had only a bed in our bedroom. The plasterers were still plastering, the plumbers still plumbing and the carpenters still woodworking!

For the next month, with this background, we led a strange life. We decided to have one hot pub meal a day, either lunch or dinner, and got to know all the pubs in Dartmouth. We could obtain water from a bathroom tap and boil water in an electric kettle for coffee or tea. For the rest, all our meals were cold, either cornflakes or sandwiches.

Yet we were happy. By selling our Leigh-on-Sea house we had eliminated a big financial worry. We could see the work on our new home developing and each day brought us nearer to a cooked meal. The smell of plastering pervaded the house, but what a relief in the evening when the workmen left and we had the house to ourselves! Out of the chaos, order began to assert itself.

2

Dartmouth

It was to be two years before we could renew our work on *Blue Pearl*, two very full years but not really part of the story of *Blue Pearl*. At the Vicarage, the plasterers moved out of our apartment to the one downstairs; the carpenters left us to finish off the woodwork downstairs; our kitchen was finished and the water, gas and electricity turned on; a painter arrived to paint the outside, assisted by Joan and myself. Inside, Joan and I tiled two kitchens, four bathrooms, two toilets and four backs of vanitory units. We painted fourteen rooms, two halls, two stairways and two landings, all including walls, doors, windows, skirting boards and radiators. We installed fitted wardrobes and cupboards. Outside, we created two large paved terraces, a tiled patio and two sets of steps; we built dry stone retaining walls and a cemented stone wall; we built a brick wall surround to a flower bed and created other flower and shrub borders. Finally, and with a new name, Leigh House was finished.

Our biggest task was the building of a double garage in the same style as the house. Our building loan had again reached six figures and interest was up to twenty-four per cent. I could no longer afford to pay to have the garage built and when the Building Inspector suggested that I could build it myself, and that he would advise me when needed, I decided to go ahead. The ground sloped backwards towards the house and this had caused damp problems. I decided to establish a slight slope away from the house and this meant lowering the surface by up to four feet. A digger and two trucks spent a day removing many tons of earth, then I was ready to level and prepare the foundation for the garage.

Block by heavy block the walls rose. I mixed my own cement

and manhandled the blocks. When it came to the roof Joan surprised me by standing nonchalantly on the joists, holding up the rafters to the ridge board while I banged in six-inch nails to secure them. Between us we heaved the heavy beams into position and the roof took shape. Joan handed up more than three thousand tiles to be fixed on the battens laid on the felt. I became careless – once I tripped and slid headfirst over the edge of the roof, to be caught and held by Joan who was standing on the trestles with more tiles. We had already passed our sixty-fifth birthdays.

But we made it. The garage was built, with the same roof pitch as the house, the same kind of tiles and the same white pebble-dash finish. Now it looks as if it has always been there and I can't quite believe we built it. I had designed it as two garages, one for the car and one that I would use as a workshop to help with the boat. Round the garage we had tarmac laid to provide parking for up to twelve cars.

Two things interrupted our work on the garage. For a fortnight in June 1985 we assisted Tom Harry, an old friend and colleague from Essex, to sail his Sadler 32 from Milford Haven to Harwich. Again this gave us the flavour of the sea and kept alive our hopes and aspirations.

The second incident, in September 1985, was more serious. I woke up one morning after experiencing a series of flashes in my right eye. I visited an optician, who passed me quickly on to my doctor. He prescribed eye drops and arranged for me to see a specialist at Torbay Hospital. There I learned that I had an unusual form of glaucoma, which had developed quickly and destroyed the nerves that control the central vision of the eye. I was virtually blind in my right eye, having peripheral vision only. At that time I did not know what glaucoma was. No one in my family had had it. The seriousness did not strike me and I waited for my sight to return.

Joan's diary records:

F not back from seeing doctor till 11.0 a.m. – pressure behind his eye. To see specialist next week. In the afternoon we fitted the window frame in the old garage. Then F worked on the door frame.

And on Monday 23rd:

F sent urgently to Torbay Hospital to see specialist. Has glaucoma in both eyes. We both worked outside when he came back, he on completing the window, while I painted the door.

Our priority, getting on with the job, was still the same as always! Nine months later, on Wednesday 25th June 1986, the new garage was almost completed, terraces and flowerbeds were well established and our home was complete, comfortable and gracious. It was time to pay *Blue Pearl* a visit.

The cockpit cover looked shabby from two winters of exposure and the teak toe-rail was green, but a hard day's work soon had everything looking clean and bright. We liked the boatyard and particularly our site alongside the River Dart. We could see the timber yard opposite, where the large timber ships delivered their cargoes, and the pleasure boats passing to and from their Totnes terminus.

Back to work in the garden on Thursday and Friday, I finished grouting the patio tiles, killed the weeds in the drive, mowed the lawn and planted the summer bedding plants. I spent Saturday at the boat, erecting my stairway to the cockpit and taking measurements. However, I was not yet ready to resume work at the boat. On Sunday, Joan's brother-in-law, Jack, and his wife, Peggy, came to help me in the house. Under Jack's supervision, I wired up the garage for power and light.

At this time several buyers came to view the flat and on 11th July an offer was made that I accepted, the seventh firm offer we had received. Solicitors' names were exchanged and a date, three weeks later, was agreed for exchange of contracts. On Tuesday 16th July the buyer withdrew his offer. On the Thursday another buyer viewed the flat and made a similar offer, which I accepted. On 5th August contracts for the flat were exchanged and on Thursday 7th a SOLD notice was put up. For the second time in two years we were saved from disaster at the last minute.

With the high bank rate, houses and flats had slumped in value and were difficult to sell and although our flat was always under offer, from seven different purchasers, it had been a year before it sold. The cost in interest that year was nearly thirty thousand pounds and we were relieved when the flat finally sold, even though it represented a big loss on our outlay. Towards the end of this time the bank was pressing to know how we would deal with our loan and we almost reached a critical point when we would have to sell or take out a mortgage. However, we survived. We had our lovely home, enough money to finish the boat and we owed nothing, not even a mortgage.

At last, two years after moving the boat from Leigh to Totnes, I was ready to resume work on her. On Wednesday 22nd October 1986, Joan's diary records: *F off to boat all day after sorting out his tools.*

The original drawings for the Oyster Mariner showed a stern cabin with a double berth on the port side and a settee berth on the starboard side, joined by a settee across the stern. An upholstered backrest ran all the way round the cabin with a shelf above it. For our long-distance cruising we needed more cupboard space and I decided to add lockers beneath the shelf, with the backrest positioned along the tops of the lockers. This was the task I now tackled and I spent all of the next seven days on it. On Sunday 2nd November, Joan records in her diary:

Day at boat. F worked on wood while I cleared water on deck and wood shavings in the boat. In the afternoon we glassed in two of the floors that had been left originally.

We were back in business!

A drizzly Monday was spent on work at home and on the Tuesday when we went to the boat we found that Sunday's glassing had not gone off. The two-year-old hardener had lost its efficacy and I was forced to rip out the fibreglass. We glued and screwed the verticals of my new lockers and prepared them for glassing, and returned home early with resin and hardener for me to test. We were at home on Wednesday, but on Thursday, back at the boat, we re-glassed the floors and glassed in the lockers with the new hardener – this time the resin set properly. On Friday the men arrived to tarmac our drive and I decided to stay at home and keep an eye on things. I used the opportunity to paint our wine cellar.

On Sunday we made an early start at the boat, glassing in the remaining stern cabin floors and berth sides that we had left prepared two years before. On Monday and Tuesday the tarmac men came to complete their work and I worked on the garden and painted a second coat in the cellar.

Wednesday was our club day. I had joined the local Probus, a club for retired professional and business people, and was due at

Stoke Lodge, Stoke Fleming, for lunch and a talk, and Joan had joined a literature group which met on Wednesday afternoons and was currently studying George Herbert. Thursday and Friday were wet, with gale-force winds and we spent these days constructing cupboards for the garage workshop and loft.

Saturday was warm, dry and sunny and we left at 8.30 for the boat and spent a long day gluing and screwing the sides of the berths and lockers and glassing them in. We arrived home at six o'clock very tired.

Sunday was wet, but on Monday we were able to spend a long day at the boat, putting further layers of glass fibre on the berths. We had developed a good routine for this. First, I measured up the sizes I needed, generally about eighteen inches long by six inches for the first layer, increasing the width by two inches for each new layer. Each layer was brushed or rolled into the angle between hull and berths, overlapping the previous one top and bottom and at one end, thus forming a strong bracket. Joan cut out all the fibre pieces and kept me supplied with made-up resin in half-litres. For years she had saved and washed margarine pots and these were now used – each lasted for two or three applications and was then discarded. The system enabled us to keep the resin fresh and 'runny'. Joan's hands were always clean when she handled the glass fibre. I wore polythene throwaway gloves over a barrier cream to protect my skin. Joan handed each sheet to me as I needed it and I was able to press it into position, paint it with resin and roller it before the last piece had started to go off. In this way we worked quickly and efficiently and established a good bond between the wood and glass fibre, and between the layers of glass fibre. In the end we probably worked as quickly as professionals and thoroughly enjoyed our shared effort.

Since we had finished the all-out struggle on the house and garage our social life had begun to develop: we attended events at the Yacht Club, meals and talks; Joan had her weekly literature class and I my Probus; and we had made an increasing number of friends who invited us to meals or drinks, and came to us by turns. Our home was finished and comfortable – the downstairs flat was sold and its occupants became our very good friends, exchanging fortnightly visits for an evening of bridge. All of this and the work on the boat made for a demanding but very happy time for us.

On Friday 28th November we left for a long holiday from work. We visited Peggy and Jack for their birthdays and met their children and grandchildren and, after a few days, went on to Essex to stay with my sister and meet all her children and grandchildren. We particularly enjoyed the visit to my nephew, Martin, who was also building his own boat from a bare hull. I visited my old college, Palmer's, where the staff greeted me warmly, and Benfleet Yacht Club, where I met Ray Walsh, retired Managing Director of Thames Marine, who had sold me my first two boats. He was building an Oyster 45 from a bare hull and we had much to talk about.

For the rest of 1986 the weather was poor, with intermittent gales and rain. I made several visits to the boat, working on the mahogany-faced linings to the berth bins. The four sides and bottom of each bin were fitted in such a way that each could be removed to give access to the hull. I worked on this principle throughout the boat so that the complete fibreglass hull was accessible from inside. Between visits to the boat I worked on the garden or in the workshop, cutting up bin linings. We had several invitations to drinks or meals, a visit to the eye specialist and our clubs. We also invited a young cadet from the Naval College and his girlfriend to stay with us. On Christmas Eve our family arrived and stayed with us until the 29th.

The first fortnight of 1987 was icy, with heavy snowfalls. We went to the boat once or twice to finish trims in the stern cabin, but the temperature dropped to minus ten degrees and heavy snow falls made driving difficult. I decided to work at home on cupboards.

On 18th January we were able to resume work in the boat and spent every day of the week gluing, screwing and glassing. On the Saturday we aimed to fit the stainless steel kingpost underneath the mizzen mast in the stern cabin. I had taken off half an inch, but even then was unable to force the kingpost into an upright position. I found a solution by raising the deckhead with a prop and car-jack. When I removed the jack the kingpost fitted nicely into position. I then removed the kingpost and took it to a local firm to have the top and bottom plates welded on.

The next month fell into a regular pattern, with me at the boat six days a week and Joan joining me for at least three of those days, usually for glassing. We glassed in the kingpost and lockers in the stern cabin, made trim for the locker openings and doors, and fitted the doors to the cupboards. Then we started on the

24

deckheads. I planned to glass in battens along the deckheads to which I would screw marine-ply panels. This was a long and difficult job, with the fitting all overhead. I devised a scheme of propping up the wood with vertical stretchers while I fitted it. When I had fitted the battens Joan and I cut out the marine ply at home, took it to the boat and trimmed it to fit. Then we screwed the panels into position on the battens, again so that each could be removed, giving access to the glass-fibre deckhead. Later I intended to remove the panels and cover them with padded vinyl.

Now we started on the teak plywood facing inside the top of the stern cabin. This was one of our trickiest jobs to date. Not only was the shape curved, but the panel itself had to take up the curve of the cabin. The panels were each some six feet long by eighteen inches deep. At each of the two corners of the cabin we had to bend the plywood to take up the ninety-degree curve and screw the panels onto battens glassed onto the cabin sides.

The windows came next. They were taken out from their temporary positions and refitted permanently in mastic, with teak trim to mask the glass fibre.

As we finished in the stern cabin I began to work on the galley area. I built a full-length wardrobe in teak at one end of the galley, next to the stern cabin. Between this and the midships bulkhead on the starboard side I constructed a framework of solid two-inch teak into which I could fit cupboards and drawers, the sink, fridge freezer and gimballed cooker. The framework was all mortised and tenoned, which made a very strong construction. Behind this framework, in the bulge of the hull and using the waste space behind the freezer and cooker, I built cupboards, one fitted to take crockery and one to take kitchen goods such as tea, coffee, sugar, salt and pepper, so that they would not rattle on passage. In front of these cupboards I fitted sliding doors of smoked Perspex. In the galley I installed a stainless steel sink, with fresh and salt water spigots, and next to it the fridge freezer, above which was the draining board. The cooker, fitted with removable fiddles, had two burners, an oven and a grill and beneath it was a gash bin, the only one I know made of teak. There was a worktop on either side of the cooker made of marine ply laminated with formica. I also used formica to line the well of the cooker as a fire precaution. Beneath each worktop were drawers made of solid teak with dovetailed corners. One of these was divided into compartments

25

for cutlery. Beneath these drawers were cupboards to take kettle, teapot, saucepans, frying pan and bread bin, designed and fitted to avoid rattle.

The galley was L-shaped, and a passage led past it to the stern cabin. On the other side of the passage was the engine room, with a large door giving access. We sanded the rough glass fibre of the deckhead above the galley and passage, and painted it with a coat of primer and two coats of epoxy paint to prevent damp penetration. Then we fitted battens and deckhead panels, similar to those in the stern cabin. We had to search for the right pattern of formica and for the stainless steel slides and smoked Perspex. We built the freezer into the hull and surrounded it with layers of insulation. I invented an ingenious ventilation system for it with a flexible tube having an outlet in the opening door beneath the sink. All this work was time consuming and laborious, but wonderfully rewarding, and Joan was delighted with her galley.

A few entries from the diary give the flavour of these times:

Monday 13th April. Day at boat. Don Campbell, of Dart Sails, and Sue came and made templates for the berth cushions we had ordered from him. We worked on the top galley lockers.
Friday 17th April. Day of glassing. Long day at boat, starting at 8.30. Started glassing-in lockers at 2.15, after morning preparation. Worked until 6.00. Too tired and too late to go to Club for video of America's Cup Races.
Saturday 18th April. Day of glassing. We worked from 10.00 to 4.15, glassing in three out of four sides. Home, meal, then bridge with downstairs neighbours.
Sunday 19th. Day at boat. Glassing from 10.00 to 4.30. Fairly sunny and warm, but windy. We were able to keep hatches open. Finished all remaining sides. Home by 5.30, but too tired to go to Club for further video. F to bed. I cooked meal and washed up, then to bed. Watched an Agatha Christie film till 10.00.

Although we wore masks, the fumes inside the boat were overpowering and contributed to our tiredness.

Monday 20th April. Day at boat for F. I did three loads of washing and finished last week's ironing. F put capping round stern cabin lockers and made templates for galley sides.

While I spent a day at the boat, Joan dealt with all the home chores, washing and ironing, beds and cleaning, gardening, shopping, letters and posting, with never a complaint and always a readiness to join me for work at the boat.

Tuesday 21st April. F decided to miss Probus. Both to boat, after cutting out formica shapes. Worked on shapes and fitting stretchers. To Tesco on the way home to shop and buy petrol.
Wednesday 23rd April. Both to boat early. Finished preparing stretchers, then applied cascamite. F mixed it with warm water and it jelled before he could use it. He bought thixafix and this worked well. We started again and got up both pieces with all the stretchers. Chris Gaynes of Gowans Sails came and we told him to come again in June. Home at 5.00. F mowed the lawn. I finished ironing
Thursday 23rd April. F to boat to take down stretchers and sort out next work on galley base. I house-worked, shopped and baked. F home at 5.30. Peggy and Jack arrived to spend ten days with us.
Wednesday 15th May. A red letter day. F and I went down to town to look for melamine crockery and found the yacht chandler offering fifty pieces, second hand, for £20.

The melamine was in good condition and just the colour we wanted – we needed it at this stage as I was about to make the fitments to take it.

Periods when I spent six or seven days continuously on the boat were interspersed with a day at home, catching up on the garden, or with visits from relatives or friends. The longest continuous spell of daily work on the boat would be from 2nd June to 25th June, twenty-four days in all without a break!

The first day at home after my long spell at the boat is recorded by Joan:

Day at home. I shopped for F in the morning while F prepared fitments for painting. In the afternoon we painted primer on the fitments. Then we sorted out wood for the doors. F's back was bad, so bath and heat treatment. Downstairs at 7.00 p.m. for bridge with our neighbours. Home at 11.00.

I had set up trestles in our loft room, which had an opening window and radiators. We brought home all the removable items from the boat, such as the fitted shelves and locker doors, to paint or varnish in controlled conditions. All the woodwork was given either a coat of primer and four coats of polyurethane paint or six coats of varnish.

Sunday 28th June. Day at home. F cut up wood for doors. I painted first top coat of Perfection on underside of fitments. After lunch we went for a walk along the Embankment, the first outing for a month, and how we enjoyed it! In the evening we painted the other sides.

In all, we spent six days at home, completing the five coats of paint or six coats of varnish on each side of our fitments, gluing and pinning the edging trim to the doors, and planning the boat's electrics.

Friday 3rd July. Packed car early with all fitments and doors. To Brixham to purchase cable from Quay Electrics. Walked around the harbour and had lunch. Then to boat in Totnes. Worked on screwing home fitments until 8.00 p.m. Early to bed.

For the next three days I continued fitting worktops and fitments and on Thursday 9th July:

Both to boat early. Fitted in plugs all round work tops after gluing and screwing their fiddles in place. Glued and screwed the backs to take the cooker gimbals.

As with most of our work, Joan and I had developed a technique for plugging the screw holes. I used any offcuts of teak to cut the half-inch or three-eighths plugs, which would be inserted in the screw holes with the grain going the same way as the wood. We used Aerolite 303, a two-part glue. Using a piece of quarter-inch dowelling, I rubbed the glue into the hole. Joan had a small container of hardener into which she dipped the plug before inserting it into the hole. I tapped it home with a light hammer. We plugged a huge number of holes in this way, often over a hundred at a time, and became proficient and quick. Later, on my own, I would cut off the protruding plugs and plane and sand them flat to the wood.

28

On Monday 13th July we had a message from Peter Lucas, saying that our masts and rigging were arriving the following day.

Monday 20th July. Both to boat. Sorted out screws and made a fresh order for Armes, our supplier. The main job was to lead the copper gas pipe from the cooker, round the back of the galley, through the wardrobe, round the stern cabin above the deckhead panels into the workshop and through to a gas bottle in a locker on the port side of the cockpit, a long job that required the removal and replacement of panels.

We spent the next day or two catching up on correspondence, home and garden, and preparing for our next big task, lining the deckhead panels with foam-backed vinyl.

Saturday 25th July. Started early at home working out how to stick the vinyl on to the panels, especially round the corners. Decided to cut triangular pieces out of the outer corners and insert an egg-timer shape on the inner corners. Completed a small panel in the morning and a large panel in the afternoon.

A main difference between a boat built at a boat-builders and one built privately is that at the boat-builders the vessel is one of a run of such boats. All the experimenting is done on the first boat and thereafter all pieces and fitments are cut to size and produced in large numbers. The carpenters in the boat simply go along to stores and draw the required pieces, which inevitably fit. Every piece we fitted had to be measured carefully, a template made if necessary, cut out and given a final trim when fitted. With the padded vinyl we had to experiment and work out our own solutions. All of our work was one-off and took considerably longer than it would a professional. To build an Oyster Mariner, we were told, took four men approximately six months, that is with all the fitments prepared for them. To build our Oyster took the two of us the equivalent of three years.

Monday 29th July. Long day at boat. Took lunch and evening picnic meals. Put up first panel, then glued vinyl round window. Started to put in panel round window, but realised that stern and ceiling panels had to go in first. Stuck on trim all round shelf fiddle.

Completed final fitting for two ceiling panels and added the small centre pieces. Home at 9.30 p.m.

Wednesday 29th July. Our wedding anniversary. Both to boat. Worked on the two panels left over on Monday. Put them in the car, then started on the other three panels. Had to put in extra battens behind each. Finished at 5.30, with still a lot to do. Home – changed – to Royal Castle for a bar meal.

Thursday 30th July. Worked all day until 6.30 on stern panels. Took the last three panels home.

Friday 31st July. At home. Finished covering all five panels with padded vinyl at 11.0 p.m. I dashed out for a quick shop at 12.15. Otherwise we hardly stopped.

Saturday 1st August. To boat at 8.30. Put up first two lined panels at stern, then two at either side, all fitting beautifully. Left at 4.30. Home, bath, then to Elizabeth's for drinks and nibblets.

Sunday 2nd August. To boat at 9.30. Put up stern ceiling panels, a very good fit. Then last one! It wouldn't go up. We had to un-stick the two corners. F had to plane a quarter of an inch off the short side and the two corners. Then we re-stuck. It fitted very well so we screwed it home. Left at 5.30.

Throughout August 1987 work continued on the deckhead panels in the stern cabin and galley area, fitting battens, measuring, making templates, cutting out panels at home, fitting them at the boat, back home to line them with padded vinyl, then back to the boat for a final fitting. During this period I made a teak dressing table for Joan, with a six-inch deep locker, to fit in a corner of the stern cabin.

It is important to avoid sharp corners in a boat, and to make a rounded corner I developed my own technique. Using quarter-inch marine ply, I bent the six-inch deep pieces in a bath of hot water, with the aid of a cramp, to form a right-angle, with the outside grain vertical to make the bending easier. I left these in the cramps to dry off. Next I took three pieces of three-ply, with the outside grain horizontal for strength, and laminated these onto the corners with an overlap, or scarf. I now had two sides of the dressing table, three-quarters of an inch thick, six inches deep, with a right-angled curve at the corner. To finish off I laminated a veneer of teak all round the outside.

On 2nd September I fitted all the finger catches to the doors.

The next day I planed and sanded all the outstanding plugs and pinholes and took measurements for the lockers in the main saloon, and on 4th September removed all the doors in the galley and stern cabin and took them home for varnishing.

When you think you have finished a cabin, you find lots of bits and pieces still to be done. It was more than a month before I would leave the stern cabin and galley. I lined the berth bins with marine ply, carefully fitting the linings so that they could be removed if I needed to get to the hull. Then I took all the linings home for varnishing. The nine openings of the berth and settee tops needed to have battens, glued and screwed, to take the flush-fitting access plugs. As they were completed we took the berth tops and access plugs home for varnishing. Two small deckhead panels that house the ventilator openings had to be made and lined with vinyl. The holes of the finger locks had to be fitted with their special trims, and I made a fitted top to the dressing table, with a hinged lid, like a school desk. We painted the hull inside the lockers with epoxy paint. At this time I also constructed the chart table with a round corner similar to that of the dressing table. Because of my previous experience this took only half the time to make.

It was not all work and no play. Very occasionally we took a day off, as on Sunday 27th September:

A lovely day on the moors. We drove through Buckfastleigh to Cross Furzes, then walked along the Abbots' Way to Huntingdon Cross and on as far as the Clapper Bridge, where we had a picnic lunch overlooking the reservoir above the Avon Dam. We explored the pre-historic hut circle there and sat in what must have been the Chief's hut, imagining what life was like then.

We had taken many pieces home for varnishing, doors, panels, berth tops and plugs, shelves and bin linings, and on 10th October we again set up our loft room for this purpose. Some of these pieces, such as the berth tops, were more than six feet long and required a good deal of space. We made a big 'U' of two trestle tables and our table-tennis table. We had developed our varnishing technique on the last boat we had built, and this had proved itself when, after nine years, the varnish was just as good as when we had painted it on. Teak is an oily wood and doesn't take polyurethane varnish. Our first coat, therefore, was of a marine gloss varnish,

31

diluted with one third white spirit, a penetrating coat, to be followed by a coat of full gloss varnish. The pieces were then sanded with a fine glasspaper on the electric sander; this had the effect of making a smooth surface and providing a key for the next coat, the first of the polyurethane gloss varnish. This was then rubbed down by hand and a second coat applied. The next coat was polyurethane with a satin finish, rubbed down with flower paper. The final coat was polyurethane satin. Before each coat was applied we dusted with a tac rag. The result was a beautiful soft, but enduring, finish.

The routine was for one side to be done in the morning, the other in the evening, repeating the process each day. In this way the successive layers jelled together. Usually Joan applied the morning coat while I went to the boat, and we both varnished in the evening after dinner. During this period I was fitting deckhead panels in the fore cabin, cutting them up at home and taking them to the boat to trim to size. Two of these pieces were too large to go through the hatch or the cockpit seat opening and I had to cut each into two smaller panels.

Monday 12th October reflects this routine:

I painted all the first side with the first coat of gloss. F to boat. He fitted side sections of deckhead, now four panels, and the two above the shelves, with battens on the deckhead to secure them. I did washing and went to town for shopping, library and more varnish. Gardened from 3.0 o'clock to 5.0, then cooked meal. F home at 5.0. After meal we varnished other side, then bed.

Friday 15th records:

F not feeling well so stayed at home. Terrible hurricane. Winds up to 110 miles an hour overnight. Damage along the South Coast. Tree opposite us lost a big branch. The garage roof in the garden below us split up and the pieces landed in our garden. To the east no electricity, telephones or trains. F and I varnished in the morning, and then shopped. Rested in the afternoon, then varnished after meal. Sunday 18th. Both to boat. Worked on two panels, fitting and securing them in place. Then fitted and screwed up central shorter piece. Heavy rain all day. Flooded all round the boat. Left at 4.30, more or less wading away from it. Still very windy.

Finishing the fore cabin was much the same as the stern cabin. The deckhead panels were finished, fitted and taken home for covering. The berth tops were given backing pieces for the openings to take the plugs, then taken home for varnishing. Doors were hung and fitted with finger catches and taken home. We dismantled the mahogany linings of the berth bins and took them home for varnishing. The last glassing was done. When the cabin was emptied of all removable pieces we painted the inside glass-fibre surfaces with a primer and two coats of epoxy paint.

Our routine now was to apply the first coat of varnish at home, then go to the boat to paint or varnish the hull and woodwork, then back home for our evening meal, followed by the second side of varnishing, When the painting in the boat was finished I continued varnishing in the boat while Joan resumed her work of varnishing at home, shopping, household chores and cooking, joining me after dinner for varnishing the second side. Wednesday 18th November records the pressure we were under:

F to boat where he worked all day. I varnished the first side of the pieces at home, shopped, ironed, washed and set hair. Attended literature class in the afternoon – Heaney's poetry. F not home till 6.0 p.m. A quick bath, then both to Janet's supper party. Home at 11.30. Began varnishing the second side at midnight.
Friday 20th. Both to boat. Dusted and tac ragged in both cabins and started varnishing the first diluted coat before lunch. Finished at 4.0. Home before 5.0. F did one side of pieces at home while I bathed and changed into evening dress. F bathed and changed into dinner jacket. 7.30 to Stoke Lodge for Probus Ladies Night. Good company. Home at 10.30. Back into working clothes to varnish second side.

At the end of November we took back to the boat a number of pieces we had been working on at home and fixed them in position, and on 16th December we began our third run of varnishing. The routine was as before. I sanded the pieces at home before going to the boat to work in the heads, where I was making a shelf and locker. Joan varnished the first side in the morning. We both varnished the second side in the evening after dinner. We finished on the twenty-third of December.

The week over Christmas 1987 was spent with our daughter in

Falmouth, in the house she and her new partner had built overlooking the harbour, but by New Year's Eve I was back at the boat, fixing the doors and other pieces we had recently varnished. Inside, *Blue Pearl* was beginning to look like a cruising boat. Only the main cabin remained to be completed.

Unfortunately, at this point first I, then Joan, went down with influenza that kept us off work for a month. It was not until 14th February 1988 that we felt strong enough to go to the boat, and our first job was to clear the leaves and wash the deck. From then on we worked hard to make up for lost time. In the next four months I spent 112 days at the boat and 10 at home. Joan was with me on 53 of those days. We began by working seven hours a day, but as the daylight hours grew we increased these to nine or ten, staying as late as seven, eight, or even nine o'clock. Moreover, there was much work to be done at home, cutting up and preparing wood. My working week, including travelling time, averaged sixty-two hours. Joan, with the addition of housekeeping, shopping and gardening, probably worked longer.

Our first task during this period was to finish the navigation area. I had built a navigation table against the port side bulkhead of the main cabin, facing aft. Now, on that bulkhead, I installed shelves with fiddles to take navigation books and navigational equipment, the fuse and switch box for the electrics, and spaces for radar, GPS, Decca, radio and a compass. The chart table was designed to take Admiralty charts, and underneath it I built a locker with a cupboard for the duty-free drinks, which could be sealed for Customs purposes, and a handy drawer to take the many odds and ends required at short notice. On the inboard side was a stout grabrail going up to the cockpit. Most of this construction was in solid teak with mortise and tenon joints or dovetails. I put much thought into it and it gave me great satisfaction. Later, on our long cruise, I had no regrets, nor did I wish to change anything.

I finished the navigation area on Saturday 12th March and began immediately on the port side of the main cabin. Two large glass-fibre fresh water tanks had been constructed by the boat builders, one on either side of the main cabin, underneath the settee berths. Now I started once more on the familiar work of taking templates, cutting the berth from a sheet of plywood at home, trimming it to fit at the boat and glassing it in. First I made the berth, then the berth top, then behind the berth a berth-length locker to take bedding, and above this a drinks cupboard, next to which was a sideboard. The cupboard shelves were cut to take bottles and glasses exactly so that they did not rattle. On our travels we gave many parties and it always gave me pleasure to see the envious looks on our guests' faces when I opened the drinks cabinet! For the sideboard, underneath the window, the boat's plans showed a single shelf. Locker space is invaluable on a boat, so I designed a cupboard underneath the shelf, with a hinged lid opening upwards, which later made a good stowage for the ship's papers. As in the rest of the boat, all the shelves and vertical sides were glassed onto the hull for additional strength.

We finished this work on Saturday 23rd April and began immediately on the starboard side. This was a repetition of what we had done on the port side, except that the cupboard was simply fitted with shelves as a food store. Joan's diary for 16th May shows how hard we were working:

Both to boat. Cleaned down sides. Vacuumed. Cut out 63 pieces of glass fibre. Did two sessions of glassing. Home at 7.30.
Tuesday 17th May. Big glassing day. Cut out further 60 pieces. Did three sessions of glassing. Home at 7.0.

We finished the berth and lockers on the starboard side on Friday 27th May and then began on the long list of miscellaneous jobs inside the boat, which took a surprisingly long time: cutting, fitting, lining and installing the deckhead panels; fitting and glassing in the kingpost for the mainmast; lining the inside of the main hatch; adding teak surrounds to the windows in the main cabin and heads; cutting drainage holes in the bilges; painting the deckhead and bilges with epoxy paint; plugging hundreds of screw holes and sanding down all the wood for varnishing.

On 30th June we took home all the movable wood for varnishing. The next day we started the routine of varnishing, one side at home, then off to the boat to varnish the fitted woodwork, then back home to varnish the second side. Wednesday 6th July records:

Started varnishing first side of eleven pieces at 8.0 a.m. at home. Then to boat, varnishing till 8.0 p.m. Then home. F varnished second side while I prepared meal for 10.0 p.m. Bed at 11.0.

I am almost sure this was our longest day, though there were several other close contenders.

We followed this with a further run of eleven pieces for varnishing, all interspersed with work on the boat in our now familiar routine. We finished and re-fitted all the varnished pieces on Wednesday 27th July. That evening Peggy and Jack arrived and the following day Jack joined me to set up the boat's electricity. Jack had been a wartime RAF electrical officer, responsible for the electrics in the Pathfinder Squadron, so he was just the man to help me. In fact, I worked to his directions. The first day we spent planning the routes of the wires and the positions of the lights and electrical equipment. Throughout the week we fitted up the wiring, behind panels and though bulkheads so that everything was hidden. Jack made me colour-code the wires with adhesive tape at regular intervals, 'for future maintenance'. We completed this work on 1st August. The next day Jack drove me to Torbay Hospital for an operation on both my eyes.

The operation, which took place the next day, was for glaucoma – a channel was to be cut at the corner of each eye to release the pressure. I woke up from the general anaesthetic in the middle of the night after the operation and, not seeing a nurse, made my own way to the toilet. Before reaching it I suddenly went blind and was completely lost. I called for the night sister, who scolded me for not calling her earlier, led me back to bed and attended to my needs. Some blood was left in my eye from the operation and this was floating around, obstructing my vision whenever I bent down. Sister was reassuring, and the next day the doctor told me that this sometimes happened and that the blackouts would continue for up to three weeks.

I remained in hospital for a week, and each day Joan made the two-hour journey each way to visit me. When I was home I spent most of the next fortnight in an armchair, listening to Brahms, Beethoven and Mozart. Whenever I bent my head, even to eat a meal, my eye blacked out. I was very dependent on Joan and tested her patience to the full. I used some of my time to clear a backlog of correspondence, dictating my letters to Joan who wrote them for me. I suffered intermittent headaches, but by Tuesday 16th August Joan records: *F walked twelve times round the lawn*! By the end of the week we had walked the length of the promenade and on the Sunday I drove us to East Prawle and we had lunch at The Pig's Nose Inn.

On Tuesday 23rd, exactly three weeks after the operation, the diary states: *To boat. F fitted deckhead panels. Home at 3.30.*

We spent a week cutting out panels, fitting them at the boat, taking them home to be covered with vinyl, and back to the boat again for final fitting – not arduous work, but enough for me at that time.

Sadly, at the end of August, our friend Michael died after a brief illness. He had been taken to hospital while I was at Torbay. We attended his funeral. On 5th September Simon Elyatt, the Managing Director of the boatyard, came to ask us about our launch date and I had to tell him it would not be until the following spring.

Our next main task was to deal with the underwater parts of the boat. The biggest scourge of glass-fibre boats is osmosis. This is caused by pockets of air being trapped in the glass fibre during layup when the hull is first manufactured. It is like a disease. Tiny holes break out all over the hull like woodworm.

Simon was a specialist in treating this and I saw many boats enter the yard looking ravaged and leave it cured, with clean, unblemished skins. The treatment was for the gel coat to be scraped away and then for the hull to be given several coats of solvent-free epoxy resin, forming a hard, impervious skin. I decided to apply epoxy resin to the underside of *Blue Pearl* before she entered the water. Simon supplied us with a special five-inch wide adhesive tape, with which we were able to stick up a skirt of thick polythene all round the boat from the waist downwards. All the work would be done in dry, warm conditions, essential to the treatment. First the hull was degreased, lightly sanded and given coats of primer and solvent-based epoxy to gel with the glass fibre. Then Joan and I applied three coats of solvent-free epoxy, using a special comb supplied by Simon to gauge the thickness. These coats were in three different colours, yellow, red and white, so that if the epoxy were rubbed away we would know to what depth and how many coats would be needed to replace it.

This work took us six days and by the end of it Jack and Peggy had arrived again. While Jack continued with the electrics, Joan and

37

I put on a coat of anti-foul primer and cut out paper patterns for the deck treadmaster. Then Jack and I both worked on the electrics. We varied the week with a trip up the Dart in a pleasure boat from Dartmouth to Totnes, a walk along the promenade and a visit to our daughter in Falmouth. Jack and Peggy left on 25th September and the next day Joan and I were back at the boat, finishing the electrics and putting the deckhead panels back into position.

Before we could lay the treadmaster on the deck we had to finish all the deck fittings, including the stanchion bases, cleats and mainsheet traveller. We also moved the shoring supports and epoxied the exposed patches. On 16th October we began to lay the treadmaster, already cut to patterns we had made earlier. We needed to work quickly, Joan applying the adhesive to the pieces of treadmaster and I to the corresponding piece of deck. We then carefully laid the treadmaster in position and weighted it down with bags of sand. I had thought of various ways of applying pressure, such as heavy objects or saucepans filled with water, none of which were suitable because of the curve of the deck. I had plenty of sand left over from our building days and I hit on the idea of loosely filling plastic shopping bags with this sand. It worked perfectly. The heavy sand took up the curve of the boat and held the treadmaster down firmly. We used up to eight bags on each piece and we could manage up to eight pieces at a stretch, enough for one day's work. We worked this in with painting the epoxy patches on the hull and replacing the deckhead panels inside the boat.

We finished the treadmaster on Friday 28th October, and on Saturday took a day off for a long walk round the Castle headland and along the coast in lovely sunshine.

Now we continued with a variety of jobs: the funnel on the anchor locker hatch for the anchor chain; the base of the oily locker, carefully fitted round hosepipes and stopcocks; hinges, pulling rings and catches; the compass on the wheel pedestal; the windlass fitted in the anchor locker; fairleads and fittings for the mizzen; waste pipes for the holding tank and the loo; ringbolts in the cockpit for the safety harnesses. All of this work was finished on Thursday 1st December and the next day we set off for New Malden, to spend a week with Peggy and Jack and share their birthday celebrations.

On 8th December we were back in Dartmouth and I was working

on the boat, the midship fairleads, foresheet runners, the main and mizzen mast shoes, the teak infills for the cockpit seats, more drainage pipes, the cockpit locker surround, and other jobs left over from previously.

We broke off for Christmas and enjoyed a visit from Jill, Rob, and Julia, our granddaughter, who stayed with us until the 29th. The next day I had a check-up at Torbay Hospital and on 2nd January 1989 I began to cut up slats for the cockpit deck, which I fitted during the next three days. On the ninth we went to the Boat Show with the Yacht Club and bought fenders and ordered our Autohelm. Back at the boat the next day, I worked on the teak main hatch surround and the cockpit deck, plugging the holes and cleaning up. I made an inlet for the mains electricity into a contact breaker in the workshop, fitted the last two fairleads and put end-stops on the genoa tracks. I installed the electrics for the masthead lights and constructed a solid teak ladder for the main hatch that could be moved easily to give forward access to the engine, and a teak folding table for the cockpit. I made the main cabin table out of teak, with a central support in the form of a locker that would take wine bottles. Most of this work was done in my workshop at home and taken to the boat to be fitted. At last I removed my Black and Decker Workmate from the boat and took it home. From now on I would use the bench in the boat's workshop.

It was now Monday 13th February and I began work on the soles of each cabin. In the boat I made cardboard templates of each section, which I took home and used to cut the deckply sections. These were then taken to the boat and fitted properly and drilled for screws, then taken home for varnishing.

The main doors of the boat were varnished at home, taken to the boat and fitted into position, a sliding door to the fore cabin and hinged doors to the stern cabin, heads and workshop. While this was going on John Rencher, of Totnes Marine Electrics, fitted our new Autohelm to the Whitlock drive and supplied and fitted a pulse charger. He also sorted out our refrigerator.

On Tuesday 7th March the man from Gowans arrived with our sails, which we stowed in the fore cabin, and on Wednesday Peter, the yard engineer, came to de-winterise and test our engine. It started at once and ran sweetly for two hours. Meanwhile, at home, Joan was varnishing the plydeck, twelve pieces in all, and had reached the sixth and final coat. On Thursday we stood the plydeck in our hall and took the last pieces of woodwork up to the loft for varnishing. This occupied the next week, with jobs like gluing and pinning trim to the edges of the table, fitting brass rails in the wardrobe, installing air vents and soundproofing to the engine room, and fitting the emergency tiller. On Monday 13th John fitted the Autohelm, which did not work – power was going into the computer, but not coming out. He came again on Wednesday, but still without success. He telephoned Autohelm, who suggested that a spring clip might have loosened in transit. He fixed the spring clip and all was well.

Pressing social engagements took us from our work – a supper invitation from Geoffrey and Marjorie, the Probus meeting, the DYC cruising supper, drinks and nibbles at Bill and Doreen's. We kept these engagements, even though they interrupted the varnishing and left us working sometimes till after midnight.

And so to the last hectic week. We still had some painting and varnishing inside the boat to finish, scrubbing the weather-stained outside teak, cleaning and polishing the hull, and two coats of anti-fouling to put on. On Wednesday we finished at 10.45 p.m., Thursday at 11.30 p.m., and Saturday at 11.00 p.m. On Sunday we began to replace all the varnished and painted pieces from home. On Monday we made two journeys to the boat with plydeck panels, the tables and the ladder, and got to bed at 12.45. The great day had arrived.

From the first entry of the log of *Blue Pearl*:

Tuesday 4th April 1989. Launch Day.
Jill and Rob arrived at 0730 and we all drove in the Marina to Totnes to prepare Blue Pearl for launching.
After a year's part time work and two and a half year's full time we were all but ready. The last week has been hectic, with Joan and I often working till nearly midnight. We arrived at 0900. Rob worked on the installation of the Calor gas bottle; Joan and I on assembling the table; and Jill went into Totnes for stores. Peter, the Yard Engineer, assembled the propeller. John Rencher came to fit the radio. The V.H.F. will have to be moved to accommodate the aerial plug.
Almost immediately Simon, the Yard Manager wanted us on

the cradle (he had told us it would be 1400 before we would be required for launching). Work stopped while the Yard took over.

At 1030 John Ellerby, an old friend from Leigh, whose boat occupied the next mooring to ours, arrived and immediately turned to rig stanchions and guard rails.

At 1100 our granddaughter, Julia, arrived. Rob found that our Calor gas bottles wouldn't fit into the gas locker provided and we would have to change to camping-gas. Rob and Julia secured the toilet screws. Julia then started on the plydeck screws while Rob spliced ropes on to fenders. I worked on the anchor and chain and found that the anchor was too big for the locker provided. John Ellerby painted the last patches of anti-fouling and then chased up the dinghy outboard engine, which had been left in the works for servicing. The yard had forgotten about it and Peter had to do a rush job on it. Joan fastened the deckhead screws and cleaned out the anchor locker, then she and I worked on the cabin table, securing it to the deck. Jill arrived back with food.

At 1230 work stopped again for the boat to be craned in, although there was not enough tide to float it. Joan performed the launching ceremony and poured the libation champagne on to the bows.

'God Bless Blue Pearl and all who sail in her.'

All the family, the boatyard people, John Ellerby, John Rencher and Dick Moby, a neighbour who happened to be present, drank a glass of champagne. The sun was shining. It was a very pleasant interlude.

Afterwards work continued as before. Joan and I now fixed the fore cabin door and the main hatch ladder. At 1430 work stopped again while we were moved to make way for another boat to he launched.

At 1600 there was enough tide to start the engine and for Peter to check that all was well. He found water in the bilge and tightened the jubilee clip on the cockpit drainage hosepipe. Later, I found that the real leak was in the water inlet hosepipe to the engine. The jubilee clip had been tightened on the pipe but not over the brass nozzle. The pipe was split for about an inch.

John Ellerby filled the water tanks. I settled the final bill.

41

At 1630 we made ready to leave. The mooring lines were taken in. I put the engine into forward gear. Blue Pearl went astern. I quickly stopped the engine and the mooring lines were made fast ashore. Peter was sent for. He found that the problem was in the Morse control and he started to work on it.

At 1800 we finally left and motored down the river to Dartmouth at six knots – very pleasant. The echo sounder worked well, but the log gave no reading except the time.

1900. Arrived Dartmouth. Dropped Joan, Jill, Julia and her friend, Paul, at the wall and took the boat to the mooring in a horrid force six cross wind with stronger gusts. At the eighth attempt we made it and made fast.

The wheel steering is tricky to handle and it was difficult to judge when the rudder was fore and aft. The head of the boathook was faulty and it fell off. It was difficult in the cross wind to get close to the mooring-buoys without fouling the existing lines. By now it was blowing seven and bitterly cold. Finally, John Ellerby fastened our mooring chains to the buoys.

Because of the leak in the bilges we closed all stopcocks and pumped out the bilges. The pump was not working properly.

We left the boat at 2015 and met our final problem. The outboard engine would not start. Rob rowed us to the wall against the strong wind and tide. Jill met us with her car, but I had already run up the hill and missed her.

A happy and on the whole successful day with everyone pulling his or her weight. Work on the boat was not quite completed because of interruptions. Rob drove Julia to Totnes to collect the Marina. Bed at 0045 after a very happy meal.

3

Working Up

As happens so often with boats, the frenetic preparations for getting *Blue Pearl* launched were followed by a long period of waiting, of disappointments, of faulty gear. It was not until 29th May 1989, nearly two months later, that we were able to enjoy our first sail.

After several delays, the masts were stepped on 8th May. A few days later we tried to hoist the sails, but the luff tape of the genoa stuck in the track of the furling gear and we had to winch it down. The tape was too thick for the track and Gowans had to collect the sail and replace the tape. When we hoisted the mizzen we found the mouse had been wound round the top of the mast so that the sail would not go up to its full height. The kicking-strap of the main boom fouled the electrics and I had to change the position of the deck-plugs.

Meanwhile we were able to clear up the backlog of work on the boat. I repaired the engine hosepipe, cleared the log paddle-wheel and checked its wiring, took down the 240-watt fluorescent lamps that had served us for so long while we were working in the boat, laid a complete set of mooring chains and warps, made and fixed the side flaps to complete the dining table, made and varnished the galley and chart-table drawers and finished the dressing table mirror-cabinet. Joan set to and made curtains for all the windows.

We had lots of trouble with our dinghy engine – a loose choke, the plugs oiling up, the starter-cord spring slipping out. I spent more time rowing the dinghy than motoring it. At length John, while manoeuvring *Blue Pearl* astern, capsized the dinghy which we were towing and immersed the outboard in salt water. I had to take it to Chris Hoyle, a specialist in outboards, for a complete overhaul.

43

Our stainless steel boarding ladder, constructed to my specifications, arrived and I fastened it in position astern of the boat. Our new spray-hood was delivered and a few days later Don Campbell brought along our berth cushions. The spray-hood and berth cushions fitted exactly and gave us much pleasure.

On Sunday 28th May our rigging was at last finished and the next day, with Mike, our young naval officer friend, and his fiancée, Clare, Joan and I left our moorings and took *Blue Pearl* out to sea for her first sail. The wind barely got up to force three, but at times we were able to make five knots in a calm sea and brilliant sunshine. The cares of the past three months were blown away by the wind.

Some adjustments had to be made to the rigging, but on 6th June Joan and I were out on our own in a force five and now we could enjoy our boat's sailing quality. We handed the mizzen and took in a reef in the main and sailed easily at six knots. The next day the wind was stronger and blowing across river onto our mooring. We were unable to get away from it without fouling our propeller, and this was to be a constant problem while moored in the Dart.

On 5th June we joined in a Club outing to Salcombe. On the way home we tried out the Autohelm, but it was lifeless. On the 17th John Rencher came to check it. He showed us a contact-breaker in the circuit, which we did not know about – all we needed to do was push the button. John took the opportunity to repair our VHF, which had not been working. Later he came again to check our Autohelm. We motored out of harbour and made trial runs on all headings, checking the fluxgate compass with the ship's compass. The compass error in the fluxgate compass was too great and John decided to move it to a better position inside the table locker.

Back at the mooring Joan and I decided to spend our first night aboard. In fact, we stayed for two nights, trying out and enjoying our domestic facilities. John came the next day and moved the fluxgate compass and checked the VHF and masthead lights, which had been faulty.

On Saturday 1st July we set out on our first cruise, to Falmouth and the south west. We enjoyed an excellent sail to Salcombe in a blustery force five wind, with a reef in the main and the genoa slightly shortened, and maintained a speed of five knots. The

Autohelm was still faulty. It worked under engine, but under sail the boat simply came up into wind and the Autohelm did nothing to stop it.

We were given a delightful mooring in the Bag, with high banks and wooded hills, sheep and birds and, the only drawback, passing motor-boats constantly exceeding the eight knots speed limit and rocking us as they passed.

After a pleasant weekend, exploring Salcombe and the estuary, we left for Newton Ferrers where we spent a night before sailing on to Fowey. There we were greeted by the harbour launch, *Zebedee*, and the harbour master, who was partial to Joan's fruit cake and who showed us to a comfortable berth alongside a pontoon at Mixtor. There we spent three quiet nights, riding out a blustery storm followed by a thick fog.

On the second day the fridge stopped working and the lights dimmed. The two heavy-duty domestic batteries were flat. I was concerned about the wiring, put in for us by a professional engineer at Leigh-on-Sea. I suspected that only the starter battery was charging. The cooker of the Westerley Centaur alongside us had broken down and we invited them aboard to use ours.

On Saturday our toilet pump broke while in use, leaving a mess everywhere. I cleaned this up, but was unable to repair the toilet. I decided to leave it until we reached Falmouth, where we tied up alongside the town pontoon at the Yachthaven. Jill and Rob invited us to a meal at their new house overlooking the harbour. The next day we sailed up to Restronguet, where we anchored and had lunch before sailing back to Falmouth. Jill and Rob stayed to dinner with us aboard *Blue Pearl*, but before that I dismantled the toilet and found that the plastic plate behind the diaphragm, which must have been faulty, had shattered.

On Monday Jill collected me in her car to take the faulty part to a big chandler's in Penryn, but they hadn't a replacement in stock. They faxed through to Blake's for a spare part and Blake's promised this by first post on Tuesday. In the meantime there were adequate facilities in the yachthaven. I was surprised to find that the showers were mixed. We had met this abroad, but never in England. I was amused when I went to take my shower: two young Swedish women had stripped off in the communal changing room and were taking their showers. As I left the showers two middle-aged men with towels approached me. 'Have those young ladies left?' they asked. They were not prepared to change while the girls were there.

Sea Drifter, a large ketch from Dartmouth, arrived and moored alongside us. Like us, Robert and Joy Wakelin, the owners, were members of Dartmouth Yacht Club. They joined us with Jill and Rob for drinks after our evening meal. Now we began to see the fruits of our labours. Our main cabin, which could seat eight, was very comfortable and our drinks cabinet duly impressed.

The next day Robert, a former garage owner, came to check our charging and declared it to be wrongly wired. I had noticed a Lloyds-approved electrician's van along the quay, servicing the Customs launch, and I asked Kevin, the firm's manager, to look at our wiring. He found three faults: the ammeter was not wired in at all; both wires from the blocking diode went to the starting battery, with no charge at all going to the domestic batteries; the wire used was too small. He corrected these faults and, for good measure, provided and fitted a three-way switch. From then on, throughout all our sailing, we never had another breakdown in the engine electrics.

The next day was spent waiting for the replacement part for our toilet pump. It did not arrive as promised so the chandler stripped a part from a complete pump and sold us that. I quickly fitted it and the toilet was in use again.

On Thursday, to re-charge our batteries, we motored up the Fal to Smugglers Cottage, once a haunt of smugglers, now a well-known restaurant. We were joined by Robert and Joy in *Sea Drifter*, who came aboard for lunch, and we all went to a barbecue supper at the cottage. We enjoyed a quiet night on the buoy and the next day took the dinghy up to Malpas, where a friendly motorist gave us a lift into Truro. We walked back along the river.

The next day we returned to Falmouth, where Kevin fitted the new switch. *Sea Drifter* joined us and after dinner Jill invited us with Robert and Joy to drinks on the terrace of their beautiful home. We had enjoyed Falmouth, explored the river, had meals out and made new friends, and this is the very stuff of cruising.

The next day, Sunday, we left for the Helford River and more delights, a beautiful and quiet mooring, a visit to the local club, exploration by dinghy of Daphne du Maurier's Frenchman's Creek and an excellent meal on the verandah of Port Navas Sailing Club, overlooking the creek. We had arrived by dinghy and at the end of our meal we picked our way on a falling tide through the rocks to our mooring.

On Tuesday we left Helford for our journey home, calling first at Fowey, where *Zebedee* greeted us and the harbour master showed us to a visitor's buoy opposite the town. From our previous visit we had earned a free night, so no charge. Joan used her 'Buoy Friend', which I had bought in Falmouth, to pick up the buoy. The fo'c'sle of *Blue Pearl* is high out of the water and Joan had found it difficult to pass a warp through the buoy ring and back to the boat. Now she had a snap shackle on the end of the boathook, which she snapped on to the mooring ring; the other end of the warp was already fastened onto a bollard on the foredeck. We were moored. In my own time I could replace this mooring line with one passed through the ring and back to the boat, ready to let go when we left. Never again did Joan worry about picking up a buoy.

On Thursday we arrived home in Dartmouth after a hard sail against an easterly force five to six. We maintained five or six knots easily, with long and short tacks. Off Salcombe the sun was shining and the sailing was good so we decided to push on to Dartmouth for a late lunch aboard ship and an hour's sleep.

John Rencher came on Tuesday to check the Autohelm, which we had been unable to use. He thought he had corrected the fault, but when we tried it a few days later we found that it still would not hold the course under sail. John Smith of Autohelm came on 3rd August to check the installation and found a pinched wire in the computer. He replaced this and checked all the soldering. We sailed outside the harbour to check the Autohelm and found it was now working properly. It gave us no further problems throughout our cruising.

On Friday 18th August we set sail again, on a cruise to the Channel Islands and Brittany. We left at 1030 for our first night passage in *Blue Pearl*. The wind was southerly, on the nose, force one, and as this remained with us we motored all the way. Joan and I resumed our old habit of one hour on, one hour off and one hour social chat, when we took it in turns to make coffee. The night passed easily and dawn greeted us to reveal les Hanois and the lighthouse, at first obscured by the cliff background then standing out clearly as we rounded the island. We entered St Peter Port, to be herded by the capable harbour officials over the sill to a crowded pontoon, where we were rafted to several other boats.

We enjoyed a week in Guernsey, with visits to old haunts in Fermain Bay, the Battle of Flowers in Suamerez Park, and a two-day car hire when we explored the island.

On Saturday 27th we sailed on to Jersey and tied up at the pontoon in St Helier. Again we spent a few days enjoying the harbour, enjoying our boat, exploring the island on foot and by car, and on Thursday 31st August we set off for St Malo. The calm, windless days of the Channel Islands were coming to an end and gales were now forecast.

We had left the Minquiers behind us and were approaching the Rade St Malo with the wind force five from astern and rising. I decided to hand the main and run in under genoa. I put the engine on, turned into wind and lowered the mainsail. Suddenly there was a thud and the propeller was no longer working. I stopped the engine as *Blue Pearl*, under genoa alone, turned down wind. With our light crew there was no way I could hoist the mainsail without an engine, so I decided to run into St Malo under reefed genoa. We tuned the VHF to channel 16 and immediately heard a gale imminent warning. The wind increased to force seven and we were moving at five knots in a bumpy sea. I did not like the thought of entering a strange harbour in a gale-force wind under headsail only and without an engine, so I asked Joan to call up Harbour Control and ask for assistance. I heard Joan's reply:

'Would you please speak more slowly,' pause, 'and in English?'

A pause from St Malo, then a heavily accented voice, speaking slowly and in English, said, 'Please give your latitude and longitude and say what is wrong.'

Joan replied, 'We are just passing the buoy before the harbour entrance. We are under foresail only and have no engine. We need assistance with mooring.'

'We will meet you in the harbour in a motor-boat.'

'Prepare an anchor just in case,' I told Joan.

As we approached the harbour launch the skipper told us he would take us to pick up a mooring, for which we prepared, then suddenly, without warning, he changed his mind and towed us to a nearby pontoon at St Servan. We had no fenders out and the wind, now force eight, was blowing hard onto the pontoon, which had a rough metal edge that badly scraped our lovely new boat. It needed four men to hold us off and all our fenders plus rubber tyres to cushion us against the pontoon in the strong wind and tide. During the night the tide dropped, the wind died and we had a good night.

The next day I tried to get the Marina engineer to look at our problem. He was not available till Saturday. I checked the Morse controls and found nothing wrong. Maybe the propeller had fallen off!

At 0830 on Saturday two boats and four engineers came to tow *Blue Pearl* fifty yards in calm water to a position alongside the wall on the slipway where we could dry out. The men immediately disappeared. I rigged warps to hold *Blue Pearl* against the wall. As we dried out all was revealed. An old and rotting piece of fisherman's warp, with frayed ends and full of marine life, was wound tightly round the propeller shaft. I cleaned this. The clutch engaged and the shaft turned satisfactorily. I took the opportunity to scrape the boat's bottom, where the large number of barnacles made me question the quality of our anti-fouling.

After a long wait, the engineers turned up in the afternoon, tapped the propeller with a hammer, put the boat into gear (total time ten minutes), and presented me with a bill for 985 francs or £98. Apart from the short tow I had done all the work! When the tide came in Joan and I motored the boat to a neighbouring and more sheltered pontoon.

The next day, 3rd September, we left in bright sunshine and passed through the Rance Barrage. The Rance was lovely, a large stretch of water, where the natural habitat had been enhanced, not destroyed. We motored quietly, listing depths from the echo-sounder, to St Suliac, where we picked up a buoy and spent a nervous evening awaiting (a) the owner's return, or (b) the fall of the tide to leave us high and dry. Neither happened and we went to bed still wondering.

St Suliac is a pleasant, sleepy village, with an old church and a butcher's, baker's and grocer's. The lady Port Superintendent was charming and told us that we were on a visitor's buoy, C15, which had been allotted to a yellow boat that had come in late and taken another mooring. She also told us that until 18th September the Barrage retained four metres of water above datum, which meant that we had plenty of sailing water and trouble-free moorings.

After two days exploring the Rance we returned through the Barrage to the Bassin Vauban in the centre of St Malo, where we expected to meet our granddaughter, Julia, who was currently working in Paris. Three-quarters of the city had been devastated in 1944 after D Day and was re-built in local granite. The old ramparts, however, had survived and, as access was only minutes from the boat, we took the opportunity to walk all round them.

While we were waiting for Julia, Don Campbell, who had made our berth cushions, arrived in his boat *Uomi*, and tied up alongside. We invited him and his crew, Mike Etheridge, a friend from Probus, for drinks and a chatty evening. We also took a coach trip to Mont St Michel, which I had last seen in 1939 when hitch-hiking across France.

Julia was not on her train and, instead of the special meal of roast beef and plum pudding that Joan had prepared to greet her, we spent a quiet evening dining alone. The night was very dark, the harbour ill-lit and we wondered if Julia would ever find us. She arrived at midnight, having had to work on Sunday morning, which caused her to miss her train. She had asked the railway to give us a message at St Malo railway station, where we were waiting for her, and for the harbour police to alert us. The railway had simply ignored her request and the harbour police claimed that they could not find the boat, although it was in a conspicuous position alongside the quay.

A late morning in bed was followed by a walk along the ramparts in a heavy mist. After lunch we set off through the Barrage to St Suliac, where we introduced Julia to our favourite harbour mistress. Then followed two delightful days, showing Julia the boat and allowing her to sail it and develop her skills.

Julia had first sailed with us, kept in check by her safety harness, when she was three years old in *Petrel Two*, our first boat, a twenty-three-foot sloop. After that she came to us every summer holiday and sailed regularly with us. She learned to steer the boat and bring her up to our mooring when she was only six years old. At seven she was rowing the dinghy freely in tidal waters. At nine she was taking the dinghy under engine on her own to pick up passengers or stores. At ten she was taking bearings and could plot a running fix. She had sailed with us in *Pendragon* and the chartered Centaur. She loved taking the helm, and the wilder the weather the more she enjoyed herself. Now, aged twenty-two, with university behind her, she came for a brief interlude to enjoy the tranquillity of the Rance.

50

At the end of her long weekend with us we sailed back to St Servan for Julia to catch the train back to Paris. Gales in the next three days kept us in harbour and we were joined by Jimmy and Jenny Langlois, tomato farmers from Guernsey, in their motor-boat *Claire Louise*. We exchanged visits and became firm friends.

We left on Saturday 6th September at 0930 in a force six wind from SSE, sailing well with one reef and two-thirds genoa at six-and-a-half knots. The wind backed and increased to force seven and I put on a preventer for the mainsail. We were now sailing at seven knots, a glorious, exhilarating sail. At 1300, south-west of the Minquiers, the wind dropped to SW force one, but picked up a little at 1415 when our speed crept up to three-and-a-half knots. We were now sailing with the preventer on the main and the genoa goose-winged, not our best point of sailing. We would have liked a spinnaker for this wind but I had not been able to afford one. We arrived in St Helier at 1450, where Jimmy and Jenny took our warps and moored us alongside *Claire Louise*. Because of the gale warnings they had cut short their passage to Guernsey. Again we exchanged visits.

On Wednesday 20th September the shipping forecast still gave gale warnings for Plymouth, but we decided to set off for Dartmouth and stop at Guernsey if the weather was still inclement. It was bad so we put into St Peter Port, where Jimmy recommended an Italian restaurant, Giovanni's, for lunch. In the evening Joan's diary records:

We slept in the sun all the afternoon. Later some Canadians came aboard for afternoon tea. F cooked a lovely evening meal – scrambled eggs on toast!

Gales were still forecast for the Plymouth area so we remained in harbour, and on Tuesday we were invited for tea at Jimmy and Jenny's home. We saw their extensive greenhouses with modern computerised control of ventilation and watering. They supplied one of the big supermarkets and their tomatoes had to be perfect.

We left Guernsey at 1800 on Thursday 26th September, missing the shipping forecast. The wind was SE force one and, with the genoa flogging uselessly and unsure of what weather to expect, we continued under reefed main and engine.

From the log:

0330 Sea became disturbed and choppy. I thought it must be the result of previous gales.

0400 Estimated position Dartmouth 145° 20 miles. Joan spotted the loom of a light that could be Start Point, more to port than expected. I was unable to see it.

Almost immediately we were struck by a great increase of wind from the south. Blue Pearl almost broached to. Wind force eight. Too much sail. Turned with difficulty into wind and got sail down. Difficult putting it to sleep because of steep, short-pitched waves knocking me about and because of the height of the boom above the deck. Joan found the boat difficult to control in the dark with the steep seas. Ran before the wind under bare poles for an hour while I secured the sail.

A small group of trawlers had been three to four miles on the port bow and another group a similar distance on the starboard bow. When all was secure we saw that the trawlers had dispersed and appeared to be making for home. We had temporarily lost our bearings and did not know which group we were now near. I thought that the trawlers ahead and on our port beam were making for Brixham so I followed them. However, they appeared to be making east of our course and at 0530 I decided that they were not making for Brixham so I resumed our course of 330 degrees, under engine. Visibility was now down to one mile.

At 0700 the mainsail blew out of its tiers and became a wild thing. It was impossible to deal with on the present course because of the pitching and rolling. Once again we turned down wind and I had a wrestle with the sail. I fixed my safety-harness to the kicking-strap eye-plate on the boom. Even so I was bruised and thrown about, once down the hatchway. Eventually I got it under control and the boat back on course. I thought that we were now well east of our course.

0800 At last we identified our position, three miles east of Hope's Nose. We saw no sign of Berry Head Light. We altered course to 210 degrees to clear Berry Head. The wind was now force eight, increasing, from the west. A small trawler on our port quarter had accompanied us most of the way since the gale struck and made an impressive sight butting into the wild sea. I wondered how we appeared to him. I was grateful for his company. He now crossed astern of us, probably making for Brixham Harbour.

0830 Sighted the Day Mark and confirmed our position. A large merchant ship lay athwart our course off Berry Head. Just as we started to go astern of him he went astern so we resumed our course.

0900 Sighted the Mewstone and steered visually to clear it. The wind was now dead ahead and had increased to force nine. The sea was steep pitched, sometimes knocking us back. Waves and spume, blown horizontally off the crests, swept over our deck continuously. I thought that our light spray hood would not stand up to it so we kept it furled and every wave took us in the face. It was difficult to spot fishing-buoys, which we felt were menacing us. The noise was a roar rather than a whistle. I put the boat on autohelm and it coped better than I did. Because of the water coming over the boat I was unable to see, but Joan did very well and managed to spot the buoys and enable me to steer round them.

1100 We thankfully altered course into Dartmouth. Once past the Castles we were in a different and much kinder world. We had no problem in picking up our mooring, though John had removed the spar buoys. For about seven hours we had been buffeted by wind and sea and were very tired. We had a hot drink and got our heads down.

I hoisted a 'Q' flag whilst on our mooring, but no Customs Officers arrived, so we took the forms to the Old Customs House.

Although the storm had been frightening at first and worrying for a time, as we gained control and saw how well the boat and gear stood up to it we began to relax and, in a perverse way, to enjoy it. The wildness made me realise that some of the pictures of storms at sea we had seen were more realistic than I had appreciated.

Much later in our cruising I realised the mistakes I had made. In gale conditions, tacking against the wind, *Blue Pearl* was much easier to sail with a tiny foresail and the mizzen. Under this rig she was much kinder to the crew.

We had intended to make one more cruise in 1989, along the coast to the south west. We left on Saturday 14th October, but ran into the equinoctial gales and after a few days in Salcombe returned to Dartmouth, where we arranged for *Blue Pearl* to be laid up for the winter at Mill Creek, ten minutes' drive from our house.

4

Brittany

At Mill Creek I asked David Heale, the resident engineer, to service our engine and provide us with a hot-water system. David, an excellent engineer, serviced the Perkins himself and the only problem we ever had with it was in Sicily when I failed to tighten a brass nut on a plastic bolt properly and let air into the fuel system. The mechanic who installed our hot-water system was another matter. David designed a system that used heat exchange from the engine so that whenever we entered harbour, as we always did under engine, we finished up with hot water. In the hot-water tank he fitted an electric immersion heater for use in marinas where 240-volt electricity was available. Hot and cold water taps were fitted on the galley sink and on the washbasin in the heads, and, as a safeguard, the spigot sea-water pump was left on the sink.

When we launched from Mill Creek and used the system for the first time we found an unpleasant taste in the cold water; the mechanic had used rubber pipe instead of a plastic pipe specially designed for cold water. The hot-water pipe leaked in more than one place because the mechanic used plastic instead of rubber and fitted the wrong size jubilee clips. A leak occurred below deck where the pipes to the galley and heads joined; the mechanic had bodged a brazen Y piece instead of fitting a proper plastic junction.

Our outboard had broken down continually and I gave it to David to sort out the trouble. He concluded that it was not worth repairing and supplied us with a Yamaha, which served us well throughout our cruises.

Whilst ashore I took the opportunity of ordering a Decca for John Rencher to fit. This gave us trouble for the first few weeks after launching, largely through my own ignorance, but John came several times and solved my problems.

Joan and I repaired the scratches made at St Malo, cleaned and polished the hull, scrubbed the bottom and gave it two coats of anti-fouling. I renovated our tender, which I had made twenty years before, replacing the teak and re-building part of the glass-fibre hull. I completed the cockpit table and fitted it, folded flat, into a stowage position underneath the main-hatch stairs, and fitted U-bolts in the cockpit that did double duty as catches for the table supports and as D-rings for our lifelines. The past season's sailing had shown us the need for more fairleads, amidships and on the stern, and for two more cleats on the stern. We fitted all these at Mill Creek.

We launched on Wednesday 8th May 1990, and spent several days trying out the new gear, the hot-water system, the Decca and the Yamaha, and correcting the faults. On the 17th we set out on a trial run to the south west, but when we found the Decca still not working we stopped at Salcombe and returned three days later to Dartmouth.

In the next ten days we dealt with problems affecting our windows at home. When our house was renovated we had double-glazing installed; all the windows in the south-facing wall had clouded over through a fault in the manufacture. The manufacturer refused to take any notice of my correspondence, so I decided to have the double-glazing replaced by another firm and sue the original makers for the cost – £1500. It was during this period that the work was carried out and I dealt with the court and the defendant's solicitor.

On 14th June we joined a Yacht Club rally to Torquay and on the 27th we left for a long cruise to Brittany. An hour after we left large drops of water were seen coming out of the heat exchange system, so we returned to harbour and sent for David. This was when he dealt with the faulty piping. It was not until 3rd July that we finally left for l'Abervrac'h.

I used the Decca to give us our position each hour on the hour, and a series of crosses on the chart marked our progress. The course to the Lizen Ven Buoy, outside l'Abervrac'h, was 202 degrees and at 1500 we were twenty-one miles from Dartmouth, two miles west of our course. When the tide turned easterly at 2200 we were driven further east. The wind had now increased and veered to

SSW. I took in the mizzen, put one reef in the main and reduced the genoa to two-thirds, ready for the night.

Shortly after 0200, with sixty-eight miles on the log, a fishing-boat, not trawling, suddenly altered course towards us and passed fifty feet ahead. I feared a collision until the last moment, but under sail we were unable to take avoiding action.

The ship's log now takes up the tale:

0300 Log 70.4 miles. Wind has increased to force six. Reduced to half genoa. Still one reef in the main. Sea becoming rough. Joan has managed two half-hour catnaps and I one. Tacked on to course of 245°.

0400 49° 71' north. 3° 50' west. Although we have logged four miles in the last hour we have made good only 2.4 miles. Wind has increased to gale force. Sea rough. Joan went below to make coffee and buttered buns, but spent too long in the galley and was sick [she was sick only twice in the whole of her sailing career]. *The coffee and buns were welcome.*

Decided to furl the genoa and put on the engine; this would enable us to steer a better course, closer to the wind.

0600 49° 5' north. 4° 2' west. Log 83.4. Made good five miles in the last hour, a combination of engine and sail and the turn of the tide. The 0555 shipping forecast has revealed our plight; there are warnings of gales in every single area around Britain and down to Sole and Biscay. There is no way we can avoid them. I briefly considered Roscoff; but on looking at the chart decided it was too complicated to navigate in the present conditions, raining heavily, sea very rough, visibility poor. Heading into the sea makes the boat slam down and, when I went down for the 0800 navigation and to grease the stern tube, the engine smell hit me and I was sick three times in the next two hours. With these conditions and if visibility were still poor as we approached l'Abervrac'h, I began to consider keeping out to sea and heaving-to to ride out the gale.

Joan and I have each managed a catnap, stretched out on the lee cockpit seat, covered by a groundsheet; we actually slept, in spite of the gale. 'George' does most of the work. The Autohelm 6000, combined with our special Whitlock drive, is a powerful instrument and copes well in these difficult conditions.

0915 Log 98.5. Wind now force nine. Difficult getting up and down the hatch. Both of us badly bruised. Decided to tack south as the wind has veered to the WSW. This will close the land and maybe the seas will be quieter.

1000 Wind easing to force seven.

1100 48° 49' north, 4° 13' west. Wind force six. Sea bumpy and difficult, but good progress.

1130 Caught sight of Ile de Balz, seven miles on port bow. Switched over to new Decca waypoint, which gave Lizen Ven Buoy bearing 238°, distance 15 miles. Tacked towards the west and continued tacking along the track to Lizen ven.

1830 Lizen Ven just to port. This confirms our Decca position, a great relief as this is the first time we have used Decca in earnest. In the past four hours the wind has remained at force six and the sea has eased. Visibility has continued to improve and the sun has come out. With all this our spirits have risen and we begin to look forward to l'Abervrac'h. We have even seen another yacht, approaching us, probably from l'Abervrac'h.

2000 Moored to Buoy No. 13. Both very tired indeed. I had a headache, took paracetamol and lay down for half-an-hour. Joan tidied up the boat and prepared hot soup. I recovered and we both thoroughly enjoyed our supper and then retired to bed and an exhausted sleep.

Next morning the wind was still force six, but the sun was shining and we slept most of it on our comfortable, six-foot-long cockpit seat cushions. In the afternoon we decided to go ashore, but in the strong wind the harbour assistant was unable to control the harbour launch. Either he bumped against our boat or failed to hold it alongside. Joan decided not to risk it. Ashore I met Fritz and Marion, from the fifty-foot Dutch ketch *Atlantis*, and invited them aboard for drinks.

Friday was a lovely sunny day and we walked up to the Centre Ville, where there was a good butcher's, baker's and grocer's. The grocer, a rugby and football fan (he had played for Mitcham FC), was full of the World Cup and Linnaker. He personally recommended the best wine to buy. I became involved in a three-way discussion. A young Dutchman, who could speak English but not French, wanted to know where to buy waterproofing for his tent flysheet. I translated both ways, English to French and French to English.

After fifteen minutes, during which all trading ceased and the usual French crowd collected, I managed to get the message across. One lady had become so engrossed that she nearly walked out without paying her bill, amidst a lot of good humour.

That evening Joan cooked a meat pie, followed by the fruit cake she had baked at home. Fritz and Marion came aboard after dinner and stayed until midnight.

The next day, Saturday 7th July, the weather forecast was bad, with the force six wind moderating but fog developing. We had a lazy day in the boat. I prepared waypoints and navigation for our next passage, to Camaret, and did some routine maintenance, and Joan washed clothes, tidied the boat and prepared another excellent evening meal – roast lamb, followed by plum crumble and washed down with the footballing grocer's claret, Chateau Fontanet 1988, a smooth, dry wine.

Later, as the wind got up and the tide ran out, because the buoys were too close to each other boats began to drift together and I spent much of the night fending off the boat next to us, on No. 8 buoy.

The next day, in a good wind, we had a sparkling sail through the Chenal du Four to Camaret. I was particularly impressed with the Decca. The Chenal du Four is a difficult, winding passage, marked out by a series of buoys. I put the key buoys as waypoints on the Decca and used them to navigate safely. Identifying the buoys was easy. This happy day was crowned when Fritz and Marion, who had invited us in to drinks on our arrival, came aboard after dinner for a game of bridge.

From Camaret we had a slow, lazy passage, in hazy sunshine and a calm sea, to Morgat, a good marina with the outer three berths on the first pontoon capable of taking our draught. That evening we walked three miles to La Roof, a restaurant recommended by the harbour assistant, but the meal was 'nouvelle cuisine' and I did not enjoy it. The next day we shopped, enjoyed the walk round the headland and had our evening meal in the cockpit on our new table.

The next day we had another slow passage in calm seas to Douarnenez, eleven miles in five and a half hours, with the wind rarely above force two. In sailing you take the smooth with the rough and use the smooth passage to relax and rest. At Douarnenez we decided to go into Treboul Harbour, where we berthed at a good pontoon, next to a fifty-foot German ketch. At 2300 a big fireworks display on the eve of Quatorze Juillet brought hundreds of spectators along the quay. We had a grandstand view from our foredeck and it was 0100 before we retired to bed.

We suffered the usual problem of not having the right connection for the pontoon electricity and walked a dreary two miles along the main road to the Rallye Supermarket to buy it, then back to Centre Ville, Douarnenez, for a pleasant lunch in a café overlooking the harbour. In the afternoon I fitted the connections for electricity and water. At last we were able to charge our batteries and fill our water tanks, and use our electric kettle and toaster and the boat's 240-volt lighting. In the evening Joan provided another excellent meal, melon, steak and plum pudding, and I provided the sherry and claret.

We left the pontoon at 0630 in a thick mist with the wind force three. From the log:

Motor-sailed for seven miles on a course of 259°. Mist thickening. Visibility down to fifty yards. Suddenly heard a Frenchman shouting that there was danger ahead of us. Immediately turned to starboard, away from land and potential hazard. Decided to give up the passage to Benodet and return to Douarnenez. Engine off. Sailed under main and genoa at four knots.

The next day:

Left pontoon at Treboul. Almost no wind. Sea smooth. Visibility about five miles. The sails would only hinder progress so decided to continue under engine at about five knots. Course 259° along the coast.

0820 Passed the jagged rocks standing out to sea at Damon, where yesterday the fisherman shouted a warning and waved us out to sea. Then we were within two hundred yards of the rocks and heading directly towards them.

0830 The mizzle came down again and stayed with us. Visibility down to less than half-a-mile. Coast barely visible.

0925 Decca brought us exactly to Basse Jaune. Using Decca waypoints steered round Pointe du Raz. The La Plate Tower and Vielle Lighthouse made a splendid, dramatic scene in the mist against the rocky headland.

Across Audierne Bay visibility improved. Suddenly a fishing-boat altered course and came straight for us. At the last minute, as I turned to avoid him, he turned away. This was another example of unprofessional conduct shown by some fishermen.

At 1630 we arrived at Benodet and picked up a delightful visitor's mooring. The next day we explored Benodet and shopped, and at 1600 motored up river to Lauros, where we anchored in a small bay. The following day we took the dinghy up to Quimper, about an hour's run, where we lunched, explored the ancient capital of Cornouaille and visited the cathedral, twinned with Truro Cathedral.

On Thursday 19th July we left the anchorage at 0600 and caught the last of the ebb down the river. We passed lovely, wooded banks with occasional chateaux, peaceful and quiet in the misty, early-morning light.

We left Benodet under full sail at 0700 and sailed the seventeen miles to Concarneau in four and a quarter hours in calm seas and a light wind. Concarneau has an easy entrance and we found a comfortable berth in the Outer Harbour Marina.

We strolled round the interesting walled city and went to a bank to cash a Eurocheque. At other French banks I had always had my passport with me, but never been asked to produce it. Following Murphy's Law, this time it was asked for and when I could not produce it the clerk refused to serve me. I offered proof of my identity with my Dartmouth Yacht Club card, Exeter Flotilla card (including photo), OAP card, bank card, RAC card and, finally, my driving licence. He studied all of these with great care. Our conversation was in French and I became sure that he could not understand a word of English. After half an hour he finally gave way, accepted my driving licence and let me have my money.

In the evening we went to a very French restaurant in the Ville Close, inside the walls. For starters I tried *fruits de mer*, expecting an hors d'oeuvre of shelled fish. I had never chosen *fruits de mer* from a restaurant in England, but when in Rome! I was presented with a platter of unshelled shellfish and a variety of utensils. I was unable to de-winkle the first winkle (there were more than twenty of them). Joan, having finished her pâté, took over the de-winkling for me while I concentrated on a slender leg of crab with the nutcrackers. French people around us were intrigued by our combined efforts and almost applauded when I popped the last winkle into my mouth.

The court case about our windows was to take place in Torquay on Friday 31st July so we decided to interrupt our cruise, sail back to Dartmouth and continue the cruise after the court case. We left on 20th July under full sail and swept through the Raz de Seine at ten knots with the strong tide pushing us, arriving at Camaret, a distance of sixty-two miles, in eight hours forty minutes, our fastest passage to date.

On Saturday we left Camaret at 1030 and were through the Chenal du Four at 1345. The wind was NE force three so we decided to make for Falmouth, course 358°, distance 90 miles. Under full sail our speed was four and a half knots. We maintained this until 1800 when the wind died and we started the engine to motor-sail. At 2310 the wind backed to the north, dead-heading us for Falmouth. With the log reading 59.2 miles we decided to make for Dartmouth and altered course to 077°. The wind was now down to force one so I handed the genoa and sailed close to the wind under main and motor. Visibility was about five miles, but clear overhead. We could see stars, but no horizon in the haze. We maintained this course throughout the night, with 'George' steering and Joan and I taking half-hour watches and catnaps, followed by half-an-hour together for refreshments and social chat.

From the log:

At 0200 a large ship steered towards us and then slowed down to our speed on a parallel course about half-a-mile distant. At first we thought he was a fisherman trawling. After fifteen minutes he turned away and disappeared.

0300 The same ship (we called him 'Charlie') again approached and laid a parallel course, half-a-mile distant. Again, after fifteen minutes, he turned away. We could identify him by three lights forming a triangular pattern on his starboard side.

0400 Charlie again. Same procedure. We now decided he was a Navy ship, training officers in interception and shadowing. We were the target. We could only see his lights and he did not come near enough for us to identify him.

0500 Charlie again. He completely spoiled my catnap as he appeared at the beginning of Joan's watch. We could now see him a little more clearly in the half-light. He appeared to be a largish merchant ship, five to ten thousand tons, with the bridge and superstructure well aft and the hull long and low in the water.

0600 I had decided to call Charlie by lamp and ask him who he was. Only he did not appear this time and we did not see him again.

Months later I was attending a Probus lecture by a Customs Officer on drug smuggling. At the end of his talk he said, 'Now, some of you are sailors. If you see anything strange will you please report it to Customs?'

I told him about our cross-channel adventure.

'Is your boat a ketch?'

'Yes.'

'Thirty five to forty feet in length?'

'Yes.'

'That,' he said, 'was the enemy.'

He asked if his colleague in the Drug Squad could come and see me. This officer wanted to know all about the episode. I showed him our log and the chart, with the position where we met the ship still marked, and drew a silhouette of the vessel. He was particularly interested in the three lights.

He told me that the ship was almost certainly a drug smuggler trying to make contact with his British tie-up and that we were the third ketch to have been approached in this manner. The other two had been blinded by searchlights and we were the first to give some description.

I told him that I had intended to call the ship by Aldis lamp and ask for his identity, but he had not shown up again.

'Just as well,' the officer said, 'otherwise you might not be here to tell the tale.'

Anyway, at 0900 the visibility was down to one mile, but the wind was increasing. At 1100 it was force five and we had a beat into a NE wind and a choppy sea. At 1330 on 2nd July we arrived at Dartmouth.

The next week was taken up with finalising our court case, which was heard at Torquay Magistrate's Court, before a judge, on 31st July. The case lasted two and a half hours. I conducted my own case, using Rob as a witness and an affidavit by the firm that installed our replacement windows. In presenting the case I had described the upset we had felt as our lovely view through the lounge windows gradually diminished. The judge told me that we could claim compensation for the emotional distress and asked me if I wished to do so. I thought about it for a minute or two, but such compensation is against my principles. I wanted only a return of the £1500 we had spent, and the judge awarded this in full with costs. The defendant was given a month to pay. We had won. It was time to resume our cruise.

On Saturday 4th August we left for Brest. The passage of 134 miles was uneventful and took thirty-two and a half hours.

On 8th August another easy passage took us through the Raz de Seine to Audierne, where we anchored just outside the mooring buoys in the Anse de St Evrette. The next day we left at 0900 for Loctudy, passing a basking shark ten feet away and a school of twelve porpoises. Off Loctudy we took the Karek-Saoz Buoy wide as directed in the Pilot and ran aground. The channel was, in fact, close to the buoy. As the tide was rising we quickly came off.

Loctudy is a pleasant fishing harbour with a good supermarket, a boulangerie, boucherie and fishmarket. We enjoyed the spectacle of the fishing boats returning en masse, racing in on the incoming tide to be first to unload and auction their catches in the fish hall. We bought fresh fillets of sole and enjoyed our evening meal. As usual, we slept soundly.

We liked Loctudy so much that we decided to stay on. At 0700 next morning we made an early dinghy exploration along the wooded banks of the river to Pont l'Abbé, a charming, small town. On the return a yacht grounded on the falling tide and we tried unsuccessfully to tow him off. Later we visited Ile Tudy and watched the wonder of the water rising and cutting off the land. After an afternoon's sleep we went ashore, again to watch the return of the fishing fleet. We bought huge, newly caught sardines in the fish market and after another very satisfying meal we tidied the boat and prepared for the next day's sail to Ile de Groix.

We arrived in Port-Tudy, Ile de Groix, at 1425 and tied on, with many others, to a single, large mooring buoy. The next day, Sunday, we went for a walk through Groix (Le Bourg) along the coastal path to Loc Maris, stopping for lunch at a restaurant at Grands Sables, a good lunch and a pleasant walk. In the evening Jean Pierre and Christian, from the next boat, gave us a glass of Bordeaux to celebrate our seventieth birthdays (due the following December) and came aboard for a chat and a tour of the boat. Jean Pierre's father was a wine producer and he told us of the excellent cheap Bordeaux wines that come from just outside the Bordeaux region.

On Monday 17th we left for Belle-Ile and moored in the outer harbour between buoys. We found this harbour dirty and overcrowded, with too many boats on the buoys bumping each other. We were glad to leave the next morning for Crouesty, Port Navalo, a big marina with limited visitors' moorings. Our pontoon was a long way from the Capitainerie and other facilities. This was our most expensive marina so far.

On a dull, grey morning on Wednesday 15th August we left Crouesty under engine in a blustery SW wind, rain and mist. We swept through the entrance to the Morbihan, with a six-knot tide pushing us, and raced to Ile aux Moins, where we anchored off the NE tip, to the east of the buoys. It was too rough to go ashore in the dinghy so we rested in the boat. That evening we had fireworks on the harbour wall. A boat named *Bambi* arrived and, to my mind, anchored too close to us. At 2300 she swung round and touched us. We were asleep, but I got up quickly and found her snubbing our anchor chain. Fortunately, the owners, who had gone ashore, returned shortly afterwards and moved their boat to a vacant mooring.

In the morning we took the dinghy ashore and thoroughly enjoyed a pleasant stroll to and beyond Le Bourg, past interesting cottages, both old and new, that blended well together, with wisteria and bougainvillea in full bloom. One lady, whose garden we were admiring, seeing our interest in her gorgeous show of lavatera, a flower we had not met before, offered us some seeds from her plants. (We grew these at home the next year and had an equally lovely show.) We decided to return after our visit to Vannes and explore further.

The course to Vannes, although twisting and turning past innumerable tiny islands, was well buoyed. We were running under headsail only, not a very manoeuvrable rig. A small yacht, under full sail and going at just our speed, gybed three times across our bows, giving us some anxious moments.

As we approached the narrows I decided to furl the genoa and proceed under engine. The furling gear jammed and the situation became quite tricky as many boats were coming out and blocking the narrow way in. Joan had to steer through them while I fixed the furling gear. In the entrance to Vannes, just before the bridge, we were too far to starboard and just touched bottom but soon came off. We were one of a number of yachts, too large for the waiting pontoon (eight metres), jilling around and awaiting the opening. When the bridge opened at last a crowd of forty to fifty yachts sorted themselves out and proceeded in an orderly fashion up the channel to the moorings. We were the third out on our pontoon and had three yachts outside us.

The next day was a relaxing one. We explored Vannes, the lanes, the cathedral and the imposing buildings. We had our evening meal in the Café aux Halles in good company. I tried to order the meal in my very best French, but the waiter seemed unable to understand me. Nor could I understand him. After a while, in halting French, he said he was '*Ecossais*'! We reverted to English and broad Scots.

'You speak English quite well,' Joan said, 'for a Scotsman.'

On Saturday morning we enjoyed our visit to the extensive market, where we bought meat, vegetables and fruit, but the wines were limited and expensive.

The bridge opened at 1610 (one and a half hours either side of high water) and we sailed to Ile aux Moins, where we picked up a buoy, but were told we were too big and must anchor. At first we had difficulty in anchoring and made three attempts before our anchor held in a better position farther away from the slipway.

The next day we took a picnic lunch and walked to the south side of the island along a path marked '*sentiers sauvages*', with a variety of wild flowers. Back aboard we found that our anchorage suffered from eddies and once or twice we turned a full circle. A good hundred metres is needed between boats.

The next morning, on the slack tide, we made our way easily out of the Morbihan and sailed quietly, under full rig, to Port Haliguen, a good marina with good facilities and close to Quiberon, which we explored.

The next day we sailed quietly to La Forêt. Charles, sailing alone in a Twister out of Kingswear (opposite us at Dartmouth), invited us for drinks and then came aboard us for a baguette and cheese lunch.

At 1700 our granddaughter, Julia, arrived to crew home to Dartmouth. On Thursday 23rd August we fuelled at the pontoon, ready for the journey. The mechanic was so interested in Julia that he allowed the fuel to overflow and flood the deck! He soon cleared it up and we sailed away under full rig in a very light wind to Benodet, where we picked up a visitor's buoy.

The next day I gave Julia some practice at picking up a buoy, then we set off under main and motor in a light headwind to Audierne, where we anchored off the breakwater.

After a quiet night we left the anchorage under main, genoa and engine and motor-sailed through the Raz de Seine, but once through we cut the engine and sailed under full rig at four knots to Camaret, good visibility, carefree sailing.

Julia chose a very French restaurant for our evening meal and it was very good, but nearly spoiled by a noisy table nearby – all English.

On Sunday we left our berth at 0700 and motor-sailed hard at seven knots to catch the last of the tide up the Chenal du Four. The wind was southerly, force one or less, and we continued motor-sailing through the Chenal, now well known to us (our fourth time that year) and on a general course of 358 degrees towards Falmouth.

In the afternoon the wind backed to the west, force two. We stopped the engine and our speed under main and genoa was three and a half knots, just right to arrive off Falmouth with enough light at dawn to see the fishing buoys.

That evening, conditions were so good that we decided to have our meal in the cockpit, three courses with wine on a properly laid table with napkins and side plates. The sun was a ball of fire in the west; the sea was calm with a glint of gold; the boat was sailing upright, with 'George' in control. Throughout our long, leisurely meal we were entertained by a large school of porpoises that had joined us as we left the Chenal du Four and stayed with us until we approached Falmouth. It was magical, one of the most memorable evenings of my life.

That night the phosphorescence from the wakes of the porpoises was dramatic as they sped to and from the boat. We saw several shoals of smaller fish breaking surface and seemingly attacking us, leaving hundreds of phosphorescent streaks.

We used a three-watch system, one hour on duty, one on standby and one off. Off duty meant an hour below and standby a sleep on the cockpit cushion, so we all enjoyed two hours' sleep out of three. Apart from manoeuvring round fishing boats we had no problems and the night passed easily.

At 0700 on Monday we picked up the Lizard Light at fifteen miles and at 0930 arrived at Falmouth and berthed in the marina. Jill and Rob joined us for supper on Tuesday and Julia left us the following morning.

The passage to Dartmouth was in easy stages, calling at Fowey, Newton Ferrers and Salcombe, and we arrived in Dartmouth on Saturday 1st September 1990.

5

Four Gales to Gibraltar

By October I had decided to leave the boat on its moorings over the winter and, to this end, I replaced the existing warps with chains to guard against the winter gales.

We were now committed to sailing to Gibraltar and the Mediterranean, and spending three or four years exploring it. All our plans and efforts would go towards this end. In November we ordered an awning from Don Campbell, specially designed for the Mediterranean, that extended over the cockpit and deck as far as the mainmast, with flaps on either side that could be lowered to keep out wind or sun.

In January 1991 I went to the London Boat Show with Alan Burwin, who sold electronic equipment in Dartmouth, and with his guidance decided on a Raytheon radar and a GPS that could be interfaced, and an Italian generator, which I could use to charge my 12 volt batteries and would also generate 240 volt electricity for my power tools. These would be supplied and fitted by Alan.

On Wednesday 9th January 1991 disaster struck. We had a telephone call from the harbour master, saying that a neighbouring boat had broken away from its moorings in the gale and crashed into ours, doing some damage. I went down immediately and found that the hull had been severely scraped along its starboard side, the gunwale was broken in two places and our new boarding ladder damaged and cracked. The other boat's owner met me, agreed that his boat was responsible and showed me the frayed warp, weakened by rust from the metal eyepiece. I privately thought that his warps were too thin to withstand a winter gale.

The owner's insurance company asked me to obtain two quotations for repairs and chose the cheaper one of £1000 from Philip and

Son. The following month this insurance company informed me that they would not cover my insurance, but would treat it as a natural disaster and therefore knock for knock. I obtained a letter from the harbour master stating that the warps used by the other vessel's owner were insufficient for the winter gales and that the gale in question was quite usual in January for Dartmouth. I sent a copy of this letter to the owner's insurance company and to my insurance company, whom I had kept informed.

When the other insurance company refused to budge I asked my insurance company to take them to court. They refused, but said I could do so at my own expense. I simply did not have the money for this. My company now took on the insurance claim and cancelled my no claims bonus, which, over the next three years, cost me over £500.

In December 1990 I had given a talk at the Yacht Club on 'Building a Boat from a Bare Hull', illustrated with slides of the work in progress. This had gone down well and in February I was asked to give it to Probus and to another club.

The other feature of the spring was the development of our social life. We had given dinner or lunch parties in the past, but now, with the prospect of spending several months abroad each year, we decided to concentrate our invitations into two big parties. The first was on 27th January, when we had eighteen to lunch. In preparation we had bought a hostess console that provided four heated containers for vegetables and a heated plate rack. We stood this in our serving hatch for guests to help themselves. The routine soon established itself and we now benefited from the design of our large living room and kitchen. Over the years the guests grew in number and eventually we catered for thirty people, all seated at tables. The kitchen and living room were linked by a serving hatch, six feet wide with a beautiful oak surround. Joan served the meat at one end and our guests helped themselves to vegetables from the hot dishes at the other. A separate table provided cold meats and salads.

As always, we shared the preparations. Joan prepared and cooked the meal, on this first occasion steak and kidney pie, fish pie and roast chicken, followed by a chocolate gateau, peach pie or trifle, while I vacuumed the room, re-arranged the furniture and set the tables with cutlery, napkins and wine glasses. We both received our guests and while Joan talked to them I went round with drinks. Joan served the meat and I served the wine. When all were served

70

we joined our guests at one or other of the tables. After the meal we all retired to the armchairs in the other half of the room for coffee and conversation.

A week later we gave a second party for twenty guests. Of course, there were return invitations. All our guests invited us back, and the large party became a feature of Dartmouth life. Our problem over the next three years was to fit our busy social life into our five months' residence in England.

During these early months of 1991 I spent many hours revising and practising my astro-navigation. I had obtained a Yachtmaster (Ocean) Certificate years before, with my navigation based on the haversine method. Now I converted to the RAF method, also used by the Royal Navy, using an assumed position and tables. I was still not confident in my GPS and wanted my sextant as a backup.

Joan and I also worked on our log of the Brittany cruise, putting together excerpts from the ship's log, Joan's diary and our photographs. We entered this for the Club's 'Best Kept Log' competition and were awarded the Tolman Cup.

Martin, my nephew, who had built his own boat and sailed along the east coast, and his wife, Jenne, wanted some deep sea experience and offered to come with us as far as Gibraltar, an offer I was glad to accept. I also put up a notice on the Club notice board inviting Club members to join us for part of our cruise. This offer was taken up by a husband and wife, Caspar and Moira, who elected to join us for the Balearics leg.

At the end of March *Blue Pearl* was hauled out at Philip's yard for the insurance repairs and we took this opportunity to clean and polish the hull and bright work, scrub the outside teak and apply anti-fouling. We serviced and greased winches and stopcocks and cleaned out the fresh water tanks; we also fitted a strong bollard on the foredeck to take the anchor chain and two more cleats and fairleads on the stern. All that was left to do was the installation of the radar and GPS.

We launched on 30th April and the pace of preparations was stepped up. We had all the deckhead panels to replace after the work on the bollard and fairleads. A leak in the fore hatch had developed and had to be dealt with. At last we were loading up with our berth cushions, sails, which I had removed for cleaning, awning, rubber dinghy, which was stowed beneath the cockpit sole, and other essentials. We bought and stowed provisions for a week's sailing and Herbert, a friend from the Yacht Club, collected our bonded stores from Plymouth. A Customs Officer sealed them in our bonded locker. We sorted out our clothes for the next seven months, Joan washed and ironed where necessary, and we transported them to the boat. I fixed ringbolts to take the lee cloths, made from strong PVC by Don Campbell.

By Friday 10th May, the radar and GPS had been fitted and Alan Burwin came to commission them and to set up the electronic device I had purchased from him for boosting the alternator.

At 1000 Caspar and Moira joined us for a pleasant two-hour sail to test the new instruments. The GPS was not working. We berthed at Dart Marina, ready for our departure next day, refuelled and topped up with water.

The next day, Saturday 11th May, Alan arrived early and worked all morning on the GPS. He sorted out all the problems except one. If the engine was switched on with the GPS working it blew the GPS fuse. This problem was never solved.

I was involved with Alan all morning, so when Rob, Jill, Martin and Jenne arrived at 1100 I had to leave the final loading of stores to them. I was unable to check and, in the rush, several things were left behind, notably the boat's insurance documents, the pump for the Avon dinghy and our bird book.

At 1715, with Jill and Rob waving farewell from the Castle headland, we left harbour on our great adventure. We were both turned seventy and a new life was beginning for us.

Our course was to the Skerries Buoy, outside Dartmouth, then 210° to clear Ushant. A note from the log:

> *0050 Large ship passed close across our stern. Started engine and turned to port to get farther away. Blew fuse on the GPS. GOLDEN RULE – Even in emergency turn off GPS before starting engine.*

We followed this practice throughout our cruise.

The first four hundred miles were fairly uneventful. The wind varied from NE to NW and, apart from a short period of one and a half hours when it reduced to force one, it remained at force three to five, giving us an average speed of five and a half knots.

We were in three-hour watches, three hours on and three off with one-and-a-half-hour dog watches. Husband and wife shared the watch and Joan and I were able to extend our rest with our usual practice of one hour on, one hour asleep on the lee cockpit seat and one hour social chat. We all felt relaxed, and Joan and I began to recover from the pressure of the past months.

Our telescopic spinnaker pole, in two sections, was very heavy to handle and really too long for our genoa, and Martin spent some time in the boat's workshop, making a wooden plug for one half of the pole, with a fitment to attach to the mainmast. We never did buy a spinnaker and the fitting served us well throughout our cruise.

Minor incidents occurred. At 160 miles our lights dimmed. We had run the domestic batteries down, probably through using the Autohelm, the navigation lights and the fridge freezer. I switched over to the engine battery and ran the engine in neutral to charge the domestic ones.

On Monday, 250 miles from home, a small finch landed on deck and enjoyed food, water and a rest before flying off. A few miles later two dolphins joined us and showed their paces. Later still we were buzzed by a light aircraft at masthead height.

At 1500 on Tuesday, log 376, we altered course to 224 degrees, our first change since the Skerries.

At 1800 there was a gale warning for South Finisterre, force seven possibly eight. From the log:

0220 Wednesday 15th May. Gale forecast. Heavy rolling seas.

0600 North 48° 53'. West 8° 30'. Log 445. Passed fishing fleet. Wind NE force six. Sea lumpy.

0700 Log 450.5. Double reefed the main.

1200 Log 478. Wind force seven, gusting eight. Gybed to course 270° to round the headland of Cape Finisterre. Put preventer on the main. Handed the genoa. Sailing at 7.5 to 8 knots under double reefed main only. Surfed down the huge, rolling sea in a welter of foam. Boat's speed touched 8.8 knots. Exhilarating.

1800 Joan asked if she should cook the roast beef for dinner. The boat was being thrown about a lot so I laughed and said that stew would be easier to cook.

After dinner in the cockpit, we altered course to close the shore and escape the excesses of the N.E. gale. Very easy to eat our meal out of the newly purchased bowls.

2300 Wind dropped to force 1 – 2. Rolling heavily in confused sea.

2400 Log 542.6. Gale forecast for Finisterre.

0005 Thursday 16th May. A heavy sea came through the open hatch. Wind rose suddenly to force eight. Speed jumped to over eight knots. Boat rolling heavily. Running under double-reefed main with preventer. There is a real danger of broaching-to. Autohelm copes well but is eating up the battery.

0015 North 42° 02', West 9° 13'. Called Martin into the cockpit and sent Joan below to join Jenne and give support. Altered course to 142° to close land and find some easing of the sea. This brought wind on the beam and steadied the boat. Left main well out to spill wind. Speed dropped to four knots. This was what we wanted in order to arrive at Bayona after dawn. Much easier in the boat. Martin and I relaxed and discussed the problems of the world.

0130 GPS position North 42° 18', West 9° 11.5'. Current is pushing us so we are not closing land sharply enough. Altered course 20° to port. This kept us on a steady approach to Bayona. Wind still force eight. Sea still breaking and violent. Spilling wind with sail well out. Motion much steadier. Sent Martin down for an hour's kip. Joan joined me in the cockpit.

0330 Main batteries weak and lights flickering. Switched to engine battery and started engine. Ran engine in neutral to charge the batteries while sail drove the boat. A very strong light marked our approach, fl 2 ev. 8 secs. Pilot records it as ev. 16 secs. Wanted to arrive at Bayona just after dawn to see our approach. Boat's speed just right for timing.

0520 Off entrance to Bayona Bay. Wind has dropped to force four. Seas easy. Arrived Bayona.

0600 Lowered mainsail and motored quietly to a pontoon. This required us to pick up a span buoy for the bows and hack into the pontoon for two stern lines. When going astern Blue Pearl kicks to the right and I failed to get it into position. As there was more space on another pontoon I manoeuvred into that, bows on, using the span buoy for our stern.

0700 Finally made fast. Distance covered 580 miles. Time 4 days, 13 hours, 50 minutes. Average speed 5.2 knots.

When we checked in at the Port Office I realised that I had neither our insurance policy nor a certificate, not even the number. We all slept until 1430 and that evening we had a meal ashore and I telephoned Jill and asked her to contact our insurance company and ask for a photocopy to be sent to Gibraltar.

We spent the next day in harbour, intending to shop and prepare for the next leg. Unfortunately it was a public holiday and the shops were closed. On our way back we met the owner of a large catamaran, *S'Magic*, and mentioned our problem. Then we had a windfall. His crew had run out of time waiting for the adverse gale to subside and were flying home to England. He had food for four men for five days, which he was going to dump. He gave us some of this and, when I returned his gift with a litre of whisky, he sent a lot more, steaks, chicken pieces, ham, vegetables, butter and cheese, about £30 worth in all. Our problem was solved. While on the pontoon I charged our batteries and topped up with water and fuel.

The next morning, Saturday 18th May, we left the pontoon at 0600 in a force one and motor-sailed at six knots until 1000 when a force three easterly wind picked up and we switched off the engine and put up full sails. We had an easy run at five knots to Leixos, where we moored alongside *Eclipse II*, a round-the-world Australian. The skipper, who made me feel one of the long distance brethren, explained the Portuguese procedure. We must first report to the police. This required two visits, one before and one after dinner, and in all took over two hours. We finally convinced them that we were honest mariners and paid the fee, 100 escudos, about 40 pence.

We left harbour next morning for a run of 160 miles to Cascais. With little wind and a flat sea we motor-sailed until 1315, when the wind picked up from the north west, force four. Under full sail we reached a speed of six-and-a-half knots, which we maintained until 2100, when the wind died and we resumed motor-sailing under main and motor. In the evening we saw our first flying fish.

At 0100, Monday 20th May, on a dark drizzly night, we were approaching the narrow passage between Peniche and the island of Berlenga.

From the log:

Approaching Berlenga. The radar showed the island and mainland perfectly on the 12 mile range with three ships in the vicinity. Our waypoint on the GPS was the centre of the channel. Because they were interfaced, the bearing and distance on the GPS were transferred to the radar and showed up as a dotted line with a circle marking the waypoint. All I had to do was to line up the ship's heading line with the GPS bearing line and continue until we scored a bulls-eye in the circle. Magic!

At 1000 we entered Cascais and anchored in the harbour, with fishing boats all round us. We rested and, in the evening, enjoyed a quiet meal in the cockpit, with a lovely sunset and a starlit and moonlit night sky. The next morning we left at 0700 under main and motor in a flat calm. From the log:

1000 Tuesday 21st May Log 17.3. Glassy calm.

1300 Wind veered to north, force one. Running with engine and main well out with a preventer. A sunny day. Visibility 15 miles.

Four porpoises passed down the side of the boat, but did not stop.

1415 A racing-pigeon landed on the mizzen boom, twenty miles from land. 'Percy Pigeon' was nervous at first and disdainfully refused the cornflakes offered to him. A saucer of water was more to his taste.

1610 Wind increased to force three. Engine off. Set genoa.

1900 We were eating stew out of our deep bowls in the cockpit when Percy joined in. At first he sat on my shoulder, then on my knee. I left him some remains and he jumped into the bowl itself and finished them off.

2100 Wind dead ahead, force one. Handed the genoa and turned on the engine to motor-sail. Percy picked his spot under the spray-hood and settled down for the night.

0200 Wednesday, 22nd May. Log 107. Tacking round Cape St Vincent. Wind suddenly increased to force seven. Sea becoming rough. Took in two reefs.

0300 Wind gale force eight. Sea very rough. Hard going tacking into it.

0600 Log 120.8 Gale force eight still blowing. Average speed over last three hours – three knots.

0900 Log 134.3. Gale easing. Wind force seven. Percival, one minute asleep with fluffed feathers the next woke up and took off on a straight line for the Algarve. He knew a thing or two. He had ridden out the gale with us.

1430 Arrived Vilamoura. Distance 164 miles. Time 31 hours 30 minutes.

Taking down the mainsail in the crowded harbour, I had not secured the topping-lift, and the boom fell on Joan, badly cutting her forehead, over her right eye. With blood pouring from the wound she went below. Neither Jenne nor Martin was able to deal with it and I was fully occupied in bringing the boat alongside in the crowded harbour. As soon as I could, I hurried below and found that Joan, who had been a wartime first-aid assistant, had drawn the wound together and covered it with a plaster.

That evening, in good spirits, we enjoyed our first swordfish steak at an open-air restaurant. Joan now had a black eye as well as the plaster. The waiter eyed me suspiciously, but paid particular attention to Joan.

We left Vilamoura the next morning, 23rd May, and experienced the difficulty Portuguese officialdom has in adjusting to the needs of visiting yachts. With nearly two hundred miles to go we had planned on leaving at 0600 and arriving, with luck, before nightfall on the 25th. Promptly at 0600 we were passing the reception berth at the entrance when we were called to the side in a very peremptory manner by an official, who looked like a policeman, armed with a pistol. Although we had informed the office the previous evening of our leaving intentions, we were now told that we must get clearance from the police, customs and harbour authority. None of these arrived until 0900 and for three hours we patiently fumed. We left at 0930 after completing virtually identical forms at each of the three adjacent offices, harbour, customs and police.

By mid-day we were sailing under full rig on a course of 125°, hard on a moderate easterly wind. Visibility was good and the sea moderate but lumpy. The dorsal fin of a shark was spotted, weaving to and fro fifty yards astern of us. He stayed with us for an hour and it was not until after the cruise that we were made aware of the effect it had had on Jenne. The following night she had suffered nightmares, dreaming that the boat was foundering, that the dinghy would not inflate and that the shark was waiting for her.

At 1300 the wind had backed to the south east, force one, and we furled the genoa and started the engine. An hour later the engine began to overheat because of a broken fan belt. To my dismay the engine spares, which had been put together for us by an engineer, revealed no fan belt. As we could make little progress towards Gibraltar we decided to return to Vilamoura, twenty miles away. Seven hours later and a mile from Vilamoura we ran out of wind. I made a fan belt of nylon cord, spliced in a long loop that went round three times, and Martin fitted it. With Jenne watching the 'fan belt', we started up and held our breaths. The engine was put into gear. Slowly, at three knots, we made good the last mile and tied up on the service pontoon at 2200.

Everyone at Vilamoura was now most helpful. The marina had offered a tow if needed and refused payment for the night's stay; the service station provided and fitted a fan belt and supplied a spare at a low cost; the police, customs and harbour officials waved us through without formalities, saying, 'Have a good journey.' We also took the opportunity of buying a dinghy pump to replace the one we had left at Dartmouth. This, I think, was partly the cause of Jenne's dream.

By 1000 we were away under motor, with the mizzen as a steadying sail, heading south into a force one wind. All day we motored in the bright sunshine, with little or no wind but an increasingly lumpy sea.

At 0400 on Saturday 25th May the log reads: *Swell getting higher. Wind increasing from the east. Altered course to close shore for some protection.*

At 0900 the wind was still increasing and the sea was becoming rougher. By 1700, as we approached Cape Trafalgar, we met the full Levanter, with the wind at gale force eight and increasing. How I appreciated Martin's strength as he wrestled with and took down the mainsail! And Joan, who remained calm throughout though badly bruised, helped by Jenne, never failed to provide hot drinks and a hot meal.

I began to think of retreating, behind Cape Trafalgar and heaving-to. Martin and Jenne had joined us for a fortnight's holiday and they were due back at work on Tuesday, following the bank holiday. It was already Saturday, so we continued on.

At 1800 I was below, working at the navigation table, when the boat was flung on its side and I was thrown across the cabin and hard against the corner of the dining table, which struck my chest. I found myself gasping for breath and immediately felt very sick. I made for the cockpit and spent the next few minutes retching. I thought I might pass out and said, 'I am feeling very sick and must lie down for a bit.' The crew looked horrified. I dared not tell them I was hurt, for I believe they were depending on me in this critical situation. I staggered below and lay down on the lee berth in the main cabin. I either fell asleep or passed out, for the next thing I remember was Martin calling me anxiously, 'Freddie, Freddie. You must come up. You must come up.' The twenty minutes' rest had restored me. The sickness had gone and, apart from the pain in my chest, I felt better.

At 1900 it was getting dark and we were approaching Cape Tarifa with the wind now at force nine and gusts recorded at force ten, directly heading us. I decided to take in the genoa completely and motor-sail with mizzen only. I kept at half throttle to hold the boat close to the wind, using the mizzen to drive it, but opened up to full throttle when tacking. I endeavoured to keep the boat moving at three to four knots. The seas were huge and constantly breaking over us and sweeping the deck. Wind and noise shattered the senses. As far as we could see in the boat's lights the spume was blown horizontally over the sea's surface.

I believed the situation had reached its climax. Sea, wind and noise had reached their peak. I felt a surge of affection for *Blue Pearl* and great confidence in her strength. The crew had done well in a very difficult situation and I knew I could now last out. I decided to tack no longer but to motor home. Again Martin showed his strength in handing the mizzen, with Joan and Jenne helping. All my concentration was on steering and throttle.

At 2130 the gale began to ease, at first the wind to force eight and then, as we passed into Gibraltar Bay and the lee of Europa Point, the sea. Quite dramatically the sea was turned off, and we were motoring to the Customs shed in Gibraltar, arriving there at 2300. The Customs Officer told us that we were the only boat to have come through the Straits that day and did we know we had come through a force ten? Our bruises told us, 'Yes.'

79

6

Costa del Sol and Costa Blanca

Gibraltar provided a much-needed break. On Sunday 26th May Martin and Jenne left by plane for England and Joan and I were able to enjoy some rest and respite from the demands of sailing. My chest remained painful and it was a month before the pain eased. Joan's forehead began to mend and eventually she was left without the scar she had feared over her eye.

We were able to look for the source of the water that had come aboard in the recent storm. We found no trace of a leak and decided that it must have come through the funnel through which the anchor chain passed from the foredeck to the chain locker. A lot of water had come over the bows and much of it must have found its way through the funnel. I made a wooden plug that slotted over the anchor chain and this solved the problem. We removed floorboards and thoroughly cleaned out the bilges.

There are two very good marinas in Gibraltar, tucked well away next to the runway – Sheppard's Marina and the town marina in Marina Bay. We chose the latter and did not regret it. On a concrete pontoon, our berth was comfortable and easily accessible, water and electricity were both available, toilets and showers were close at hand, and all the staff were kind and helpful. Moreover the charges were only £7 per night, among the cheapest we were to find in the Mediterranean. Nearby were two good chandlers and an excellent but inexpensive restaurant, Bianca's.

I looked forward to our first stroll round the town, which I had visited three times, the last in 1942 when I spent several weeks waiting for a passage to England after the invasion of North Africa. On another occasion, in 1941, I recalled I had bought a branch with five hands of bananas, which I nursed all the way home. I

81

remembered the curious stares as I carried these now-ripe bananas through the streets of London to Joan's house. Bananas were not seen in England in those days. I also remembered the slabs of cherished chocolate for my family and the silk pyjamas for me bought from an Indian whose shop flowed onto Main Street, then a dirt road with horse-drawn gharries.

Gibraltar had changed considerably. High-rise blocks now bordered the extended runway; the dirt road and gharries had been replaced with a tarmac road and many cars and taxis. A few Indian shops still overflowed onto the pavement with displays of silks, cottons and rayons; there were still enough bars to satisfy a fleet, though the bars, like the docks, were mainly empty.

On Monday we had a day of rest. On Tuesday we walked round the town re-visiting old haunts: the Bristol Hotel, where as young naval officers we met for drinks or lunch, was still there. On Wednesday we walked across the frontier to La Linea, a much bigger town than I remembered. On Thursday we took the cable car, from which we had a panoramic view of the empty docks, to the summit of Gibraltar and had refreshments in the restaurant there. When I had last been in Gibraltar there was no cable car and no restaurant. Then we had walked to the top to see the Barbary apes which were roaming wild; now we found that they were still there, penned up in a den with an entrance fee to see them. It was well worth the visit. One of the apes had just given birth and was being guarded from the young males by her grandmother. A zoologist, who happened to be visiting, explained to us that this was the custom among these apes. Joan was soon on friendly terms with grandma and had a long chat with her.

On Saturday 1st June we were ready to go and, for the next week, made our way north-eastwards in easy stages in a prevailing light wind. We spent one night in Estepona, a developing town that was already beginning to look squalid as bad drains had caused the recently laid tiles to crack; another in Benalmadena, a good harbour with an easy entrance, excellent facilities and good services; and a third in Marina del Este, a lovely, small private marina, surrounded by rocky hills, with good services and the best showers and toilets to date. We shared our pontoon with an Oyster 39, *Larboard*, and an Oyster 63.

On this leg, along a rugged and grand coast, we saw dolphins and flying fish. A fishing boat passed across our track, half a mile ahead of us, and a few minutes later we ran into hundreds of small dead fish, jettisoned by the fishing boat. Fish stocks were declining in the Mediterranean and, no doubt, this type of action contributed to the decline.

On Tuesday 4th June we reached Adra. From the log:

1330 Arrived Adra. There were no boats anchored in the harbour and no room on the Dique de Levante because of numerous fishing boats. Approached Club Nautico for a pontoon berth. These generally seemed to be too small for us. Attempted to tie up against a large German yacht at the end pontoon. He waved us away and we made the difficult turn between the pontoons and tied up alongside another large yacht. A man from the Club Nautico told us that we could not stay there and there was no place for us on the pontoons. After some sign language, however, he indicated that we could anchor in the middle of the harbour. We tried twice, but the anchor dragged. At the third attempt, more towards the entrance, we were successful. We inflated the dinghy and rowed ashore to register, to be greeted by a friendly policeman, who settled our business on the quayside.

We enjoyed two days in Adra. The shopping was good and the harbour peaceful; the fishing boats did not disturb us.

The next day we left harbour with no wind and a choppy sea, motoring all the way to Aguadulce. Unlike our last port this was a beautiful and helpful marina. We were greeted by 'sailors', who helped us to berth. The English-speaking girl in the office was courteous and helpful. We told her we intended to visit Almeria and she warned us about pickpockets and thieves.

In Almeria we were walking through a poor part of the town, just behind the main shopping street, trying to follow the route to the castle. We came to a square where many young men were lolling about, either drugged or drunk. Perhaps influenced by the marina girl's warning, 1 thought the situation looked dangerous, even menacing, when two men began to walk towards us, so we did a quick left turn down a side street into the High Street, only two hundred yards away. We did not visit the castle.

When we arrived back at the boat we found that the wind had got up and torn our awning, which had been taken down by a friendly German and his wife in the next berth.

83

The next day, Saturday, we left harbour in a light southwest wind and a heavy swell under genoa and motor. The wind soon died completely and we motored the rest of the way to San José, a small but very pretty harbour. 'Sailors' helped us to berth. Our water terminal did not work, but Jean, a helpful Frenchman from *Transmed*, joined our hose to his and we were able to fill up. I also had to join an extension lead to our electricity cable to reach a terminal that worked. In the evening Jean came aboard for drinks, and gave us good advice on future ports.

We went out to a local taverna for our evening meal, which turned out to be one of the most unusual we had ever experienced. The proprietors did not speak English and we had no Spanish. I drew a nice picture of a large white fish, say a sea bream, to show them what we wanted – and we were each served with a dozen small sprats, dried bread and no garnish or vegetables. As a meal it was a disaster so, to make up for it, we ordered chicken, which turned out to be fried bones and little meat. For sweet we chose one of those luscious Spanish ice-creams; we got a small cube of vanilla, straight from the fridge, served on a stick. At £22.50 it was an expensive if deplorable meal, but it was served with politeness and good humour and we saw the funny side of it.

In the afternoon we turned to, took down some deckhead panels and repaired the mainsheet traveller end-stops, which had been damaged in the storm approaching Gibraltar. At 1900 we had been invited to Jean's boat for drinks and the Monaco weather report. From him I bought up-to-date Greek and Turkish pilot books for £20 each and two older Western Mediterranean pilots for £5 the two. We returned to our boat, where I had some English money, and in passing it across to Jean I dropped a £20 note into the harbour and watched it slowly sinking. Jean was very quick and successfully fished it up with a boathook.

Jean was an engaging host, but he kept us too late and it was 2230 when we returned to our boat to put back the deckhead panels, with curses from me and pacifying noises from Joan. Then we enjoyed an extremely good meal that Joan had somehow managed to prepare.

On Monday we again had no wind, but a pleasant, easy motor-sail in a placid sea took us to Aguilas, our next port of call, accompanied by flying fish and a Finnish yacht that stayed with

A huge empty shell (Chapter 1)

Stretchers to fix teak linings (Chapter 1)

Blue Pearl at Benfleet, showing stairs (Chapter 1)

Working in the main cabin (Chapter 1)

Joan on the joists of the garage (Chapter 2)

The finished garage (Chapter 2)

Leigh House (Chapter 2)

The view from our living room (Chapter 2)

The launching of
Blue Pearl
(Chapter 2)

Joan offers the libation
to the gods (Chapter 2)

The galley
(Chapter 3)

The chart table
(Chapter 3)

Stern cabin
(Chapter 3)

The dressing table
(Chapter 3)

Main cabin
(Chapter 3)

Fore cabin
(Chapter 3)

Blue Pearl at Smugglers Cottage (Chapter 3)

Blue Pearl on
the Rance
(Chapter 3)

Two dolphins joined us (Chapter 5)

A light aircraft buzzed us (Chapter 5)

Rolling seas (Chapter 5)

Percy Pigeon (Chapter 5)

Gibraltar: The cable car (Chapter 6)

Joan and the ape (Chapter 6)

Marina del Este (Chapter 6)

Cala Calabra, Majorca (Chapter 7)

ontanelles: Dining in the cockpit (Chapter 7)

Alicastre Bay: Porquerolles (Chapter 8)

Monte Carlo (Chapter 8)

The Sanguinieres (Chapter 8)

Tarxien temple, Malta
(Chapter 13)

Mdina, Malta
(Chapter 13)

Tranquil Bay
(Chapter 14)

Vliko Bay
(Chapter 14)

Abelike Bay,
Meganisi
(Chapter 14)

us all the way, forty-eight miles in ten hours. Aguilas is a good port of call, though berths are few. We were well received by the harbour master, who had no office but always seemed to be on hand when boats arrived. The toilets and showers were good and we enjoyed shopping and seeing the town, a pleasant, clean seaside town with little industry.

On Wednesday we set off at 0730 for a typical day's sailing in this part of our voyage. The wind was north east force one; our course was 075°; we motor-sailed under main and motor. At 0800 we set the genoa, sheeted hard in, but an hour later the wind backed and we handed the genoa. The sea was lumpy, but the mainsail steadied us.

At 1045, just after passing Mazarron, we were buzzed by a helicopter and sea spray from its downdraft came over us. At 1200, off Cabo del Aqua, we were circled closely by a large Spanish Customs boat.

At 1810, after tacking close to the wind under main and motor in a lumpy sea, we arrived at Cabo de Palos, a tricky harbour with a dogleg entrance. As we entered, a Welshman in a boat alongside the harbour wall called a warning to us of 'a rock in the middle of the harbour'. He directed us to steer to the starboard side of the channel. We followed his directions – and grounded. This was simply the shallow side of the channel; the deeper side was to port, near a red buoy. We soon hauled off and tied up to the wall.

We enjoyed one of our best meals to date at La Tuna restaurant, recommended by Jean. There was no charge for our night's stay. As we returned to the boat in the darkness a large motorboat entered the harbour and tied up ahead of us, with four young men aboard. 'What place is this?' we were asked. They had arrived from Majorca with no charts, no radio, radar or GPS, and had simply steered north east until they hit land then sailed along the coast until they found a harbour entrance.

A thunderstorm passed over us and we had a restless night, disturbed by the strong swell that surged into the tiny harbour and kept us bumping against the wall. The next day we were again motor-sailing, with the main hauled right in, in a light wind and bumpy sea, just holding our northerly course to Torrevieja.

Torrevieja is a large harbour with a good, but expensive marina. Anchoring is free so we decided to berth one night and anchor the second. The town was excellent for shopping, with a good supermarket and good shops in the main streets. We bought a travelling iron to add to our amenities.

On Saturday 15th June we left harbour at 0700 for Villajoyosa, a small harbour with few berths, all full. There was no room to anchor so we departed rapidly for Altea, five miles along the coast. There was no *muella presidente*, as described in the pilot, so we tied up at the fuel berth where we were told there was no room in the harbour. However, the fuel master rang up the Club Nautico who found a berth for us for the night for £12.50, one of our more expensive nights.

On Sunday 16th June we left harbour in a south west wind, force three, under main and genoa, sailing at last. At 0945 the wind was south west force six and we were running at six knots under genoa only. At 1030 the wind decreased to force four and we re-set the main, with a speed of five knots. At 1235 we arrived at Morayra, twenty-two miles in 6 hours 35 minutes.

In the evening we walked round Morayra, a small pleasant town with good shopping facilities, butchers, bakers, two greengrocers, two small supermarkets and a wine shop where you could taste the wine and buy from the barrels at £1 per litre, in your own bottle. We decided to stay an extra day.

The next day was dull, overcast and cold and we were glad to be in harbour. We had sailed four hundred miles along the rugged coasts of Costa del Sol and Costa Blanca with the high Sierra mountain ranges in the far distance. The winds had generally been light, forcing us to motor-sail most of the way. Sometimes the sea had been tranquil, but often it was disturbed and unpleasant.

On Tuesday 18th June we left the Spanish mainland for Ibiza. The forecast wind was north force three to four, but the actual wind, when we started at 0615, was east force one. The sea was lumpy, and once again we were motor-sailing under main and motor. The log recalls the events of the morning: a young man in a fast fishing boat came too close and rocked us violently; two yachts passed in the opposite direction; a cruise liner passed astern of us and a large tanker ahead; a large cargo vessel over-took us and forced us to increase and turn away; we saw two dolphins.

At 1245 the wind suddenly backed to the northeast and increased to force five. The sea became lumpy, but at last we were sailing again. Fifteen minutes later the GPS failed. I switched off and on and this cured it. At the same time the wind increased to force seven. From the log:

1430 tacked to clear Isla Conejera. Wind force 7. Ibiza shrouded in mist. The sea a mass of white water.

1500 Tacked to course 078°. GPS failed again. Over to dead reckoning and radar. Radar picture good – showed the numerous islands and the main coast and entrance.

1630 GPS okay. A difficult situation resolved. GPS and radar gave a clear picture. Mist disappeared and revealed all. Sun came out. Coast gradually blanketed the wind, and the sea subsided as a result. An easy entrance into San Antonio.

1825 A friendly official waved us into an empty berth and took our mooring lines. There was also room for anchoring in the large harbour.

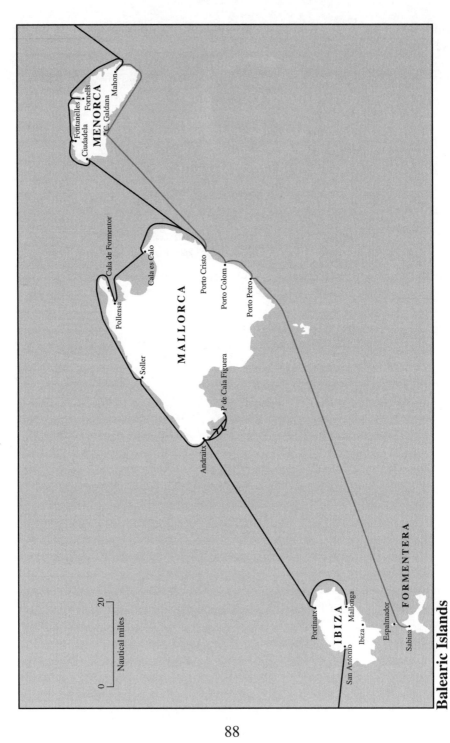

Balearic Islands

7

The Balearics

After a quiet, restful day in harbour, we left San Antonio at 0915 on Thursday 20th June, under main and genoa in a force four south-west wind. We were making six knots, but as we passed between the islands the gusts gave signs of a stronger wind to come and I should have taken in a reef while the sea was still calm, protected by the islands. We turned the corner round Isla Conjera and were headed by the full force seven from the south west, throwing up a lumpy sea. We continued sailing with the sails sheeted right home.

At 1130 we rounded the Blada Islands and were unable to lay our proper course, so we furled the genoa and motor-sailed 30 degrees off the wind, continuing with tight tacks in a stroppy sea until we rounded Isla Vedra at 1330. The engine was switched off, the genoa unfurled and we enjoyed good sailing on a beam reach, through Freu Grande, past Espalmador, into Ibiza Bay. We arrived in Ibiza at 1750, forty-eight miles in ten hours.

We berthed in Puerta Ibiza la Nueva to face the exorbitant charge of £28 per day or £141 for the week. I decided on the week. I telephoned Caspar to confirm our arrival and arranged for him and Moira to join us on Monday 24th June.

On Saturday I serviced the engine, changed the oil filter, and cleared the air and fuel filters. The air filter was completely choked and I wondered if it had been touched when we had last had the engine serviced in Dartmouth. I repaired buttons on a berth cushion and made a safety strap for the galley where, in rough weather, Joan had found it difficult to keep her feet.

On Sunday morning we worked on the boat and in the evening took a quiet stroll round the large town. We noted the good shopping facilities, but thought it over-commercialised and expensive.

On Monday I continued working on the boat and found the source of a leak in the bilges, a badly made union in the fresh water system, bodged up by David Heale's man when he installed our hot water system, which I replaced with a new Y junction. We cleared the fore cabin and emptied the lockers ready for Caspar and Moira's arrival at 1830.

The next day we spent shopping and seeing the town and fitting a plug on our new iron. On Wednesday our toilet seized up and Caspar and I stripped it and cleared it. The exit pipe had furred badly and this had caused the seizure.

On Thursday 27th June we left harbour and sailed to Puerto del Espalmador, a lovely sheltered bay with a sandy beach. In the high season this anchorage is crowded with pleasure craft from Ibiza, holiday makers and a beach café. Now, in June, we were the only boat in the anchorage. The water was clear and we could easily see the sandy bottom, with occasional patches of weed. It was too good to resist and before our evening meal we all had our first swim of the season.

That evening we began what was to become our standard practice – drinks followed by dinner in the cockpit on the lovely teak table I had made, set out formally with place mats, napkins, glasses for wine and water, and cutlery. The meals were usually four courses, on this occasion melon for starter, chicken breasts stuffed with grapes, fresh beans, carrots, broccoli and new potatoes, plum crumble and custard, biscuits and cheese. Joan and Moira took it in turns to cook the meal, while the men prepared the table and washed up afterwards. Dinner was taken in a leisurely fashion, usually lasting two hours from first drink to last coffee, with the sun setting in the west turning the sky to gold, to pink, to purple. The only movement was the ladies getting the next course or the men refilling glasses. The only sound was our quiet voices and the occasional chuckle of water as a small wave passed.

The next day was a make-and-mend and, after a lazy morning and lunch in the cockpit, we strolled along the beach, which we had to ourselves, to the Trocados headland. A brief siesta was followed by a swim and a salad meal, again in the cockpit. We had noticed a large plank floating near the boat, and during the swim I brought it aboard. It was solid oak, about eight feet long, a foot wide and an inch thick, just what I wanted for a gangplank! I stowed it along the stanchions on the starboard quarter.

On Saturday 29th June we enjoyed a sparkling sail westwards of Formentera and back to Puerto de Sabina. We had fun with the showers. I put in a 25-peseta coin and turned the water on, soaped myself thoroughly – and the water ran out, with me covered in soap. I discovered that your 25p purchased water for one and a third minutes, so either it had to be a quick shower or you needed a stack of 25 pesetas. When Joan came out I discovered that she had had a similar experience.

We liked the marina and the little town of St Francis, which we walked to next day. The walk itself was flat and uninteresting. We also enjoyed dinner at the Hotel Bonavista.

Next day, under main and genoa, we sailed to Cala Llonga on the island of Ibiza, nineteen miles in four hours twenty minutes. We anchored in fifteen feet, in clear water, near a sandy beach, many holiday flats, hotels and restaurants and a busy and noisy town. We spent an uncomfortable, bumpy night in a swell from the south west and, the next day, motored to Santa Eulalia, six miles away. My pulse charger had developed a fault in Sabina and after a long effort I had been unable to repair it. In Santa Eulalia I walked for miles searching for a trickle charger with no success.

On Thursday we left harbour at 1030 with the wind north east force five, increasing later to force seven with gusts to force eight. We had one reef in the mainsail and two thirds genoa. It was a cracking sail, reaching 6.5 knots as the wind increased. We tacked inside Isla Tagomago, a lovely island anchorage, but rather exposed in the gusty, uncertain wind. Caspar saw his first flying fish. We tacked into San Vincente, but again the anchorage was too exposed. The wind eased and we shook out the reefs, still sailing at 6.5 knots to Cala Portinatx, a good anchorage in the north-east wind and reasonably sheltered.

Again we enjoyed a swim from the boat. For us the beautiful bay was spoiled by high-rise holiday homes and very loud disco music that came from several different directions until the early hours of the morning. Nevertheless we spent two nights in this anchorage.

We were up at dawn on Saturday 6th July and at 0615 we left harbour under full sail, main, mizzen and genoa, in a light wind that increased later. We sailed the fifty miles to Andraitx in Majorca in nine hours with some help from the engine for two hours when the wind died on us. At the pontoon the berth master insisted that

I backed into the berth, a manoeuvre that I had not yet mastered. My difficulty was that when going astern the boat veered to port, with a hard kick as I went into gear. The problem here was enhanced by the strong wind blowing in. The boats on either side of us were only nine feet apart and our beam was twelve and a half feet. I tried, unsuccessfully, three times under the eagle eye of the berth master and the critical eyes of my crew. However, I found a solution, if a temporary one. I got into position by going astern, then straightened up by putting the gear ahead so that we were lined up and approaching the two boats. Then with the crew fending off on either side I gently eased the boat astern, forcing a space for us to fit into. Later in our cruise I developed a much better method and backed with confidence with just Joan as my crew.

I took this opportunity to fit out the oak plank from Espalmador so that it could be lowered or raised from the stern with our mizzen halyard. It bridged the gap nicely between boat and pontoon and we all, including the ladies, soon became adept at walking the plank.

We thoroughly enjoyed Andraitx, perhaps because of the sparkling sail, perhaps because of the lovely sunshine, or the excellent berth, electricity and water, showers and toilets, perhaps because of the large supermarket where we replenished our stores, or the patisserie where we bought fresh bread and open tarts, but I think mostly because of the Club Nautico swimming pool where we enjoyed a long swim followed by a rest on a lounger and soft drinks. That evening we enjoyed dinner in the privacy of our cabin, followed by coffee in the cockpit.

On Sunday we left harbour at 1400 under main and genoa for an anchorage between the islands of Illatas, but as we rounded Punta de Cala Figuera we liked the look of Cala Sol de Mallorca so we entered it, turned to port and anchored in fourteen feet in the south west corner of this lovely, sheltered bay, with its narrow, protective entrance. Our now familiar swim was followed by our evening meal in the cockpit.

On Monday Caspar, Joan and I rowed ashore in the dinghy and explored some Phoenician caves with, nearby, a small restaurant with toilets and showers. We took the dinghy to the small harbour of Puerto Sol de Mallorca on the north side of the bay and decided that it was too small for *Blue Pearl*.

The next day we sailed quietly at three knots under genoa, with our large awning up to protect us from the fierce sun, to Islas Illatas, looking for an anchorage, but it was too exposed to wind and swell. We furled the genoa and motored to Puerto Portals where we were told that no berths were available, although several were empty. Our reception was cold and indifferent and they appeared to be interested only in large and expensive yachts. Grudgingly they allowed us to stay for one night on the waiting pontoon for £25.

The next day Joan and I caught the bus, after half an hour's wait, to Palma, which dropped us an hour's walk away from the cathedral, our destination. The walk was a pleasant one, partly through pedestrian precincts, but when we reached the cathedral at 1215 it was closed. We made a long, hurried walk to a chandler where we had been recommended to buy a trickle charger. Our small map led us to walk half a mile past the chandlers and when we finally arrived at 1315 it was closed until 1630 for the siesta. Now, very hot and bothered, we gave up and returned to the boat with probably a quite undeserved dislike of Palma. At 1710, leaving the awning up we motored back to Cala Sol de Mallorca for another pleasant and refreshing night.

On Wednesday we returned to Andraitx and anchored in the harbour. In the evening we went to the Miramar restaurant for dinner, a rip-off: an indifferent meal for four cost £95.

On Thursday, in a flat calm, we motored to Cala Llado, a tiny cove on Isla Dragonera, and found a beautiful anchorage, surrounded by rugged cliffs, that could take only four or five yachts. We explored the cliff walk and saw several rare lizards and, as the water was warm and clear, we enjoyed two swims from the boat, one before lunch and one before dinner. A pleasure boat arrived in the afternoon, during our siesta, and we were entertained by a quintet playing flamenco and jazz music. I drifted into sleep, thinking of Jill's first marriage to Pépè, a well known jazz guitarist who sometimes played flamenco music.

As evening approached we were surprised to see all the other boats depart. In the middle of our evening meal we discovered the reason: a strong wind and heavy swell got up, making the anchorage untenable and even dangerous. We had to take up our anchor and motor to San Telmo, three miles away on the main island, where we finished our meal and had a quiet night.

The next morning, after a walk ashore and coffee in a restaurant overlooking the bay, we left the anchorage under full sail, tacking at three knots in a force one to two wind. By 1400 the wind had dropped to less than force one and our speed to one and a half knots. An hour later, hardly moving, we handed the mizzen, started the engine and motor-sailed along the rugged coast. We looked in at Foradada, but the anchorage was open to a rising swell, so we continued to Puerto de Soller and anchored in fourteen feet in this wide, natural, circular harbour.

In the middle of the night the wind died completely and I was awakened by our yacht touching the next. The yachts lay in all directions. I took in some chain and put fenders out on both quarters. Caspar volunteered to stay in the cockpit, but when I went up three times in the night to check the situation I found him, not surprisingly, fast asleep.

In the morning we moved to a spot with more room. We tried three times before our anchor held. After lunch Joan and I rowed ashore to shop and collect water in jerricans from a fountain. At teatime the skipper of a French boat, whom we had been chummy with in Llada, and his wife rowed over to us with huge cuts of a tuna they had caught while spear fishing in Llada. Joan cooked them in butter and lemon and, with fruit cocktails as starters and a plum crumble for sweet, we enjoyed another splendid meal.

We left Soller early on Sunday 4th July and motored to Cala de la Calobra, a good harbour with dramatic, if gloomy, mountain scenery. We continued to Cala Vincente, a lovely cala with clear water. We shopped and had a drink ashore in a hotel at which Caspar and Moira had once stayed, and when we returned to the boat we found that a swell had got up and we were rolling heavily. We decided to move on to Isla Formentor, where we enjoyed a good night in a cala surrounded by trees and half-hidden hotels.

The next day we sailed to Puerto Pollensa. The Club Nautico would not allow us inside the harbour and we were given a berth outside the harbour wall for an exorbitant £20 for the night. We had a particularly bad night. A party of Germans in the cockpit of the boat next to us sang noisy, drunken German folk songs until two in the morning, when I went out and asked them to break it up – surprisingly they did so at once. In the evening we anchored for nothing in the bay, fifty yards from where we had berthed, and enjoyed a peaceful and quiet night.

On Wednesday we left our anchorage and had an excellent sail

94

under full rig across Pollensa Bay, but as we crossed Aleudia Bay the wind died and we took in our sails and motored to Cala el Calo, a small fisherman's harbour, for a quiet night.

After our customary swim and breakfast we motor-sailed to Puerto Costas de los Pinos, an attractive anchorage by a pine forest, for lunch, followed by a swim and a siesta, and then, keeping our awning up in the hot sun, we sailed under genoa and mizzen to Porto Cristo, where we found an excellent berth in the Club Nautico. In the evening a German motorboat came alongside and I helped them to berth. Unfortunately, a young woman jumped from the boat to the pontoon and twisted her ankle. Joan, a wartime-qualified first-aider, treated her and put on a cold water bandage.

In the morning Moira's family, on holiday in Majorca, came aboard and they all left for lunch ashore and an afternoon swim from the beach. The German came to tell us good news of his casualty and brought us a bottle of wine.

On Saturday 20th July there was no wind when we left Majorca so we motored the thirty-five miles to Ciudadela, the old capital of Minorca. There were no anchorages and no berths in the Club Nautico, but we were able to raft up alongside *Leila of Cowes*, an Oyster 48, on the Muella Commercial, at a cost of only £6.15. In the evening we visited the cathedral and walked round the attractive old town.

The next day we left under genoa and mizzen and a spatter of rain and sailed to Cala de Algayerens with its three smaller calas. We chose Fontanelles, with woodland behind a pleasant beach, clear water, a sandy bottom and very good swimming. As usual we enjoyed dinner in the cockpit and a quiet night.

We left Fontanelles the next day under full rig, tacking into a headwind to Cala Rotja for a swim and lunch, after which we continued to Cala de Fornells. We took our sails down as we approached the narrow entrance, motored well into this long, broad cala, and dropped anchor at the head in eleven feet.

After a quiet night we motored *Blue Pearl* to an anchorage opposite Fornells village. This has grown considerably since Robin Brandon wrote his Pilot and now has two supermarkets. We returned to our original anchorage, where the anchor dragged in the night so that we had to re-anchor.

The next day we left our anchorage under full rig, and a good sail brought us to Mahon, where we were given a good berth at the Club Maritime. Caspar and Moira, who were leaving us in Mahon, went off to find hotel accommodation, while Joan and I pursued our favourite occupation of walking around the street restaurants to decide on our evening meal. In the end we settled for the Club restaurant and the four of us had a farewell dinner on the terrace, our best restaurant meal of the month, for a modest £60, including wine.

We had enjoyed having Caspar and Moira with us, I because of Caspar's help with sailing and maintenance, and Joan because Moira shared the cooking. We also found the shared expenses of fuel and berthing a help. We had settled on a routine of swim, meal and siesta, which Joan and I would develop throughout our Mediterranean cruise. Yet, strangely, once they had gone we were glad to be on our own, to feel free to do our own thing in whatever way we wished. Certainly, on our own we tended to talk more to neighbours and make friends with the owners of other boats.

We liked Mahon, particularly the walk along the Promenade, with its beautiful waterway on one side and street of cafés on the other, and the broad steps up to the city with its excellent shops. We promised ourselves that we would call here on the way home to England.

A gale was forecast in the Golfe du Lion, with heavy seas expected, so we delayed our departure. We motored round to Cala Teulara for a quiet night at anchor and on to Fornells for another swim and another peaceful night. Then it was time to leave the Balearics.

8

Cote d'Azur

On Monday 29th July 1991 at 0615 we took up our anchor, set
the main and, as we left harbour, the genoa. The two-hundred-mile
passage from Menorca to Toulon took thirty-four hours fifteen
minutes. I wanted to arrive before nightfall the next day and that
meant an average speed of not less than five knots. The wind was
south force one to two when we left Fornells so, with the main
goose-winged, I kept the engine ticking over to give us a good
start at 6.5 knots.

The light wind veered steadily and at 0830 we had both sails
out to starboard on a broad reach. At 1600 the wind veered to the
north west and increased to force five. I switched off the engine,
still maintaining a speed of 6 knots. The sun was so hot that the
helmsman carried a sunshade. At 1900 the wind was force 6 and
I rolled in the genoa a little, sailing comfortably at 5.5 knots. The
boat's motion was quite violent and Joan spilled a cup of hot coffee
over her arm.

At 2000 we took a reef in the main for the night. Immediately
afterwards the wind eased to force three, and when I went to unfurl
the genoa the roller reefing jammed. I soon cleared it and with
full genoa and reefed main we were able to maintain 6.5 knots.

At 2100 we started our one-hour watches. This was our wedding
anniversary, which usually occurred on a cruise and was celebrated
with dinner in exotic surroundings. This was the first time at sea.
The visibility was good, with almost a full moon, and we had the
sea to ourselves.

Dawn was very bright with a red sky. At 1100 the wind headed
us and dropped so we started the engine again and motor-sailed,
hard on the wind. Half an hour later the wind increased to force

five, so we stopped the engine and continued sailing at 5.5 knots. At 1500 we were in the Rade de Toulon when the wind increased to force six, heading us, so we motor-sailed into port, tacking hard on the wind, arriving at 1630 – two hundred miles in thirty-four hours.

A friendly harbour official directed us into a berth between two English yachts on the Quai d'Accueil, where we could stay for four nights at £7.50 per night. We showered, had a long rest, a late evening meal and then a deep sleep.

The next morning we walked round the attractive city, through the excellent street vegetable market, through the fish market, through the Carrefour supermarket near the harbour, the largest we had ever seen, to the tourist office and the bank where we drew French money.

We returned to the boat for a late lunch and a siesta. Our neighbours were very friendly – Malcolm and Bobbie, in a Nicholson 48, both from Bristol University, on our starboard side, and Mike and Pam Bird to port. Mike and Pam came in for a drink and recommended a restaurant for our belated anniversary dinner, a small one called Celanche, where we enjoyed an excellent Chateaubriand for two, lovely vegetables and French fries, ice cream and coffee, a simple but hugely satisfying meal.

By Thursday the mistral, which had been building up since our arrival, was in full blast. It usually lasts for four days. We were glad to be in harbour and decided to stay until it was over. We had gale force winds all day. It was bumpy in the harbour and we were touching the pontoon so I slackened the stern warp and tightened the bow warp to hold us off. We shopped in the street markets and the Carrefour.

On Friday we took the cable car up Mount Faron, where we had a magnificent view of the harbour and Rade right out to the Porquerolles. We spent an hour in the museum and saw a film and a diorama of the allied invasion of Provence and the liberation of Toulon and Marseille in August 1944. Then we had lunch in the Mount Faron restaurant and returned to Toulon to shop. We spent some time with Malcolm, who was keen on weather forecasts and had high-quality, up-to-date equipment.

On Saturday we made some final purchases in the Carrefour and looked at trickle chargers, which were too expensive and inadequate for our batteries. We left our berth at 1045, took on a hundred litres of fuel and motored to a cove in the Rade, near Hyeres, recommended by Malcolm. The wind was light and heading us and we were glad to use the engine to charge our batteries.

We arrived at the anchorage, in a wide, wooded bay, at 1415. There was some swell at first, but this eased as the faint, offshore wind died. I enjoyed a swim, although the sea was five degrees colder than in the Balearics, and we had a peaceful night.

On Sunday we left our anchorage at 1030 and motored, in a flat calm, across to the Bay of Alicastre in the Porquerolles, a lovely, open, wooded bay with a large number of boats anchored close together. We both enjoyed a swim in water that was much warmer than at Hyeres.

On Monday we took an early morning stroll along a wooded path, then motored round the coast to Plage d'Argent Bay where we anchored but were disturbed by three motorboats that arrived, rafted together on one anchor yards away from us, and were left by their crews to drift to within a few feet of us. Again we enjoyed a walk through the woods, to Langoustiere Bay, which we liked so much that on our return we left our anchorage and motored round to it, anchoring well out to avoid the large number of boats.

We were up early next morning for a walk through the woods to a headland on the south side of the island. Back at the boat, we enjoyed a swim and then, in a flat calm, motored round to the small town of Porquerolles. There were no berths vacant in the harbour so Joan shopped while I anchored the boat in the bay opposite the entrance. In the evening we took the dinghy ashore for a very good meal in the pizzeria. The starter was a small pizza, cooked in the restaurant on a charcoal grill. I have never liked pizzas but I changed my mind with this one, cooked and served individually to us with a flourish by the chef.

The barometer was falling again and the weather forecast was *Storm in West Provence with winds force 8–9, locally 10*. We decided to cross over to the shelter of Hyeres and not go on to Port Gros as intended. At first we were told there were no vacant places until 1500, but eventually they fitted us in. For the sixth time we needed a different water connection from those we had, which we had to buy in Hyeres. We liked the small town and the berth was well protected. During the night we had thunder and lightning as the storm passed over.

By Friday the forecast was good for our area. We went ashore to change our Gaz bottles and take two loads of washing to the laverie and on our return found that our ensign had been stolen from the stern jackstaff close to the jetty.

We left the berth at 1215 in a force one wind and motor-sailed to St Tropez, where we anchored in the bay. St Tropez is the home of motorboats of all kinds, most of which spent the day charging around us at twenty knots, making the water oily and quite unsuitable for swimming.

The next day we sailed to Anse de l'Argent Faux, a lovely anchorage surrounded by cliffs and woods with one or two large houses. The water was warm and we enjoyed our swim. During the day there were only five other yachts but many small motorboats. In the evening all the yachts withdrew and we had the bay to ourselves for an uncomfortable night with little wind but an unpleasant swell.

On Sunday 11th August, after an early swim and breakfast in the cockpit, we sailed to Monaco. I had always wanted to visit Monte Carlo and this was the main purpose of our sail along the Riviera. We put up the courtesy flag we had bought specially in Hyeres and entered Monte Carlo Harbour, only to be told that there was no room for visitors, although we could see many vacant berths.

We sailed on to Menton, where we first tried the Vieille Port, which seemed cluttered, small and with no reception point, and then to Menton Garavan, a modern marina where we were well received and helped into our berth. The facilities were good and the cost only £12.50 per night, so we booked in for two nights.

The next day was a very full one. We walked along the promenade and explored this attractive Victorian/Edwardian town with its strong English influence and many English hotels, obviously a holiday centre for the English since Victorian times. We had lunch in a pleasant restaurant then took the train to Monte Carlo.

I was familiar with Monte Carlo only through films and literature and very much looked forward to exploring it. We walked round the cathedral and the palace grounds and joined a very dull organised tour of the palace that relied on recordings in French to describe each room that were too quick for us to understand. The cost was £3 each and we did not enjoy it. This was followed by the most expensive orange squash we had ever met – £4 per glass!

We walked back to the boat from the station, had tea, a siesta and a shower and followed this with a pleasant meal in the Marina Club, salad, pizza, ice-cream and a litre of Provence rosé for a total of £20, including the gratuity.

9

Corsica

On Tuesday 13th August we left Menton for Corsica. From the log:

1400 Left harbour. Wind less than force 1 from SE. Retained awning and motored. Co. 144°, speed 5.5 knots. Sea calm. Hazy sunshine.

1530 Wind SW2. Set mizzen and genoa. Left awning up and motor-sailed.

1600 Log 10.

1730 Wind SW3. Took down awning. Set main. Engine off. Beam wind. Speed 5.5 knots.

1900 An enjoyable supper: cold chicken and salad, followed by cake that Joan had baked in preparation. Log 30. Wind SW4. Took in mizzen, ready for the night. Speed still 5.5 knots.

2100 Speed up to 6 knots. Took in three rolls in genoa to improve all round visibility. Boat very comfortable at an average speed of 5 knots. This will bring us to Corsica two hours after dawn.

2300 Log 44.5. Several ships about, probably fishing vessels. Joan and I on one hour watches, though sometimes disrupted by shipping.

2400 Log 48.8. Position – North 43° 05', East 8° 15'. Difficulties with fishing trawlers. Engine on and evasive action. Turned to starboard to clear one, then to port to avoid another. The second trawler settled on a parallel course to ours one mile ahead.

Wed 19th August 0100 Log 54. Engine off.

0345 Log 64.4. More problems with trawlers. One, not

trawling, stayed with us for an hour, and then crossed ahead of us. Another, not trawling, overtook us and crossed 100 yards ahead. More evasive action. Slowed down by spilling wind from mainsail. Escorted by trawlers for next three hours, not trawling and slowing down to our speed as they caught up with us.

0700 Log 73.3. Shook out rolls in genoa.

0830 Wind dying and going ahead. Handed sails and motored.

0900 Arrived Calvi and anchored at the head of Golfe de la Revellata. Total distance 90.8 miles. Time 19 hours.

We had the anchorage to ourselves and, after a quiet day and a peaceful night followed by a swim and breakfast, we motored round the corner to Calvi harbour. This was full so we anchored amongst the hundred or more boats outside the harbour.

Calvi is full of history, dating from before Roman times. It was reputed that Christopher Columbus was born there and Napoleon took refuge in the citadel. Nelson captured the town, but lost an eye.

Most of the shops were closed as it was a Saint's Day. When we returned to the boat we found that the anchor had dragged and the crew of *Smithereen* had re-anchored us, using their own kedge anchor to support ours. There were no good vacant spots in the anchorage so we returned to Revellata and anchored in Anse de l'Oscelluccia, a small bay in the north west of the gulf, for an even more peaceful night than the previous one.

On Friday 16th August, after a morning swim, we returned to Calvi for shopping. We did not have enough cash with us to pay for all the stores we bought at the supermarket, so I left Joan guarding them under the eye of a suspicious official while I returned to *Blue Pearl* for more money. After lunch and our siesta we decided not to go on to Ile de Rousse as intended but to return to Revellata for a swim, dinner and another good night.

The next day, after our customary swim and breakfast we had a pleasant sail, under genoa and mizzen along a rugged and attractive coast to Ile de Rousse, with our awning up to protect us from the hot sun. We anchored just outside the harbour, and enjoyed the rest of the day in the somewhat crowded and bustling town.

At 1015 on Sunday 18th August we left our anchorage and motor-sailed in a very light wind along a dramatic coast towards Florent. We looked into several anchorages, all open to the swell from the south west, and finally settled on Anse d'Orlando, a beautiful bay surrounded by tree-covered hills, with clear water, a sandy bottom and good swimming. By nightfall, however, although there was little wind, an uncomfortable swell developed and we had our worst, rocky night of the cruise.

On Monday, with the wind north north west force five, backing and increasing, we left for Florent, with one reef in the main and several rolls in the genoa. There had been white horses in the anchorage. Now we ran into big, tumbling seas from ahead. I decided to go the other way and run before them to Calvi. We altered course to 240 degrees, but the genoa would not set until I poled it out and goose-winged the main with a preventer to hold it. Three hours later the wind dropped to north east force one and we were making little headway in a very lumpy sea. I put the engine on and motored to our favourite cove in Revellata for yet another comfortable night.

The next day we motor-sailed in a light wind to Girolata. We had intended to anchor off the beach, but the heavy south-west swell portended a bumpy night so we put into the crowded Girolata harbour, and dropped anchor among some fifty other boats. Another fifty or so boats arrived and anchored with fenders out in the tiny, packed harbour. Fortunately, there was no wind or swell and we enjoyed a quiet and undisturbed night.

In the evening we strolled up to what once might have been an attractive, picturesque village, with old streets and houses. Like so many such villages its attraction was its undoing. The harbour suffered from a constant stream of vedettes, catered for by numerous cafés and restaurants, with dirt and litter everywhere.

The next day, Wednesday 21st August, at 0745 in a light wind we sailed under full rig through the Sanguinieres, where we furled the genoa and started the motor, through Ajaccio Bay to Ajaccio, where we moored in l'Amiraute Port de Plaisance at 1445.

We jilled around in the marina at first, but as no help was forthcoming we decided to take an empty berth, bows in because of the difficult wind. We made fast to a friendly, neighbouring boat. Our stern buoy was missing, but the next one was free, so I used the dinghy to take a warp out to it. While I was doing this, an impatient French boat arrived and tried to take our buoy. I told him in French to go away and find his own buoy. Eventually it was sorted out and all was well.

We enjoyed a lovely five-course meal in a street of cafés, all out on the pavement, separated by shrubs and lit by fairy-lights, with a background of talk in many different languages, very French, very popular and full of atmosphere.

On Thursday, while Joan did the washing, I searched fruitlessly for engine oil among the chandlers and garages. After dinner a 35-foot Beneteau came next to us and Jerome and Natalie from Paris and their friend, Elaine, came aboard for drinks.

The next day, while Joan shopped I again searched for oil in the old port, this time successfully, and began to service the engine. Not having the right tool, I was unable to remove the oil filter. I made a Spanish windlass, but was still unable to turn it. Jules, a Dutchman from two boats away, came to help and, with his strength and my windlass, succeeded.

I sent a fax to Malta Shipyard reserving a berth for the winter lay up. In the evening Jules and Marlene, from Amsterdam, came aboard for drinks and we had an enjoyable chat.

The next day we left our berth and motored to the fuelling berth, where Bruce and Michelle, from the catamaran *Double Worries*, helped us with our mooring and came aboard to look at *Blue Pearl*.

We had an easy sail to Pointe de la Castagne, a small bay sheltered from the north west. We were the only boat left at anchor and just eating our evening meal, with plenty of room available, when a large Italian boat chose to anchor a few feet away from us and finished up broadside across our bows, only twenty feet away with the wind blowing him on. I left my meal and hurried forward to deal with the expected collision. However, he put on his engine and moved a few feet further on, still a hazard. After an hour he pulled up his anchor and moved further away.

On Sunday I cleared the log, which was choked with barnacles, and at 1015 we left harbour under main and genoa for Campo Moro, a wide bay sheltered from the west and south west. A swell developed in the afternoon but lessened in the evening and we had a quiet and peaceful night with a lovely full moon.

After our pre-breakfast swim we thoroughly enjoyed the fresh croissants brought out to us by a friendly Corsican baker. I re-wired the boat for a 240-volt 13-amp plug in the galley to come off the mains system. I used our 13V/240V generator for the power drill and kept it on 240 volts for Joan to do her ironing and test the new system. We had a late lunch, a siesta and a walk round the village with its baker, two grocers and several restaurants.

On Tuesday 27th August we left the anchorage at 0730 under mizzen and motor. The wind was negligible so we kept the awning up. By 1130 the wind was getting up from the south west so we turned the engine off and continued sailing at 4.5 knots. By 1145 the wind was increasing and the sea becoming lumpy so we took down the awning. From the log:

1215 Arrived Figari. Wind force 6. Motored to head of the long inlet. Just past the jetty the soundings changed suddenly from 12 to 6 feet. We backed off and tried south of the jetty. Again alarming changes of depth, suggesting big rocks underneath. Depth went down to 5 feet 9 inches, so our keel was just missing the bottom. We tried north of the small island as recommended in the Pilot – a depth of 35 feet, shelving suddenly. Wind now force 6–7 and blustery. Dropped anchor with two other boats, but we dragged and so did they, so we all moved off. We anchored by the tower, again recommended, but again dragged. Wind now force 7–8, possibly a mistral. Decided to leave this difficult anchorage and make for Bonifacio.

Leaving Figari unexpectedly, with Joan below, 'George' on the helm and me tidying fenders and warps, I suddenly saw a single rock 50 yards dead ahead. Emergency turn to starboard to clear. In the strong wind we had been making 20 degrees leeway without my realising it.

We proceeded to Bonifacio, a pleasant harbour with easy access between towering pink cliffs dotted with caves. There were two possible anchorages on the left: the first was not tenable; the second required a stern line ashore, which I was not ready to try in the strong wind. It was easy to berth in the pontoon and the charge was reasonable – £12 per night. However, the below-standard showers and toilets were expensive. We enjoyed a peaceful night after a tiring day.

There were shops and a supermarket along the quay and we spent the morning shopping, followed by lunch aboard, a siesta and a shower. In the evening we walked up to the citadel to explore the old town with its narrow alleys, church and flying buttresses.

Then, down at the quayside, we had a good meal for £8 each at the Restaurant Bonifacio.

On Thursday with the wind forecast north east force five, we decided to move to Anse de Paragnano, a bay two miles back along the coast, sheltered from the east. We shopped for four days' supplies and tried for Italian lire, but the exchange would not deliver.

At 1315 we left harbour and motored to Paragnano. The wind was west force four, blowing into the bay and setting up a strong swell. The holding was poor and we dragged our anchor twice before settling. We dragged again and re-anchored in the central channel in twenty-six feet. All the other boats had left. Later, a motorboat anchored outside us. We had an anchor alert every two hours, but otherwise a quiet night.

In the morning I woke with a sense of urgency. The wind had increased to force six from the north east and we were dragging rapidly on to the motorboat. We started the engine, took up the anchor and cleared out from this troublesome anchorage.

The wind was now north east force seven, gusting eight, and we set off for Sardinia under mizzen and half genoa at a speed of six knots. With the wind increasing, I decided not to go on but to make for Bonifacio, where we knew there was a good, safe berth. We quickly found a berth opposite our last one, into wind so berthing was easy. I paid the Capitainerie for a further night and we went to the bank to draw more money. This time the young cashier suggested a method of drawing Italian lire. He cashed a £100 Eurocheque in sterling, from which he paid £35 in French francs and £55 in Italian lire, charging us £10 for the transaction.

After dinner on board we walked up to the citadel for a concert given by the Young Philharmonic Chamber Orchestra of Cologne, including 'Spring' from Vivaldi's 'Four Seasons', concertos by Bach and Mozart and a piece by Paganini, held in the church with a very appreciative, cosmopolitan audience, mainly from the yachts – French, American, German, Italian, Dutch, British and others – a moving experience that well repaid our return to Bonifacio.

On Saturday 31st August the forecast was wind north east force four to five, moderating to three to four so we decided to leave for Sardinia. On the way out we were stopped by a Capitainerie boat and told by the official in truculent tones that we had not paid our dues. I said we had paid and the official became quite aggressive. I asked to speak on his mobile to the Capitainerie. They had booked our third night as a continuation of our first two nights instead of as a new night after one away. With this cleared we were allowed to leave.

10

Sardinia

At last, at 1130, we reached the harbour mouth. The wind was north east force five gusting six. Our course was 149°. I set a reefed main and two-thirds genoa. The sea had many white tops and a few big waves, but I thought it was reasonable and our speed was 5.5 knots. At 1230 I was hardening up to the wind and at 1305 the wind was heading us, so I took in the genoa and motor-sailed.

At 1400, south of Spargi, we altered course to 112° and I was able to unfurl the genoa and turn off the engine. At 1440, three miles north east of Punta Sardegna, I decided to go to Cala Francese. It looked good so we anchored at the head of the bay in twelve feet, with fifty feet scope of chain.

The pretty little anchorage, with pink rocks and shrubs all round, was almost full with seven boats. The holding seemed to be good. We had a quiet, undisturbed night, followed by a most interesting day. It started with a swim and the Corsican on the next boat calling out, 'Do you have to do that?'

'As an Englishman, yes. Are you coming in?'

'As a Corsican, no, not likely!' he said, and he upped his anchor and left.

The Italians on the jetty prepared to leave. They looked long and anxiously at the boat next to us and then took out a long third anchor line and dropped it almost across his anchor chain. He was ready to leave, but was so concerned that he dived in and inspected it. Apparently all was well for he quickly left.

The Italians then contacted me and intimated in Italian and gestures that they wished to leave. The previous night they had dropped their anchor almost on top of ours and now we were lying across their chain. I obliged by motoring out to the extremity of my chain. The skipper gave the third anchor rope to two girls to haul in, having taken it out of its fairlead so that there was no bight in it. He then motored towards us, releasing his mooring line from ashore. The girls could not hold the anchor rope and dropped it in the water where it disappeared from view. The skipper overrode his second anchor and kept coming at us, while I retreated until I was at the end of our anchor scope. Fortunately, as it dragged forward, his anchor came up. He then stayed over our anchor chain for ten minutes, debating with his number two. It was difficult for me to keep out of his way. At last he left us and anchored farther off. Then the two men returned in their dinghy with scuba gear and efficiently recovered their anchor.

The next episode was the arrival of a fleet of seven small yachts from a sailing school. They all intended to lay out an anchor twelve feet from me and drop back to the jetty. The first three achieved this. Then a squall approached with an increase of wind to force six. The others tried many times, but only one more made it. One nearly hit us, but I had a large fender ready and fended him off. The remaining three anchored in mid-harbour.

The wind increased to force seven and changed direction by 180 degrees to the southwest, blowing us towards the rocks on the northeast side. This was accompanied by thunder and lightning and heavy rain. Joan had prepared our lunch, so we sat under the cockpit hood eating it, keeping an eye on our anchor and watching the large yacht accompanying the sailing school drag its anchor and re-anchor four times.

Before the wind returned to the north east a large fishing boat came in and tried to anchor between the three yachts. Having nearly hit the large boat, he went farther down the bay. His young son came over in a dinghy to borrow a pump because the dinghy was flabby. Ours did not quite fit, but I jumped in and held the nozzle while he pumped – and it worked.

We had begun to settle down for the night when a Corsican boat with four adults and six children aboard arrived and anchored close to us. When the wind turned he put out a stern anchor and his boat was exactly over our chain. We had a sleepless night. In the morning we had to ask the Corsican to move his boat while we got under way, which he did with a cheerful smile.

We left the anchorage at 0830 and motor-sailed round to Villamarina on Isla San Stefano, about three miles away. It has a disused wharf, but we did not like the derelict buildings, old machinery and piles of rubbish, so we tried anchoring at the head of the bay. We were too near the sides for swinging, so we tried the west side, which looked good, but we grounded on rock while sounding in. We soon came off and finally anchored in the middle of the fairway.

In the afternoon a large ferryboat, carrying two dustcarts, crashed through the anchored boats making some of them move out of its way. It off-loaded the carts in seconds and departed with equal haste. We all breathed easily again, including the Corsicans, who had arrived and again anchored just across our anchor chain. An hour later *Jolly Ferry* came back, in the same mad rush, and collected the carts.

The wind, which had been north east force four all day, increased to force six and we, in company with most of the boats, departed. We decided to make for Porto Palma, on Caprera Island, three miles away. The wind increased to force seven and the sea became rough. The anchorage was in a lovely wide bay, well protected from the north east. We anchored in company with two other boats from San Stefano. The wind died and we had a peaceful meal in the cockpit in an ideal setting. Then the storm clouds came over and the wind increased. We packed up and went below. During the night there was thunder and lightning, but we had a peaceful night.

The next morning, Tuesday 3rd September, we sailed to Cala Gavetta, Maddalena. There were no places available in the marina so we moored on the East Quay, in a deserted ferry berth. For the first time ever we dropped an anchor and backed into a berth, and it was very successful.

At 1200 we saw a berth in the marina being vacated so we hurried across and took it up, bows in. The laid stern line was a little too short for us. A German and his wife, Wulf and Ann, from *Baleja 11*, Hamburg, helped us to moor, and after our evening meal they came round and chatted.

On Wednesday we enjoyed a quiet day in Maddalena, a pleasant town with adequate shops but no toilets or showers in the marina. There was no charge for mooring, but we paid £5 for water.

In a telephone call Jill told us that she needed to contact us by fax, and we were unable to find fax facilities in Maddalena, so the next morning we left for Porto Cervo. Porto Cervo is the hub of the Aga Khan's Costa Smeralda, a millionaire's playground, reported to be very expensive. However, when we arrived, we found an excellent, buoyed, free anchorage, where we dropped in fifteen feet. The Yacht Club would not allow us to use their fax machine, but when we asked at the marina the girl told us she would have to ask her boss. She returned to tell us the boss had agreed and there would be no charge.

On our return to the boat we found that a *Sunsail* charter boat had anchored too close. After a peaceful night we had to motor to the extent of our chain to let him out. We then took the dinghy over to Porto Vecchio, the Old Port, where some fifty old sailing boats, mostly sixty to eighty feet in length, were moored for a rally. Back in the marina we collected Jill's fax, telephoned Peggy and Jack on their golden wedding anniversary and returned to the boat for another peaceful night.

The next morning we went ashore in Porto Vecchio and walked around the newly constructed 'old fishing village'. Unexpectedly we found it attractive and restful, if very expensive for shopping. Later in the morning we motored round to Cala de Volpé for a quiet night and then on to Porn Island for another, and so to Olbia, where we arrived at midday on Monday 9th September.

At the Yacht Club I was given an unpleasant and unhelpful reception. The Capitainerie was more accommodating and told us to berth alongside a large Corsican yacht on the wharf next to the diesel pump. When the owners, Mauro and Shakura, a young couple who spoke fluent English, returned they invited us aboard for drinks and came back to us for a return in the evening.

Ashore for shopping the next morning, we bought fruit and vegetables in the open market and meat in the covered meat and fish market. I managed to replace our paraffin lamp, used as a riding light, which had cracked and broken.

Back on board, we exchanged visits with *Moby Dick II*, a couple from Northampton who were on their way home after four years in the Mediterranean. We connected up to a water tap on the wharf to top up, and immediately a green unmarked van drove up and the man demanded 10,000 lire for the water. I told him that we had only topped up with 100 litres and refused to pay. 'Okay,' said the man, 'nothing then,' and drove away. We thought he was not an official but someone trying it on.

We left Olbia in the afternoon and motored in a light headwind between Isola Tavolata and the mainland, avoiding the numerous rocks with visual navigation. Tavolata is a spectacular island, rising sheer from the sea to a great height, with light and shade where the sun outlines the ridges and crevasses.

At 1620 we arrived in Porto della Taverna and anchored in the southern corner in twelve feet, well protected and with a magnificent view of Tavolata and its tall cliff, with the sun glinting like snow on its summit.

After a peaceful night, a morning swim and breakfast in the cockpit, we motored five miles through the islands to Cala Coda Cavallo, a small, sheltered anchorage behind an island and a reef. The strong wind lasted all day but died as night fell and we slept peacefully.

On Thursday, in a wind from the east that increased steadily through the day to gale force, we sailed to La Caletta Harbour. We were guided to a downwind berth by a harbour official, but were unable to hold the boat so came alongside the pontoon. We were told that the wind, now force eight and veering to the south, was a sirocco. Several people helped us, particularly Urve from *Treekeeper*, a large old Danish fishing boat. We warped the boat's head out, using the engine to bring the head round, while Urve pulled the bows out on the mooring line and made fast. With the mooring line taut, we dragged onto the pontoon and I had to hold us off with the engine.

We were now directed to an upwind pontoon, where it was much easier to moor the boat head to wind. I set breast and stern lines to the pontoon to steady the boat and hold us off the next boat. Altogether, it took an hour to moor. Later, Urve came aboard for a drink and we had coffee aboard his boat. He was refurbishing it in handsome style and we compared notes on boat building. In the evening the wind backed to the south west, still force eight, with a violent electrical thunderstorm.

The next morning, Friday 13th September, the French boat next to us picked up a weather forecast saying that the sirocco was expected to last two more days, so we booked two nights in Caletta, £12.50 the first night and £7.50 the second. Caletta was rather a run-down place and we did not find an attractive restaurant, so we had dinner in our cabin. Ilse and Sigurd, from a Danish boat on its way home after four years in the Mediterranean, came aboard for pre-dinner drinks. After another thunderstorm we had a quiet night.

The next day we sailed to Gonome and tied alongside a sixty-foot barque. In the evening we tried an Italian pizzeria, but it lacked the sparkle of the French restaurants and the meal was not brilliant.

Early on Sunday morning, with the wind north west force five to six, we set reefed main and genoa and had a good sail to Arbatax. We moored stern-to with an anchor chain out forward, helped by Peter and Sylvia from a forty-foot Atlantic, *Spirit of Lundy*. Later Peter, who had a bicycle, used it to help us carry water in plastic jerricans from a tap a hundred yards away. In the early evening we took down our awning in a violent thunderstorm and heavy rain. After this, Peter and Sylvia, who were from Bideford, came aboard for drinks.

At 2400 we were awakened by a bang. A huge ferry had arrived and berthed fifty yards away. His wash had driven us broadside on to the wall. Peter and I put on our engines to hold us off. Both boats had dragged their anchors, so we both took them up and motored to vacant places on a commercial wall on the other side of the harbour, where mooring was forbidden. The remainder of the night passed peacefully.

11

Sardinia to Malta: In the Lap of the Gods

At 0700 the next morning we left Arbatax for the island of Ustica, 30 miles north of Palermo and 180 miles away. At 2130 the storm began. Since the beginning of September we seemed to have run foul of the gods, with strong winds, often of gale force, dragging anchors, harbours with no available berths and several electrical storms.

This current storm continued throughout the night, with sheet lightning, forked lightning and a dangerous-looking type like a pillar of light that came straight down from the sky to the sea. We saw a number of these, at one time three together, only a mile or two away from us. The gods were indeed angry.

At dawn an ominous, black, evil-looking cloud, belching lightning, was coming from astern and slowly catching us up. Ahead was a smaller but equally unpleasant cloud coming towards us.

'What happens when the two systems meet,' I said to Joan, 'particularly if one is charged positively and the other negatively? Let's get out of this!'

I put the motor on at full throttle and turned at right angles to the line of approach. The two systems met in a swirling mass of cloud with a loud clap of thunder. The black clouds were illuminated with continuous lightning, sheet, forked and pillar.

Then I heard Joan cry, 'Look! There is an aeroplane right in the heart of the storm!'

She pointed to a vapour trail, which we took to be an aircraft, that emerged from the heart of the cloud and followed an erratic course across our stern. The weaving became more pronounced and the vapour trail began a shallow dive and plunged into the sea a mile astern of us.

'We must look for survivors,' I called, and turned *Blue Pearl* towards what looked like a maelstrom where the vapour trail hit the water. From this emerged a thick pillar of water vapour, rising to a height of a hundred feet, which moved towards us at great speed. Puzzled at first, we then perceived it to be a waterspout with a circular motion on the sea and the pillar weaving back and forth and from side to side, like a huge dancer – or goddess. Was she the source of all our problems and was she angry that we had dodged the clash of the storms? It was easy, in a situation like this, to see and feel how the legends of the ancient Greeks and the trials of Ulysses had been born.

I told Joan to get her camera while I took evasive action. I first turned to port on full throttle. The waterspout turned to starboard to intercept. I turned 180 degrees to avoid. Again the waterspout turned to intercept. It was as if there were an intelligence controlling its movements.

Joan emerged with her camera. The waterspout, a towering, ghostly figure, was about a hundred yards away. Just when I thought we must be engulfed, it stopped, turned back on itself and slowly collapsed and subsided into the sea.

I do not think we had been in great danger. The spout seemed to be more vapour than water, and the churning water beneath it was not threatening. We saw no sign of a crashed aircraft, but I believe we had witnessed the birth, life and death of a waterspout caused by the clash of two storms. There is probably a physical explanation of the phenomenon as well as a reason for the apparent ability of the spout to intercept us, but I do not know what it is. I was, however, very conscious of ancient traditions on this 'wine dark sea'. Joan was not successful with her picture – she had run out of film!

By noon we had anchored stern to wall in St Maria, the capital, indeed the only town, of Ustica, Homer's Island of Winds. St Maria is a pretty town with white-walled houses painted with colourful murals. The square, shaded by trees and exotic shrubs, has a lovely church at its northern end.

Even here the gods still afflicted us with petty annoyances. A large diving-school boat tied his bow to ours without putting out his own bow anchor. The strong wind on both boats caused us to drag our anchor until it became necessary to re-anchor, using the full one-hundred-and-eighty-foot scope of our chain. We had decided to stay two nights in harbour but, because of the noise of bulldozers and cement mixers on the wharf, we thought we would depart after breakfast and early morning shopping. However, at 0700 a man came to tell us that a big crane ship was docking on our wharf in five minutes. We had to move quickly, and decided to berth at the fuel wharf, have breakfast, shop, refuel, then leave. Just as we started to back into the berth a fishing boat rushed in and took the only available place. We gave up and set course for Palermo.

At 1425 we arrived at Palermo after an easy sail, took in fuel, and backed stern-to at the end of the fuelling wharf. We needed to telephone Jill later, and the fuel man told us that the nearest telephone was in the market, about half a mile away.

At 2200 we left to make our call. In the darkness, the wharves we were walking along were eerie. A pack of about twelve wild dogs, with staring eyes, rushed past us but did not attack. A few minutes later, in the seediest part of the dockland area, we came across a group of youths aged about eighteen, standing talking on a street corner. The talking stopped as we approached and, knowing Palermo's reputation, I feared the worst.

'Take the bull by the horns. Get them on your side,' I thought. I walked up to them.

'Mercato!' I exclaimed. 'Dov'è il mercato? Where is the market?' This was one of the few Italian phrases I had learned.

The menacing face of the leader broke into a beaming smile.

'Ah, si. Mercato,' and he broke into a torrent of Italian, with many gestures, pointing out the direction.

They were on our side, helping us, and who can harm anyone they are helping? I shook my informant's hand and thanked him, and we parted with gestures of good will. In the market I was able to telephone Jill and also the shipyard in Malta to confirm our reservation for a winter lay up.

The next few days provided the one pleasant interlude in this part of our cruise. We met some friends of our daughter, Bryn Thomas and his Sicilian wife Francesca, who took us for the weekend to their lovely mountain home outside Palermo and showed us the surrounding countryside. We became aware of how Sicily was steeped in history and of the influence of the Greek, Phoenician and Arab cultures. We particularly liked the cathedral of Monreale with its golden mosaics reflecting Arab influence, and our introduction to Sicilian ice-cream in its twenty varieties. Francesca's mother

119

invited us to an Italian meal in her penthouse flat in Palermo, ante pasta, pasta and post pasta, and we learned something of the dangers of the young mafia.

We enjoyed taking *Blue Pearl* to Cefalu, a pleasant, small harbour with a big cathedral, where we were joined by Bryn and Francesca and their small son for lunch aboard, followed by a swim from their favourite beach.

Our next port of call was Capo d'Orlando, described by our pilot book as a new harbour being built. It was an old harbour in a bad state of disrepair. We dropped our anchor well out and backed into the broken stone quay on the north side. At one o'clock in the morning we were awakened by a spectacular and severe electrical storm with tropical rain.

Porto Roso, our next port, was a rip-off. It was a new marina village, supposedly offering excellent facilities at £25 per night. We were given a berth a mile away from showers and toilets. In the village the supermarket, laundry and bank were all closed, although all were advertised and our main reason for going there. We had paid a high-season price for low-season facilities.

Our next port was Messina. We were back in the world of Ulysses and ancient legend. As we came towards the Straits the wind got up to force six from ahead, and with the current against us we could visualise the desperate attempts of Homerian sailors to navigate through, past the whirlpools of Scylla and Charybdis, to gain access to the Ionian sea and so to Greece. Although we once turned ninety degrees in the eddies of Scylla, the whirlpools offered no problems, and I had to think they must have been more menacing in the time of Ulysses. Perhaps our Perkins engine made all the difference!

Messina was difficult and inhospitable. The pilot book mentioned a yacht quay as being most suitable for visiting yachts. We located it easily, but were shouted away by a local official. The quay was for local people only. We toured the harbour twice, looking for a safe patch in the heavy swell that beat against the harbour wall. With difficulty we tied up against some large tyres, only to be told that we must vacate our berth at 0800 next morning as it was required for a cruise ship.

Next morning we set off for Reggio Calabria on the Italian mainland, where, in the marina, we were again unlucky, being allocated the end berth that was very uncomfortable in the heavy

120

swell. In the afternoon we walked into town for shopping, on the way passing a street vendor selling baskets of grapes for the equivalent of £5.

'We'll buy some on the way back,' I suggested to Joan.

On the way back the man was still there, but packing up his wares. I explained that I only wanted a few grapes, about half a kilo and offered fifty pence. Taking the money, he pushed the whole basket of grapes into my hands – about five kilos. It was grapes with everything for the next few days!

In the evening Stewart Brett and his wife from *Bluebird*, Essex, came aboard for drinks and brought a bottle of excellent Greek wine. Our GPS had been giving problems, sending a signal 'No antenna'. In the morning Stewart went up the mizzen, unscrewed the module and inspected the antenna, but could not find the fault. However, the GPS was cured.

Again we decided to stay only one night and next morning left for Taormina Bay where we thought to spend two nights, giving us a chance to visit the old citadel at Taormina and the ancient Greek port of Naxos nearby. By midday the northerly wind had increased from force one to force five. At 1300 a sudden gust from the north east alerted us and we quickly took in the mainsail and shortened the genoa to one third. The wind was rising all the time and we found ourselves travelling at 6.5 knots under our tiny foresail in a gale force wind. By 1420 the wind had eased to force six and we continued with half genoa at 5 knots.

The short gale had set up a big swell with breaking waves that made the Taormina anchorage untenable. The open harbour at Naxos was no better. The big incoming swell was crashing against the inside harbour wall and it was impossible to berth. We continued at 6 knots under partly furled genoa to Riposto where at last we found shelter. Even here we were told that we could stay only until 0800 the following morning, and so early the next day we made a quick passage to Catania. For the first time in a Sicilian harbour we were made welcome and given a good reception – by the Club Nautico. An official took our line and saw that we were accommodated with water and electricity.

That afternoon, Saturday 28th September, we made the conscious decision to make Catania our last port of call before Malta. Since the beginning of the month the gods had been against us and we had suffered a number of small setbacks. We would enjoy the amenities of our berth, arrange to join the expedition to the summit of Mount Etna on Sunday, and miss out Syracuse and Porto Palo, our intended last ports of call. We had a feeling of euphoria, of a good, happy cruise nearing its end. The upsets of the past four weeks were forgotten.

That evening we strolled into Catania to a main shopping street, looking for a bank to use a European credit card. We stopped at a bank mentioned in our Eurocheque document, but it displayed a message that the system had broken down. While we were at the machine a man, who had been standing behind us, told us of another bank further along the Liberta Viala. Walking along the street I thought I saw another bank displaying the Eurocheque sign and I hurried ahead of Joan for a better view. Suddenly I heard her cry out. She had been viciously attacked, in full view of all the people about us, by a young ruffian aged between twenty and twenty-five. He had made a rugby tackle on her from ahead, throwing her backwards onto the ground. Then he had snatched her shoulder bag containing my wallet, all our money and several papers such as cheque card and driving licence.

I turned and saw the man running off with the shoulder bag and immediately chased after him. Round two blocks I chased him, hardly losing ground. As I ran my thoughts veered from 'This isn't happening to me' to 'When I catch up with him I'll knee him in the groin and as he doubles up I'll get his arm in an arm lock behind his back and if necessary break it.' He came to a motorbike leaning against a wall. As he kick-started it I got to within three yards, but he was away, with the bag looped over his shoulder. I stared after him, but I did not see a number plate.

I started to move back the way I had come, when I saw my wife coming towards me, looking white and shaken and clutching her shoulder in great pain. She was hurt badly. Not one person in that crowded shopping street where the attack had occurred had offered her assistance. Now, in this poor back street, a crowd gathered round us and someone brought out a chair for Joan to sit on.

I have never felt so desperate in my life. I had no money, not even to telephone for an ambulance. Neither of us could speak Italian. We were surrounded by some twenty people, all speaking a language we could not understand and many wanting to touch Joan's shoulder. And all I could do was fend them off.

Then a young lad offered a coin, exclaiming, 'Telephono, telephono.' I asked him to come with me to telephone, but he was too fearful. He had made an instinctive gesture of sympathy. Now he backed off and disappeared into the crowd. Then a miracle occurred.

'I'll telephone for you.'

The voice was that of a young girl, aged about ten, speaking good English. She took me to a telephone and rang the police. She spoke fluent Italian. We returned to my wife and waited. And waited. Nothing. No sign of police or ambulance.

'I'll get my mum,' said the child.

Ten minutes later, Veronica, a Scotswoman and widow of a Sicilian marine officer, arrived.

'I have telephoned the police. They did not believe my daughter and were taking no action,' she said. 'The ambulance will be here in a few minutes.'

She told us that she would accompany us to the hospital and translate for us. She had lived for sixteen years in Catania and spoke Sicilian like a native.

First we were interviewed at the hospital police office, permanently staffed to deal with crime. We were told that this was the young mafia and the police would be unlikely to act for fear of reprisals. The last policeman to arrest a thug had had his wife savagely attacked.

We waited at the hospital for three and a half hours, mostly without a chair for Joan to sit on, while an X-ray was taken. Joan had three breaks in her shoulder and a damaged arm and hand. Her shoulder was twisted out of alignment and a later X-ray showed a broken thumb and finger. At the end of that long, weary period the doctor bound up her shoulder and told us that nothing could be done that night as it was Saturday. We were to come again at nine o'clock on Monday morning when they would arrange for treatment. Not having any money, we were left to walk the long two miles back to the boat.

An anxious weekend followed. Many Club Nautico members came to express their sympathy and to tell of similar attacks they or their friends had experienced. The club sailing master and his assistant were particularly helpful. They told us that the club was preparing brochures for their visitors in English, French and German. Would I put the English version into colloquial English? This I agreed to do, and one paragraph I wrote up read like this: 'Ladies must be very careful when walking in Catania. Thieves are particularly vicious and will not hesitate to attack a woman. Women should not carry shoulder bags. It is better for them to carry a cheap handbag, containing nothing important or valuable, which they should let go as soon as attacked.'

On Monday Veronica came at 0700 in her car to take us in good time to the hospital. Another long wait was followed by an altercation between the doctor and Veronica. She explained that the doctor was saying nothing could be done for ten days. The friendly policeman from Saturday joined in, gesticulating and shouting at the doctor. Veronica told us that he was telling the doctor he should be ashamed. Here was a lady visiting their country, attacked by one of their citizens and hurt badly and nothing could be done!

The policeman personally shepherded us past the doctor up to the physiotherapy department. Again we met a doctor who refused to do anything. Our policeman pushed past him and into the surgeon's reception room. A long argument followed. I said that if we could get no service in Sicily I would get my wife on a plane for England where they were more civilised. The two doctors finally agreed to prepare Joan for such a journey. She was strapped in a special elastic sheath that immobilised her arm yet supported the shoulder.

Veronica took us to two travel agents, but we were unable to book a through flight to Gatwick or Heathrow, where Joan could be met, until the following Friday, and that at a cost of £400.

I determined to take Joan to Malta on *Blue Pearl*. I knew I would get more help there. Joan said that, although she could not help in sailing the boat, she would give me an hour's rest during the night so long as I slept in the cockpit. Unfortunately, the weather had turned against us. With a force five wind from ahead it would have been dangerous for Joan to be aboard in a lumpy sea.

Neither aircraft nor hovercraft to Malta were available so we decided to take the next ferry, on Tuesday morning. This involved a nine-hour passage, arriving at 1800. I still had my Euro chequebook, but had been unable to obtain Maltese money in Catania and the ferry did not provide an exchange facility. A friendly Englishman on the ferry offered to take us in his taxi to his hotel, The British Hotel. He introduced us to the taxi driver, Toni, a robust fifty-year-old, full of vitality and drive, and straight out of an American film.

Toni took over. The British Hotel was full, but he deposited us at a neighbouring hotel that provided us with a room and bathroom for the night at a reasonable cost. He telephoned the airport and ascertained that the first flights out were at 0600 and 0700 the next morning. He called for us at 0500, settled our bill, and drove like James Bond to the airport where, in Maltese, he talked us through reception and customs and Joan on to the only available unclaimed seat on the 0600 flight. The cost of the flight was £200.

Toni then took me to an all-night bank to cash a Euro cheque and on to a telephone centre that was supposed to remain open all night. It was closed. Undaunted, Toni banged on the door until it was opened, swamped the male receptionist with his demands and had me inside the telephone booth before I could get my breath back. A call to Joan's sister in New Malden ensured that she would be met at Heathrow and taken straight to Kingston Hospital for the much-needed attention.

Hardly giving me time to complete payment for the call, Toni had me back in the taxi roaring away to the docks to catch the same ferry on its return trip to Catania, leaving at 0900. By 1800 I was back in Catania, arranging to leave in *Blue Pearl* at first light. In vain the Club Nautico tried to find a crew for me. The club's secretary formally expressed the club's sympathy for our plight, waived the five days' fees and, as a token of regard, presented me with a club burgee.

I missed Joan terribly. We were used to working together and knew each other's ways. Now, in addition to worrying about her, I had to think of her tasks as well as my own. I nearly came to grief as I eased stern-first out of our berth. An anchor, projecting out to port on the next boat, hooked under one of my fenders. However, once out in the harbour I found it not too difficult to hoist the mainsail with the boat under Autohelm.

The wind was north east, force four, and we were soon romping away at six knots under main and genoa. The cloud over Etna looked very much like a brooding, malevolent Zeus, an old god with a long beard sitting on a cloud. He remained in sight for twenty miles until we rounded the headland at Syracuse. With that, the cloud lifted, the sun came out, and my spirits lightened. I felt I was out of that sinister influence.

I began to enjoy the strange experience of sailing *Blue Pearl* alone. In the afternoon the wind dropped to a gentle breeze and the sea became calm, leaving me in a tranquil mood. Working the boat, cooking a meal and writing a long letter to Joan kept me sufficiently occupied so as not to brood on recent events.

Porto Palo seemed a strange place as I entered it in the gathering darkness. It was occupied entirely by fishing boats, with not a yacht in sight. An ice factory stood starkly in a prominent position and the smell of fish and diesel fuel was everywhere. I thought that this must be what a whaling station in the Antarctic looked like.

I could not see a place to moor, so I carefully motored to beyond the fishing boats until I was close to the beach in two metres, where I dropped the hook. Immediately I was approached by a large rubber dinghy with four young Sicilians in it, which circled me several times while its occupants seemed to be jeering and taunting me.

At one to clock in the morning I was awakened by a beam of light. A car on the beach had its headlights shining on me, and the same dinghy with the four youths was approaching. I went below, grabbed my heavy, long steel emergency tiller arm, and stood waiting for them in the cockpit. The dinghy came straight towards my stern – and went on to an adjacent fishing boat, which the youths boarded.

A night's rest at Porto Palo was followed by a vigorous sail to Malta, where I entered Marsamxett Harbour at 1600 on Friday 4th October, twenty-one weeks after setting out from Dartmouth.

I had called up the Harbour Authority on the way in and was told to report to Customs. It took me more than an hour, on my own, to settle the boat and pump up the dinghy, and it was after five o'clock when I knocked on the door of Customs House, now locked. An official opened up and told me the Customs Officer would not be very happy.

I was shown into his office, where he sat at his desk, in uniform, with two bars on his shoulder. He was very angry.

'What do you think we are?' he cried. 'You arrive here after hours on a Friday night and expect an instant response. It will take me two hours to deal with you.'

By way of an apology I explained what had happened to my wife and why I was late.

'My dear chap,' he exclaimed. 'I am so sorry. Let me get you a whisky.'

While I drank the whisky he stamped my documents without examining them.

Everyone I met in Malta was kind and encouraging. The yacht yard on Manoel Island gave me every assistance in berthing and hauling out. Yvonne Grima, the yard secretary, was particularly kind, offering coffee whenever I called at the office for help, arranging telephone calls and fax messages to my wife and daughter, and organising my flight home and a taxi to collect me. Fifty years earlier I had been of service to Malta when escorting a convoy through the Mediterranean. Now I felt I was more than repaid by the generous help given to me in my hour of need.

Were the phenomena we had witnessed and the bad luck we had experienced the result of natural causes? Or had we come under some malevolent influence of an ancient god? Whatever the reason, I understood more clearly how legends were born.

12

Dartmouth Interlude I

On Friday 11th October I flew home from Malta and was met at Heathrow by Joan and her brother-in-law, Jack. Apart from bandages and a sling, Joan looked remarkably like her old self. Peggy and Jack had looked after her well.

Joan told me that when she left me at the airport in Malta she had been well looked after by two fellow passengers on the plane. She had been met at Heathrow by Jack and Peggy and taken immediately to Kingston Hospital, where her wedding ring had to be cut off because of the bruising and swelling. The surgeon told her that the treatment in Catania was wrong and her shoulder might have to be broken again and re-set. Further X-rays were taken to reveal the extent of her injuries.

I had been fortunate in Malta. With the co-operation and help of the yard, things had gone well. I had scraped off the barnacles and cleaned and serviced the boat, then taken all the dirty linen, including sheets and pillow cases, table cloths and napkins, and our personal clothes, to the laundry in three loads and had it washed and ironed, ready for our return. I left instructions with the yard to look after the batteries, service the engine and clean the jets, and remove the boarding ladder they had provided and replace it for our return. I removed the faulty pulse-charger, ready to take home with me for servicing in England. Time passed swiftly and I was able to leave two days before I had anticipated.

On the evening of my arrival in England Jill telephoned, in near despair, to say that a client owing over a hundred thousand pounds had declared himself bankrupt and she and Rob were facing ruin. I decided to pay a quick visit to Cornwall to see what I could do to help. I left the next day and returned the following Wednesday, interrupting my return journey with a quick visit to Dartmouth to check that all was well there.

The next day Jack took Joan and me to the hospital where she saw the specialist. He was pleased with the progress Joan had made with the simple pendulum exercises he had prescribed and now thought that further surgery would not be necessary. It would take her at least a further three months of physiotherapy to recover. He agreed to transfer her to Dartmouth and gave her her X-rays and a letter to her doctor.

The next day we caught an early train to Totnes and arrived in Dartmouth at lunchtime for weekend shopping and a taxi home. We both needed a siesta and that evening I cooked a meal for us both.

Now began a strange time for us. We were caught up in a series of activities in Dartmouth that put all thoughts of *Blue Pearl* out of our minds. It was as though we were leading two different lives, one belonging to the boat and one to home. Our friends rallied round us and there were numerous telephone calls asking for news of Joan. Mary, from the flat below, baked a sponge and another cake and later sent up a pâté and a beef casserole.

Extracts from Joan's diary show how things went:

Sunday 20th October. F worked on papers all day, particularly Julia's bank account and Jill and Rob's affairs. Telephone calls from Joy Wakelin, Richard Westlake and Jeffrey Tomlinson about my shoulder.

Monday 21st. F spent morning writing letters. Lovely foliage plant arrived for me from F's sister. I saw Doctor Fenton who arranged physiotherapy at Dartmouth Hospital. F saw the Bank Manager to arrange a large loan to Jill.

Tuesday 22nd. F to Optician. Needs new glasses. To dentist. Needs filling. My Literature Class. F to Probus.

Thursday 24th a.m. F worked on letters. p.m. To Dunkirk Nursery for wallflowers. None left. On to Stokenham Farm for 'pick and buy' fruit and vegetables and wallflowers.

Friday 25th. Torquay Hospital Fracture Clinic for X-rays. Confirmed fracture in thumb and forefinger and that shoulder was mending. Sent to Physiotherapy Department and set exercises.

Saturday 26th. Letter from Julia's Bank. F planted wallflowers. Martin telephoned and had long talk about the cruise.

Sunday 27th. Evening – dinner at the Tomlinsons.

Monday 28th. F to Plymouth for Jill and Rob's meeting at the Official Receiver's re their client's bankruptcy. Trustee appointed. I resumed housework. Did a load of washing.

Tuesday 29th. F to see the Harbour Master to sign a letter to the Insurance Company supporting his claim.

Thursday 31st. Both wrote letters all day. F wrote to the Tax inspector re my tax.

Friday 1st November. F to have skin graft for skin cancer. F to John Rencher with pulse charger for servicing. Mary to meal cooked by me with F's help.

Sunday 3rd. Lunch with John and Irene.

Monday 4th. To Dartmouth Physio Clinic for exercises, manipulation and weight lifting. [She had to lie down and lift a two-pound weight several times with her damaged arm.]

Tuesday 5th. To Physio. F to Library. Both to Stokenham for fruit and vegetables. Annual Bridge Club lunch followed by Chicago bridge.

Wednesday 6th. Evening. To Creswells for supper.

Thursday 7th. To fracture clinic at Torbay Hospital. Picked up Flymo we had left for servicing. Had lunch at a new Pizzeria owned by Mary's son.

Friday 8th. To Physio. F back to optician. Probus Ladies Night. Dinner at Stoke Lodge. Dinner-jackets etc.

Saturday 9th. F gardened. I shopped. Jill telephoned. One of their clients is proceeding with a building. Their Building Society becoming difficult. Afternoon tea with Whittakers.

Monday 11th. A wet day. I ironed. F worked on papers. In the evening to Kay and Richard for supper and bridge.

Tuesday 12th. Gale force winds. To Physio clinic. Up to three pounds weight. Called at Missions for Seamen's fair and bought Xmas cards.

Wednesday 13th. F to Probus lunch.

Thursday 14th. To Physio. Both had 'flu injections. F to Exeter Flotilla, R.M. Lympstone, for supper and talk.

Friday 15th. To Torbay Hospital for F's eye check-up. Xmas shopping at Trago Mills. Fermoys's Pick and Park for lunch on the way home.

Saturday 16th. Yacht Club Commodore's Ball at Guildhall.

Sunday 17th. Wet and windy. Rested all day.

Monday 18th. To Physio clinic.

Tuesday 19th p.m. Bridge Club. Evening – to Mary's for supper.

Wednesday 20th. My literature class. F had huge bonfire of tree cuttings etc. Evening – Tom and Nesta came to supper and bridge.

Tuesday 21st. To Stokenham Farm for fruit and vegetables, then to Stoke Lodge for seminar on investments.

Friday 22nd. Physio. Able to spread hand more easily. Put on to pulley. Evening – Cancer Relief bridge-drive.

Saturday 23rd. F spent all day cutting back a huge buddleia and other overgrown shrubs.

Sunday 24th. Gales all day. A rest day for us.

Monday 25th. F gardened until rain came. In the evening Kay and Richard to bridge.

Tuesday 26th a.m. Cancer research coffee. Evening – bridge club.

Thursday 28th. To Torbay Fracture Clinic. The doctor is satisfied with my progress, but I may still need surgery to get full mobility. Will decide at next visit. On to Sainsbury's opening of new supermarket.

Friday 29th. Peggy and Jack arrived.

Saturday 30th. Peggy and I to Dartmouth Hospital League of Friends Fair. Freddie and Jack walked along Promenade. Mid afternoon – Jill and Rob arrived. Evening – lovely family meal, followed by Jill's video of Blue Pearl *leaving harbour for the Mediterranean.*

Sunday 1st December. Happy morning looking at photographs. Jill and Rob left after tea.

Monday 2nd. Early to Stokenham Farm pick and buy. Then to Start Bay Inn, famous for its fried fish. Then to my Aunt Jessie – in a nursing home after a fall. [Joan and I had become engaged during the war when on a visit to Jessie's farm on Dartmoor.]

Tuesday 3rd a.m. F and Jack cut down the huge elderberry tree. They all went to meet me after my physiotherapy and we walked along the Embankment.

Wednesday 4th. Jill phoned early. Trouble with clients. F to help with a cheque for £2000. Evening – after our meal we all settled down to newly purchased scrabble.

Thursday 5th. Peggy's birthday. Drove to Red Lion at Dittisham for a lovely pub lunch. Then to see Aunt Jessie in Brent.

Saturday 7th. Peggy and Jack left.

Wednesday 11th. My literature class Christmas lunch. F's Probus Christmas lunch.

Thursday 12th. Yacht Club Senior Members lunch. Freddie's birthday.
Friday 13th. F began clearing ivy in the garden. [This had run riot, climbing up and through trees and shrubs, often with stems an inch thick.]
Saturday 14th. F spent morning on ivy. Jill telephoned. The Trustee says that their 'retention clause' will not stand up in court. They will consult a barrister for his opinion. Evening – Tom and Nesta to supper and bridge.
Sunday 15th. My birthday. To Red Lion, Dittisham for an excellent roast beef lunch. Jill rang the pub to wish me a happy birthday. In the evening a concert at the R.N. College.
Thursday 17th 6.30. Drinks at Anne and John's. Then up to Pat and Ralph [also cruising in the Mediterranean] *for more drinks and sandwiches.*
Friday 20th. F began writing an article, 'Four Gales to Gibraltar'.
Monday 23rd. Torbay Hospital. Discharged. No surgery needed. Evening – to Mary for drinks party.
Thursday 24th. Jill, Rob and Tina arrived for traditional Christmas. Big turkey dinner on Christmas Day. On Boxing Day walk round the Coastal Path followed by roast beef evening meal.
Friday 27th. F spent morning with Jill and Rob, working on their court case.
Sunday 29th. F and Tina worked on her case. Posted a letter asking for postponement. Then Tina left. Buffet lunch party at Trish and Pip's.
Monday 30th. I did three loads of washing and vacuumed. F worked in the garden. I had tickle in throat.
Tuesday 31st Cold day again. F worked for an hour in the garden, but he has signs of a cold, too. We decided not to go to the Yacht Club's New Year's Eve party.

The year 1991 was one of the most eventful of our lives. A new life had begun for us at seventy, with the crossing of the Bay of Biscay and our adventures in the Mediterranean. Since returning to England we had little time for relaxation and we did not want it.

Joan's chief aim in life was to get fit for the cruise the following year. At first she had been unable to move her left arm or the fingers of her left hand. She was put on a course of heat treatment and daily manipulative exercises, including weight lifting, then the pulley. I rigged a tackle in the games room, suspending a pulley from one of the overhead beams, so that she could force her left arm to move upwards by pulling the rope through the pulley with her right arm.

For the weight lifting she had to lie on her back and lift a weight several times with her left hand to the full extent of her arm. She started with a two-pound weight, gradually increasing this to five pounds and increasing the number of times she lifted it. Sometimes I saw her with sweat pouring from her face as she passed the pain barrier in her determination to recover in time for our cruise in the spring. She was rewarded when after five months of daily efforts she was discharged, fit, from Dartmouth Hospital physio clinic.

My main efforts were in the garden. Our large garden had been neglected since we bought the house. Scrub alders and elders, old buddleias and other shrubs had all grown enormously and filled the shrubbery. Huge lianas hung from the treetops, and brambles an inch thick roamed everywhere, along the ground and up into the trees, fighting for their existence with ivy. Nettles were rampant. The undergrowth extended to our seventeenth-century wall and some of the roots were penetrating it. Along the south wall there was what had once been a sunken path. This was full of briars, ivy, nettles and small trees, and the dry-stone retaining wall was collapsing.

In the last three months of 1991 I spent as much time as I could on the work of clearing. In 1992 it became my main task, occupying several hours a day – increasingly, as her arm grew stronger, with Joan's help.

Once I had cleared out the unwanted vegetation, digging out the roots of old trees and sometimes using a wire tackle to pull them out, I began on the path. I extended the sunken path alongside the wall on the east side for a further eighty feet, digging out and removing earth and shale and topping it with gravel and coarse sand and building a dry-stone retaining wall. I created an azalea border and a new shrubbery, divided by a crazy-paving path that linked with the sunken path alongside the wall. I built a concrete raft on which to stow the dinghy. It was just like old times, only this time with sand and gravel and a concrete mixer instead of wood and glass fibre. Again, Joan and I were amazingly happy as we worked together to create our new garden.

134

One difference, particularly in the four months after our return, as the diary records, was the vast increase in social activities, and these took up much of our time. We found that we were compressing a year's activities into five months. These were interrupted for a fortnight early in 1992 when we both succumbed to influenza in spite of our 'flu jabs. We were both given a course of antibiotics and told to stay in bed. We cancelled some engagements, rested in bed and recovered, taking it in turns to get up and cook. By mid-January we returned to our normal busy routines, with intense gardening efforts, club and social activities, four more lunch or dinner parties and our own two lunch parties, the first for fourteen and the second for twenty guests, in which we returned the hospitality that had been shown to us.

In February we paid a visit to Peggy and Jack in New Malden and to my sister in Rayleigh. Martin and Jenne, who lived nearby, invited us to dinner and we re-lived the journey to Gibraltar. I took the opportunity to visit Palmer's, my old Sixth Form College, which was opening new buildings to meet the increasing numbers, and met and talked to Ken Clarke, the Chancellor of the Exchequer, who was guest of honour. In March Peggy and Jack came down to us.

We had tree doctors in to prune and shape four of our biggest trees and a stone mason to repair and point our 'listed' wall. Jill and Rob came to see us and supplied a number of shrubs from their nursery to fill the gaps made by our clearance. We returned to visit them at Falmouth and took the opportunity to see their nursery, Tresawsen.

Our time in England was rushing to a close. On Monday 13th April I had the last of several huge bonfires in the garden. On Thursday 16th April we caught a night flight from Exeter to Malta.

13

Malta to the Ionian

We arrived at Manoel Island Yacht Yard, Malta, at 0255 on Friday 17th April. The arrangements I had made six months before with Yvonne Grima, the yard secretary, had all been carried out: the gate office was expecting us; a trolley had been provided to carry our luggage from the taxi to the boat; a boarding ladder had been fixed to the boat ready for our use. I plugged our cable into the mains socket provided and we were in bed by 0345.

We slept until 0930 and when we awoke we were told by people from neighbouring boats that, as it was Good Friday, all the shops were closed. However, Conrad Jenkins of *Piper's Dream*, the boat next to us, provided eggs, bread and butter for breakfast and food for lunch and our evening meal. Even more important, his wife lent Joan a key for the ladies loo, which was kept locked.

On Saturday, on a cold and blustery day, we began to settle in. Shopping for essentials was our first priority and we stocked up with meat, vegetables, fruit and groceries, and returned the gifts of our neighbours. A workman from the yard returned our batteries, but when I fitted them the domestic battery did not work. At 1900 Joan recorded in her diary: *we had a light meal, stewed lamb and vegetables, cherries and cream, biscuits and cheese and half a bottle of fizzy wine.*

On Sunday we again awoke late to another blustery day. I cleaned out our water tanks and then John, from *Marianne Rose*, came to check our batteries with his tester and found them fully charged. Joan and I then checked our wiring and soon found the fault, a loose negative wire on our engine battery. We tried out our repaired pulse-charger and found that it was working well.

On Monday I installed and checked all our electronic gear and found that the GPS was still not working satisfactorily. In the afternoon we explored the excellent supermarkets and again had an early night, determined to make an early start next day.

At last, on Tuesday, the weather was sunny and bright, with a light wind. We were up at 0630. I scrubbed the sides of the boat, while Joan cleaned the deck and cockpit hood. I hosed the boat down and refilled the water tanks. A yard engineer came to de-winterise our engine and remove the injectors for cleaning. After a long busy day we felt that we were back in the routine of working up.

Wednesday was still sunny but windier. We were at work shortly after 0800. I applied a teak cleaner to all our outside teak and scrubbed it in, with Joan washing it off. Finally we hosed it all down. In the afternoon we walked to Sliema to find the Raytheon Agent for our GPS repair, in a shop called 'Blitz'. I was to take it to the shop the next day.

On Thursday we delivered the GPS to Blitz and were told that the power board would have to be sent to Harlow in England for a replacement, which would take ten days. Then back to the boat where Joan began polishing the stainless steel while I applied Polyshine to the hull. Already we were beginning to make friends with other boat owners. Sue and Mike, from Harlow, came for coffee and stayed to lunch, and at 1800, after an afternoon's work, we showered and changed and walked round to Msida Marina for drinks with Muriel and James in *Drake's Passage*. This social life was a feature of the yacht yard, with many people living aboard their boats, exchanging visits and information and from time to time helping each other.

On Friday we continued polishing the hull until we finished at 1330, when we collected anti-fouling paint from the yard stores. Polishing a hull is an exhausting job and we were so tired that we spent the afternoon in a deep sleep. At 1605 we went to the chandlers to buy a 25-pound kedge anchor and replace three Gaz bottles, all of which we were to collect the following Monday. We bought trays and rollers for anti-fouling.

On Saturday the engineer came at 0745 to replace our injectors. After breakfast we paid a visit to the mini-market and bought food for the weekend meals and, to our great delight, found a stall that sold second-hand books. We bought twelve. We also bought an electric kettle, to replace the one we had given to Veronica, and an electric toaster. After morning coffee we continued cleaning the hull. We rested after lunch until 1500 then completed cleaning the hull, ready for anti-fouling, and polishing the cockpit coaming and the remaining stainless steel.

On Sunday we caught the bus to Valetta and wandered up and down countless stalls in the large, attractive, open market next to the bus terminal. It offered clothes, shoes, household linen and materials, no food of any kind, and we bought sailing hats, shorts and cotton trousers.

After lunch we applied our first coat of anti-fouling. Ours is a big boat and it takes us three hours to apply a coat, Joan rollering the sides while I get underneath and do the bottom of the hull and the keel.

On Monday we booked with the office to launch on Wednesday. In the morning we shopped and went to Blitz, had a rest after lunch and then applied the second coat of anti-fouling, finishing at 2000.

On Tuesday I discovered that my RYA Small Ships Registration expired at the beginning of April. This is an essential document if you are not registered with Lloyds. I tried telephoning the number on my documents and found it was no longer in use. I tried Directory Enquiries and was told the RYA did not have a telephone number. Finally I sent a fax to Jill and asked her to sort it out. We removed the masking tape and completed the Polyshine on the waterline band and in the afternoon started on the stopcocks. All of them had to be freed and greased. The toilet stopcock refused to move and I had to leave it for a yard engineer.

On Wednesday an engineer came to release the toilet stopcock and to check that our engine was running, and at 1330 we were launched. We left the yard at 1410 and motored quietly to Msida Marina, to be helped by many willing hands into our new berth.

We felt wonderfully relaxed and happy to be afloat again after the traumas of the previous autumn. We had enjoyed the ten days in the yard, making many friends and completing our preparations, but a boat does not feel right until it is afloat. Now life really began again for us. The marina is bordered by flower beds and cut grass, the showers and toilets are good, we had a snug berth, and there was a good bus service to Valetta.

We soon made new friends: Bill Richards in *Captain Kettle* invited us for drinks and gave us local information; Gerald and

Rosemary in *Excalibur*, from Poole, moved into the berth next to us and became great friends. We were plugged into the mains electricity and enjoyed the full amenities of our boat – dinner in our spacious cabin, with napkins and full cutlery, a sherry before dinner and another of Joan's gorgeous meals, steak and kidney pie with a full range of vegetables, washed down with a good red wine, St Martins 1987, followed by fresh fruit salad and cream, and cheese and coffee.

Friday 1st May was a public holiday. We chatted with Gerald and Rosemary for a while across our guardrails and then caught the bus to Valetta. Our first visit was to 'The Malta Experience', where we were fascinated by a visual history of Malta under the Arabs, Romans, French and British. Then we walked to St Elmo's Bastion and St Julia's Bastion, overlooking Grand Harbour. St John's and St Paul's Cathedrals were both closed and would have to wait for another visit. Back at the boat we bent on our mainsail and had Gerald and Rosemary into drinks for a very pleasant evening.

On Saturday we shopped in the morning and had an early lunch aboard. A fax from Jill arrived which told us that our SSR certificate had been sent here and that the new house they were building would start on 5th May. After lunch we bussed to Tarxien to see the megalithic temples and their very ancient statues. In the evening I visited Ann and Bob on *Ichabod* and bought their short wave radio for £M15.

On Sunday we caught an early bus to Valetta Market and bought a length of lovely material to make a bedspread and cushion for our cabin, some heavy white material to extend our awning, and two lace tablecloths, a Malta speciality, for presents. We walked through the town to St John's Cathedral, admired its splendid ornateness and gazed in wonder at the two paintings by Caravaggio.

On Monday we went back to Blitz – still no GPS. We shopped in the supermarket, rested in the afternoon and enjoyed a pleasant evening on *Excalibur*.

A rough night, with a force seven wind, was followed by a blustery, cold, unpleasant day. We were glad to be in harbour. I returned to Blitz, but, although Harlow had posted a new power board a fortnight before, it had still not arrived. The manager decided to remove a power board from a new set to repair our GPS.

Meriel and James from *Drake's Passage* came aboard for drinks in the evening. They were an elderly couple who had sold their house in England to buy their boat, had spent seven happy years cruising the Mediterranean and now wished to return to England. They were worried that with the rocketing price of houses in England they would no longer be able to afford one.

It was again a rough night with gale force winds and a scend in the harbour. We decided to book for another week in the marina. Another visit to Blitz produced the repaired GPS, but when we tried it on board it did not work. Tests revealed that ROM, RAM and antenna were OK, but we were not picking up the satellites. I telephoned Blitz and their man came at 1645 with a new set and cable, but still 'No satellites'. He told us to leave the set on, as perhaps the satellites were out of action, and thirty minutes later all five satellites were operating.

On Friday I tried to interface the GPS with the radar, with no response. I telephoned Blitz and was told that a man would come at 1400, so we went shopping and on to Manoel Island to check whether our SSR certificate had arrived. In the afternoon Joan worked on the mosquito netting. At 1600, as the man from Blitz had not arrived, I telephoned the shop and at 1630 their sales manager arrived and soon made the interface work by pressing a button that had been set by Allen Burwin when he installed the set, but about which I knew nothing. In the evening we left a message on Jill's answerphone to say that the SSR certificate had not arrived.

On Friday we made an early start and caught the buses to Valetta and Mdina. We explored the quiet, elegant town, with its beautiful, sandy-coloured houses, and the cathedral and natural history museums. We enjoyed a sandwich lunch in a pleasant restaurant and then moved to Rabat, where we saw the Catacombs and St Paul's Grotto. We were back at the boat in time for tea. Two faxes from Jill and the SSR certificate had arrived. It was Gerald's birthday so, in the evening, we joined him and Rosemary for a fish platter in Vince's Bar, Sliema.

On Saturday we went to the Four Aces Supermarket for our big order to be delivered to the boat, including many bottles of Maltese wine, sherry and liqueurs, all at remarkably cheap prices. After lunch we made minor repairs to the mizzen sail and mizzen boom. Joan completed the mosquito netting and I re-stowed the fore cabin and made several more sail ties.

On Sunday we visited the small island of Gozo, to the north of Malta. We looked around the citadel and the cathedral in Victoria, the capital, and walked along the Bastion Wall, then back to the basilica. We returned to Mgarr for lunch and then strolled around the little harbour with its three pontoons and limited anchorage until it was time to catch the ferry. A lovely, simple, pleasant day ended with another of Joan's special meals.

Monday was our last day in harbour and it followed a familiar pattern of finishing last-minute jobs. Joan shopped at the butchers opposite the marina and bought some of the best meat we have met on our voyaging, fillet steak, chump chops and a boned shoulder. I set up the new kedge anchor with ten metres of chain and a shackle to attach to our thirty metres of warp. It was kept ready for use in a bucket attached to the pushpit. Joan finished off bits of washing. We then walked round to Customs to obtain our clearance and on to Yvonne Grimond at the yacht yard to ask her to return the copy of our SSR certificate that had not arrived and to enclose a thank you from me for their help. Then we proceeded to the Tower Supermarket and the chandlers for last-minute shopping and to the launderette to collect our laundry. Back at the boat we posted several cards to family and friends. Our last jobs were emptying the bilges, clearing the log propeller, taking in our landing board and, finally, singling up the mooring lines ready for slipping in the morning. Our early night became 2230.

On Tuesday 12th May 1992 we resumed the cruise that had been interrupted by the events in Catania seven months before. We left harbour at 0545 with the wind north west force one and the sea slight. At 0700 the wind increased to force three, so we turned off the engine, but half an hour later it died again and we motor-sailed the rest of the way to Porto Palo, arriving at 1515. I was interested in this fishing port that carried stark memories of my last visit. Now it was sunny and pleasant and we dropped anchor in twelve feet of water, inside the fishing boats, on the western side. We were soon joined by one other yacht.

The next day we weighed anchor at 0845, in a light north-east wind, and motor-sailed to Syracuse, arriving at 1315, and moored alongside the quay in Grand Harbour. We were greeted by a man with a van who offered to sell us diesel fuel. He would take us to the diesel company to arrange delivery. Instead, he took us a short distance to the Port Office. He asked 10,000 lire (£5) for the short trip and required a further 10,000 lire to take us to the diesel supplier. I realised that it was a con, paid him 2000 lire and dismissed him. In their usual cheerful manner, the officials did not stamp our passports, saying, 'Not necessary.'

Our mooring berth was delightful, with water on the quay and a pleasant promenade into the old city. We strolled round this in the cool of the evening, along ancient Greek and Roman streets, to the cathedral, built on the site of an ancient Greek temple.

We would like to have stayed longer, but were told by the police that we must leave early the next morning. So at 0630 we left our mooring in a force one wind from the north and a slight sea and set off, under main and motor, for Saline Joniche, fifty-eight miles away. This is a small, little-used industrial port on the south west corner of Italy and, as the wall where yachts berthed was full, we anchored in twenty-eight feet and enjoyed a quiet, undisturbed night.

The next morning we set off, again in a force one wind and slight sea. At 0900 we rounded Cape Spartivento, the 'Toe of Italy', in misty weather. We made three attempts to set the genoa, but each failed through lack of wind. At 1400, as we approached Rocella Ionica, the wind backed and increased and we had thunder and lightning. We arrived at 1500. Rocella Ionica was a new marina under construction. The harbour walls had no berths, so we anchored west of the centre in sixteen feet, and enjoyed a peaceful night.

The next day, Saturday 16th May, we weighed anchor at 0600 in dull, grey weather, a light wind and a slight sea. As we crossed the Gulf of Squillace the sea became bumpy and by 1100 was rough. We made a long tack into the Gulf to find an easier sea. At 1500, a mile offshore, the depth decreased rapidly to twenty-two feet, so we turned 15 degrees to starboard to find deeper water. At 1730, after a bumpy passage, we arrived at Crotone, anchored stern to the mole in Porto Vecchio, and decided to stay two nights.

Luckily we found a small supermarket open and bought meat, fish and vegetables, necessary after four days afloat. After four days of motor-sailing our fuel was low and on Sunday we took on 208 litres at a cost of 100,010 lire (£105). We walked through a large open market to the town, but we found litter everywhere and were not impressed. Renee and Jeannot Lane, an ex-Swiss airline pilot, from *Coquagne*, came aboard at 1800 for drinks.

We left Crotone at 0515 the next day to cross the Gulf of Taranto to Maria de Leuca, sixty-nine miles away. The wind was north west force one, the sky a clear blue and the sea slight. Under main, genoa and motor our speed was 6.3 knots. At 0700 the sea was choppy and a school of dolphins joined us for a short while. By 1000 it was again fine and sunny and the wind had almost died. At 1430 we had a squall, with the wind on the nose and thunder and lightning. We arrived at 1615 and, after being moved on by a fisherman, we tied up alongside an Australian, *Lady Catlin*, and enjoyed a peaceful night.

On Tuesday 18th May we left Leuca at 0600 under main and genoa, with the wind north west force two to three. At 0730 the wind veered and increased to force five and we were sailing at 5.5 knots on a fine reach – at last. At 0845 we passed through a fishing fleet. At 1320 the wind died and we took in the sails and started the engine. We arrived at Orthoni at 1400 and anchored in twelve feet. At last we were in Greece, though only an island outpost. Our port of entry was to be Corfu.

14

The Ionian

We had carefully read Rod Heikel's Pilot, 'Greek Waters', particularly his notes on the Northern Corfu Channel:

> *From the north pass between Peristerai Island and Corfu and proceed with caution into the channel until the stone beacon and the buoy are sighted. Leave both the beacon and the buoy to starboard. In so doing you pass between the rocky shoal which the buoy marks and the extremity of Albania – you are less than a mile from the Albanian coast. Although some yachts may have been confiscated by the Albanian authorities for straying too close to their coast, all the yachtsmen I have spoken to who have put in there because of bad weather were hospitably treated and allowed to leave when the weather moderated. Nonetheless I would not like to test the Albanian authorities myself since it might involve confiscation of the yacht and that is too high a price to pay for being curious.*

We left our anchorage in Orthoni at 0645 on Wednesday 20th May. At 1015 we rounded Cape Akateria in Corfu. The log takes up the story:

> *1115 Thunder and lightning. Very heavy rain. Visibility 500 yards. Navigating by radar.*
> *1200 Entering Albanian Channel by radar. The curtain lifted, showing us the Albanian Coast, Corfu Coast, the island that marked our turn, and the beacon we were looking for – and an Albanian gunboat half-a-mile away on a parallel course and speed.*

145

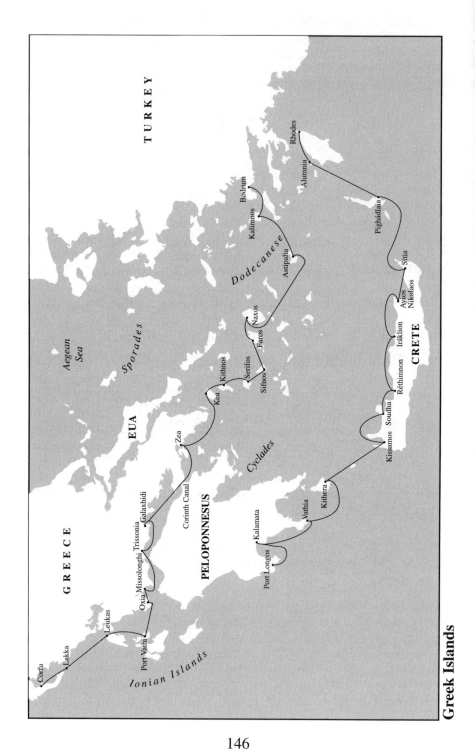

Greek Islands

1230 The gunboat turned away towards Albania.
1330 Corfu still just visible at half a-mile distance.
1400 Entered the Commercial Harbour and tied up at the
Customs berth.'

I reported to Customs and produced our ship's papers and passports and was asked to 'prove' we had come from Italy – an impossibility as nowhere in Italy had our passports been stamped. I said, 'Impossible. The Italians do not stamp passports.' We stared at each other for perhaps thirty seconds. Then he said, 'I believe you', and stamped the passports.

From Customs I proceeded to Immigration where I purchased a transit log, essential to enter any other harbours in Greece. Whilst there, I noticed a little man, not in uniform, in the corner (the Gestapo?), who eyed me suspiciously. Suddenly, while I was signing documents, he jumped up and shouted, 'Are you British?'

'Of course,' I said.

'You don't sound it!' he exclaimed. 'You have a very foreign accent.' (Perhaps he had never heard an ex Navy, ex Cambridge accent!)

My last visit was to the Port Office, where I paid for a three-day stay in Corfu.

I returned to **Blue Pearl** *to find the main hatch closed. When I asked why, Joan said, 'The fuel man told me I must move the boat. I told him I couldn't without my husband, who was dealing with Customs. He said I must, so I went below and locked myself in.'*

We found that neither fuel nor water was available that day, so we motored round to the Old Harbour, where our pilot informed us we would find a mooring. This harbour was almost completely occupied by fishing boats and pleasure boats. The only place vacant for yachts had a large, prominent notice, NO YACHTS. It was occupied by a raft of four yachts – we became the fifth. As the log concluded, *so much for our first experiences of Greece!*

The boat we tied alongside was *Vin*, a Moody, sailed by George and Barbara, naturalised Australians. Barbara was an old girl of Palmer's Girls' School, one of the schools that became my Sixth Form College.

The next day, Thursday 21st May, was Independence Day, a

147

bank holiday, so no shops were open. We enjoyed a walk in the narrow lanes of the Old Town. George and Barbara came aboard for drinks and later we enjoyed our evening meal in the Greek restaurant, Avenof.

Friday, from Joan's diary: *a.m. Ashore to bank, laundry and supermarket, and then to butcher's, greengrocer's and back to boat. F tried to get rubber for forward hatch, but no chandlers open, so he worked on it with a rubber compound. After lunch to launderette and other supermarket for bread and long-life milk. In the evening – drinks aboard* Vin *with George and Barbara. Telephoned Jill. All well except for a little insurance difficulty.* A very normal day in harbour.

On Saturday we watered at Customs Quay and at 1010 left Corfu harbour. In calm and sunny weather we motored to Port Lakka, in Paros, and anchored in twelve feet. Nearby was *Excalibur*, and Rosemary and Gerald came aboard for drinks and exchanged news since leaving Malta

On Sunday we had a walk around Paros and had lunch in a waterfront taverna, overlooking *Blue Pearl's* anchorage. At 1415 we left Lakka in a north west wind, force three, and sailed under main and goose-winged genoa to Mongonisi.

On Monday at 0715 we left for Levkas. At first we motored, as the wind headed us, but at 0830 the wind veered 20 degrees and we set the main and genoa, hauled in tight. We tacked, following the wind as it backed and veered. The sea eased and the sailing was good. We arrived at Levkas canal, waited a few minutes for the bridge to open, and then entered the canal and proceeded to Levkas town, where we moored stern to in a difficult cross current.

Heavy rain fell during the night and in the morning the wind reached gale force and we had to adjust mooring warps, fenders and the dinghy to avoid damage. In heavy wind and rain we used our dinghy as a bridge to cross to the quay so that we could visit the bank, butchers and bakers. Some boats got away in a break in the storm, but we waited until 1430 when we had a window and motored down the canal and out to sea. We sailed under genoa only in peaceful conditions at 3.5 knots to Nidri where we arrived at 1615 and anchored in Tranquil Bay. The wind was getting up again to force six blowing into the bay which was not so tranquil as its name suggests.

That evening, unusually, I cooked the meal, steak and onions, tomatoes and peas, French fries, fruit and cream, and Joan thought it was 'lovely'.

The next morning we motored into Vliko Bay and anchored on the east side in front of a landing area. After coffee we paddled ashore in the dinghy and met a pleasant Greek girl who lived in the house by the taverna, who showed us a walk round the bay. We walked for an hour along this track, with the scent of bougainvilleas and olive trees that bordered it and accompanied by a variety of colourful butterflies – a magical world.

Back at the taverna we enjoyed our favourite lunch, shandy and a Greek salad with feta cheese. We chatted to a charming Swedish couple at the next table, who had lived in Nidri for seven years. In the afternoon I had my first swim in the hottest sun since we had returned to the Mediterranean and we put up the awning for the first time. That evening we had our first meal in the cockpit and watched the sun go down over Vliko Bay. Life for us was very good.

In the next four days we explored the islands, Levkas, Mongonisi and Ithaca. Port Vathi, on Mongonisi, was a quiet fishing village with a quay, occupied by a charter fleet. Abelike Bay, also in Mongonisi, was a beautiful, secluded anchorage, surrounded by wooded slopes, which we had to ourselves. Sivota Bay was a deep inlet in the south of Levkas, with a double column of Sunsail charter boats, where we enjoyed lunch at Stavros restaurant. Then we went on to Frikes Bay, in Ithaca, where we enjoyed dinner in Penelope's restaurant, a three-course meal for two and a bottle of wine for £17; and finally Port Vathi, capital of Ithaca, the island where Ulysses was born. All of these passages were short and at each anchorage we enjoyed a walk, a swim, and dinner either ashore or in the cockpit – a charming, idyllic life.

Shortly after arriving at Port Vathi we were joined by *Excalibur*, with our friends Gerald and Rosemary, who tied up alongside us. It was time to leave the Ionian and it was our intention to stop at Oxia Island on the way to the Gulf of Corinth. We arrived at Oxia on Wednesday 3rd June, and anchored in twenty feet, with a stern line to a boulder ashore. At 1600 a strong wind suddenly developed with sudden violent gusts in all directions. We were dragging our anchor so we decided to leave at once for Missolonghi in the Gulf of Patras. The wind was now force seven, gusting eight and nine, with stroppy seas against which we made little headway. There was no chance of reaching Missolonghi before darkness so we decided to turn back to Ithaca, and ran under genoa only at 5.5 knots. We covered the twenty-four miles to Port Vathi in four-and-a-half hours.

The next day, Thursday 4th June, we left Ithaca at 0730 in a force one wind, misty visibility and a moderate sea. We made good progress, under main and motor, past Oxia Island, to the Gulf of Patras. From the log:

1300 1 mile off the lighthouse on Cape Sostis.

1315 Turned, in hazy light, to look for leading marks or buoys into Missolonghi when we grounded. Unable to back off. Took down sails. Tried hauling out boom and crawling along it to heel the boat. No luck. Wind beginning to get up and the keel bumping on the sandy bottom. Little or no tide here, so could be dangerous. Began to get out kedge.

Fishing-boat came along and offered help. He tried hauling us off with our engine helping, first forward and then astern. No luck. Then, at my suggestion, he took our spinnaker halyard and tried to pull us over to port. I didn't like this. Starboard would be better. As he came round our bows the halyard caught the port light on the pulpit and pulled it off. The fisherman rescued it. I think no damage – merely the wire broken. He then motored away to starboard, pulling our masthead halyard. This pulled the boat on to its side and I motored easily into deep water.

The fisherman told me that the sands here were frequently shifting and the channel marker buoys no longer marked the channel. He offered to escort us in and asked 20,000 drachmas (£70) for his assistance. I accepted. One of them came aboard to guide us in.

1430 Arrived Missolonghi and tied up alongside the Quay.

Had we been stranded for the night on the shoal, our situation could have become serious, particularly if the wind got up. I thought £70 was reasonable for the help given us and for the peace of mind it brought us.

We had gone to Missolonghi because of its association with Byron and his death. We were disappointed. Apart from a statue there was little to commemorate him. Our berth alongside the north-

150

east wall was comfortable but noisy, with local boys swimming alongside and a Greek band playing and singing on the green nearby. We found good shopping in a road just off the quay.

As we left Missolonghi the next day at 1000 our echo sounder was on the blink, but I soon cured this with extra castor oil. With a force one wind from the south east we motored with the main and genoa hauled well in. At 1245 the wind backed to the west and increased to force three. I turned off the engine and we were running, goose-winged, at 4.5 knots. At 1400, going through the Kioni Channel, the wind increased to force five and our speed to 6 knots. By 1500 the wind was up to force six and we were running, still goose-winged, at 7 knots, with the boat not handling too well under Autohelm. I took over the helm for the rest of the passage. Off Trizonia I furled the genoa and we ran in under main at 4.5 knots. At 1655 we anchored in the bay off Trizonia Island in front of 'Lizzie's Yacht Club'.

We invited Paul of *Westerling*, a lone sailor with twenty-four years' experience of sailing the Mediterranean, to join us for dinner in the club, on the verandah overlooking the bay. We had a very good meal with wine for a total of £14. We were able to change seven of our paperbacks for six from the club at no cost. The next morning I went aboard Paul's boat and he mapped out a recommended route for us through the Aegean.

The next day, Saturday 6th June, we motored to Galaxidhi in a force one wind. Because of the ledge against the quay we lay stern to, twelve feet off. This was too far for our plank, but Wendy and Gerald in *Jeanne*, next to us, invited us to use their boat, which was bow in and therefore nearer to the quay.

The next day, Bill and Suzanne, a young Canadian couple crewing a 38-foot catamaran, joined us on the bus to Delphi. Home of the famous oracle, Delphi is set high in the hills with a spectacular view of the valleys below. Inside, we followed a route past the ancient treasuries and the Temple of Apollo to the wonderful amphitheatre. It was said that a whisper from the stage could be heard anywhere in the auditorium. I tried it out with a speech from Hamlet, which I declaimed in little more than a spoken voice. I was amazed when a ripple of applause from all round the amphitheatre broke out at the end of it. We enjoyed a pleasant lunch in a taverna in the village before returning to the boat. In the evening Bill and Suzanne came aboard for drinks. We were tired, but we had enjoyed a fascinating day, made all the more pleasant by the company of our young friends.

At 0715 on Monday 8th June we left Galaxidhi under main, motor and genoa in a force one wind and a fine mist. At 1130 the wind increased to force two to three. I switched off the engine and we were soon sailing at 5 knots. At 1400 we arrived at the west end of the Corinth Canal and jilled around until told to follow a large tanker through the canal, a deep, narrow, straight cutting, just over three miles long.

When we arrived at the east end of the canal the Canal Authority refused to accept that *Blue Pearl* was eight tons, although it was on the architect's plans which we produced. My Small Ships Register certificate did not state the registered tonnage as a Lloyds certificate would have done. As we had no proof of our registered tonnage we had to pay £130 not £50, the correct fee for a boat of our size. I refused to pay and asked to see the manager. He would not be available until the next morning. They gave us a poor berth for the night alongside a rusty tanker. In the morning I saw the 'manager', then his superior, and then the top man. None of them would budge. The top man came to see our boat and said, 'I agree that it is a very small boat,' but he would not agree to reduce the charge. I finished by telling him that it was a rip-off and that when I returned to England I would take it up with the Greek Embassy. I never did – but three miles unescorted for £120!

15

The Aegean

On Tuesday 9th June 1992, as a quiet day with little wind was forecast, we left the Corinth Canal for Piraeus towing our dinghy. Once out of the shelter of land we found a brisk wind from the west and we were soon sailing at 6.5 knots under genoa only. At 1140 the wind died completely and we switched on the engine. A shark passed us, going in the opposite direction. At 1300, as we rounded the southern tip of Salamis Island, the wind veered to the north east and increased to force five to six. I switched off the engine and we were again sailing at 6.5 knots under genoa. At 1400, eight miles south west of Piraeus, the wind suddenly backed to the north west and at 1430 increased to gale force eight. I reduced to half genoa and, with the wind on the port beam, we were still sailing at 6 knots. Several moored tankers to starboard began to get up steam and we saw one dragging its anchor. Suddenly our dinghy, on a long tow-line, flipped over three or four times and then flew out to starboard like a kite, turning over and over. Our front floorboards flew out and were lost. It took me fifteen tense minutes to bring the dinghy under control, using all my strength, while Joan sailed the boat. At length I had the dinghy tamed, hauled up to the pushpit with only the stern brushing the water.

There was no chance of finding our floorboards in the wind-racked sea, so we continued to Zea, a marina very close to Piraeus but just round the south-east corner and therefore sheltered by land. In the lea of the cape the seas eased, and at 1600 we enjoyed that dramatic and satisfying moment of entering the safety of the harbour, getting our sail furled quietly in the crowded space and tying alongside an Italian boat on the outer mole.

The next day, Wednesday, the barometer was still very low, but the wind was quieter and we decided on a make-and-mend, with Joan doing the washing and I repairing the navigation light and servicing the engine. Again I was unable to remove the oil filter.

We enjoyed a quiet night, and the next day I bought a chain tool in the marina and removed the filter. However, I had to walk two miles to an industrial estate to buy spare filters. We found a good launderette and, in the marina, unisex showers and toilets. I stood on guard while Joan used the toilet. I enjoyed my shower, but Joan decided against the shower.

On Friday we made our long-planned visit to Athens and the Acropolis. Apart from the magnificent structure of the Parthenon, most of the buildings were in various states of ruin and we had to use our imagination to re-create the glory of ancient Greece. At the Porch of the Maidens, in a good state of preservation, I climbed over a low wire fence to take a closer picture. Whistles blew and uniformed guards arrived to escort me off the patch.

Back at the boat that evening we met a Frenchman, Michel, whom we had last seen in Ustica a year before. He came aboard for a drink and we exchanged stories.

We had arranged for mail to be sent to Zea, but a Greek postal strike deprived us of this facility and we had to leave without it. However, a fax from Jill did come through and, in the end, we came to rely on faxes rather than mail. At 1100, with a stiff wind blowing onto the mole, we achieved the difficult manoeuvre of springing off and, under mizzen and genoa, set off for the island of Kea where, after an easy sail, we anchored in Voukari, Nikolaos Bay, a fine anchorage with many other yachts arriving. The next day I swam and, from the dinghy, cleaned off the filthy oil round the waterline that we had picked up in Zea, while Joan cleaned the hatches. Before lunch we called at the taverna for a shandy. From Joan's diary:

No Sprite, so Heineken for F (500 drachmas) and orange for me (300 drachmas). When the bill came it read, '500 dr., 300 dr., (36%) + 500 dr.', a total of 1300 dr. F had put only 1000 dr. in his pocket so he rowed back to the boat for more money and his spectacles. I just sat and waited for twenty minutes. We both examined the bill and when the waiter came we showed him the two prices on the tariff. He became very agitated and said the 500

154

marked as % was for the Heineken and the bill was only 800
drachmas, a clear case of fraudulent overcharging. F paid the 800
drachmas and, needless to say, did not give the waiter a tip.

On Monday 15th June we weighed anchor at 0830 and set off
under main and genoa for Fikiadha, on the western side of Kithnos.
However, at 1030 as we reached Cape Tamelos, the wind went
round to the north west and increased to force five, and I decided
to make for a sheltered bay, Loutra, on the east coast. With main
and three-quarters genoa we sailed at 6.5 knots, touching 7 knots
in the gusts, excellent sailing. Then, as so often in the Aegean, at
1200 the wind died. We arrived at Loutra at 1310 and anchored,
as directed by the pilot, in 10.5 feet, but when the boat took up
the chain the depth was only 8 feet. We took up the anchor and
looked into lrini Bay first for anchoring and then stern to the quay,
but neither of these was satisfactory, so we returned to Loutra Bay
and anchored in 13 feet, an unfortunate choice as an unpleasant
swell got up which we were lying across and this gave us a most
uncomfortable night.

We left Loutra, the next day, in a northerly force two wind and
sailed quietly to Livadhi on the island of Serifos. We arrived in a
force five wind, anchored in 20 feet, and enjoyed a swim in the
warm water and a meal ashore in the Hotel Cyclades.

After a quiet night, we shopped in the mini-market and caught
the bus up the steep hill to the chora, or main town of the island,
that overlooked our anchorage. Donkeys were used to carry goods
up the hill and we passed one man using his donkey's tail to haul
himself up. The chora consisted of several churches, two tavernas,
four stores, a post office and a number of houses, all painted a
gleaming white, clustering on the hilltop. Our afternoon siesta was
followed by a swim and a long, lazy meal in the cockpit, with the
chora and mountains as a background and more boats arriving in
the fading light. This was a magical evening. That night our sleep
was disturbed by mosquitoes until just after midnight when we got
up and fixed the netting that Joan had made. After that we had
no further trouble. We used this netting successfully, in mosquito-
infested areas, throughout our cruise.

We spent the morning cleaning the boat and went ashore to the
Hotel Cyclades for lunch. When I had paid and told the owner we
would be leaving the next morning, he told me to wait a minute

while a waiter brought us three iced peaches, a traditional Greek gift to parting guests. Again we enjoyed a siesta, a swim and dinner in the cockpit.

The next morning, Friday 19th, a strong south-westerly wind was forecast. We left at 1100, but shortly afterwards, with the wind force seven heading us, we decided to turn round and go back to Serifos. That evening Paul, whom we had last seen in Lizzie's Yacht Club, arrived and we invited him to dinner in the cockpit, a pleasant meal, exchanging news of our travels. The weather became cold and threatening and a swell set up in the strong wind, but soon died and we had a quiet night.

On Saturday we left Serifos in misty weather and little wind and motor-sailed to Port Vathi, Sifnos. We moored at the quay by the church and went for a walk along the sandy beach, and a swim. We enjoyed the swim, but there was much oil on the sand and I had to clean our shoes with petrol. We had a salad lunch in the local taverna, followed by a siesta, swim and meal in the cockpit, a ritual that was now becoming a way of life for us.

Because of the oil we decided against staying a second night and the next day sailed quietly under genoa to Faros, seven miles away, on the south-east tip of Sifnos. This was an attractive harbour with tavernas and villas and a rugged cliff all round. The wind got up that night and, as I was not sure of our anchor, I put out a second one and felt much happier.

The next day we walked to a little church on the headland and had lunch in a taverna overlooking our boat. A Norwegian had anchored too close to us and as we swung round in the wind I put fenders out in case of a collision. The Norwegians returned and immediately weighed anchor and left. That evening an elderly couple in a rowing boat laid fishing nets across the harbour, one over our anchor. Fortunately, they collected them at first light before we left.

On Tuesday 23rd we left Faros at 0815 under main and half genoa, sailing at 5.5 knots. At 0935 the wind eased to force three and we shook out the rolls, still maintaining our speed. We arrived at Paroikia, Paros, at 1315. We liked this small, very clean town, with good shops and facilities. That evening we enjoyed our best meal so far on the cruise in the Argonauta restaurant for a total of £15, including a bottle of wine. In fact we returned next day for lunch.

On Friday 26th June we sailed on to Naxos. The small harbour was full so we anchored in the bay, but when an unpleasant swell got up in the afternoon we decided to leave and sail on to Aghios Georgis, an attractive bay with deep, rocky sides, where we anchored with two stern warps to a tiny mole. We had an uncomfortable night in the swell.

The next day we decided to move on, and motored to an adjacent island, Ekhinoussa, where we anchored in Missini, a bay open to the south and sheltered from the northerly winds that had been troubling us. It was more open than Aghios Georgis and less attractive, but there was more room and soon we were joined by several boats. One, a German, anchored close to us. We walked up to the chora, where we had some good views of the islands, and on our return enjoyed our customary swim, siesta and dinner in the cockpit.

The next day we decided on a make-and-mend, and went ashore for lunch at the local taverna. On our return we found that we had dragged our anchor; there was little wind and no current and I felt sure that it had been caused by the German boat that must have disturbed our chain when he left. We re-anchored and put out a second anchor.

The next day the wind was near gale force from the north west and the sea very rough. We decided to cut out our visit to Amorgos and stay a further night in the comfortable harbour.

As so often, the next day was lovely, fine and sunny, with good visibility, a force three wind from the north west and a moderate sea, perfect conditions for the long, fifty-mile stretch to Istapalia. We left at 0730 and by 0845 the wind had died and we were motoring. At 0935 the wind increased and we were sailing again. This happened three times on the passage, not untypical of the Mediterranean. We arrived at Skala, the capital of Istapalia at 1640.

This was not the first time I had been to Istapalia or, as I had known it, Stampalia. In 1940 I was an observer midshipman in the Royal Navy on my first mission, a dive-bombing attack on the naval barracks and headquarters of the Italian Eastern Fleet. As we flew over the Mediterranean in our Swordfish aircraft, the islands in the moonlight were like gems set in a necklace of pearls against a silver background. It seemed a sacrilege to bomb them, and I told my pilot that one day I would come back in my own boat to see the islands as they should be seen, from a small boat. The

157

bombing was devastating and RAF photographs showed the barracks and neighbouring village, occupied by naval staff, flattened. I had planned this visit over fifty years before and *Blue Pearl* was built specifically for it. It was to be the highlight of our Mediterranean cruise.

Soon after anchoring Joan and I went ashore to the Tourist Office. I could not remember exactly where we had bombed and needed more information. I spoke carefully to the Greek girl behind the counter and asked if she could give me some information about the naval headquarters that had been bombed towards the end of 1940. She said she would speak to an old man outside who might remember it. She came back and told me of two ruined Italian sites, one at Kastelano and one at Maltezana. I congratulated the girl on her good English.

'It should be good,' she said. 'I *am* English.'

The next morning, Wednesday 1st July, we had an interesting walk to the chora, up steep steps to the ruined medieval castle. In the afternoon we motored round to Maltezana Bay. I noticed that the anchor was dragging in the strong wind so I put out more chain and a second anchor. We went ashore to look for the ruined headquarters, but saw no sign of them. I remembered vaguely that there had been a seaplane base here. The village was pretty and the countryside fertile.

At 0930 the next day we motored to Agrilithi Bay. What happened next I wrote up in the ship's log:

1015 Arrived Agrilithi, a long narrow bay with a bottleneck entrance. Put out two anchors.

1000 Went ashore to search for the ruined Italian headquarters. First we climbed an unmade path that joined a dirt road climbing the mountain. The mountain was covered in scrub with occasional low trees.

We walked towards Kastelano, climbing to a height of about one thousand feet. Then, round a bend, we suddenly came upon the site. The ruins of the old headquarters could be seen clearly and some temporary demountable barracks had been put up on the parade ground. They were completely deserted, except for goats. The walls were daubed with faded camouflage. The iron poles supporting the boundary wire stood stark and lonely. The wire had long-since rotted away. The Italians had

158

planted shrubs round their huts and, amazingly, some had survived, providing a splash of colour. Everywhere was the sound of bells, making an orchestra of music, or the pipes of Pan as Joan said. The bells were attached to the hidden goats. Beside the road and opposite the ruins was a small memorial, probably in memory of those who lost their lives in our attack.

It was easy to see where we had approached in our aircraft, round a steep hill, and escaped, down the valley and over our bay and Blue Pearl*'s anchorage. I felt sadness for the victims and strangely at peace with myself, because this was a place of peace, a journey's end.*

We continued along the road, looking for Kastelano, but it had disappeared. We saw a cluster of ruined stone houses on the side of the road opposite the barracks and concluded that this must have been the village, also destroyed by our raid.

It was very hot. There had been no shelter from the midday sun or from the glare and we were very thirsty. We were not going to find the village or a taverna. We saw a small farmhouse and called there to ask for a drink. There was no-one at home, only pigs, chicken and a cat. We turned back towards the boat and were glad to sit in the shade of a small tree for ten minutes.

We arrived back at the boat at 1415, three and a quarter hours after leaving it, very weary, but content. We had a long drink, a cooling swim, lunch and the oblivion of a deep sleep.

On Friday we had a make-and-mend and a rest. The wind got up in the night and we were glad of our second anchor.

The next day, Saturday, we weighed anchor at 0745 and enjoyed an excellent sail to Kalimnos, at first hard on the wind in a lumpy sea and then, as the wind backed to the west and increased to force six, a broad fetch at more than 6 knots, riding across the seas rather than going into them. We anchored stern to the quay and found Kalimnos to be an excellent harbour with many shops and taverns. We chose a very Greek restaurant for our evening meal, recommended by Bob, from *Beach Bum of Rye*, who had helped us to moor.

The next day we motored in a light wind to Kos and again moored stern to the quay. Unfortunately there was a noisy disco opposite the yacht quay and we had little sleep. We were glad to leave early the next morning for Bodrum, our Port of Entry for Turkey.

16

Turkey

We arrived at Bodrum at 1345 on Tuesday 7th July for what was to become the favourite part of our cruise. It did not begin well. The 'entering Turkey' procedure was laborious and slow: first we registered in the marine office, then we walked the long, hot, dusty mile to customs on the other side of the harbour, where we were told that our visas, £5 each, could be paid for only in English pounds – we had only Turkish money on us so back we walked to the boat for English money and back again to customs. The next stop was in town where we satisfied the health authority and the police, then we walked back to immigration next to customs to purchase our transit log. Finally we walked back to the town centre to satisfy the port authority that we had carried out their procedures in the correct order. In all, the procedure took three hours.

Now we were able to enjoy the excellent facilities of the marina, the lovely marina building with paved terraces, café, shops and chandlers, and water and electricity on the pontoons. We were invited to drinks aboard *Beach Bum* with Bob and Angelique and enjoyed our evening meal aboard *Blue Pearl*.

The next day we thoroughly enjoyed our walk through the town, past the minaret, past the line of attractive gulets and the mosque to the Old Town with its narrow streets, hanging carpets and colourful shops and bazaars. As we entered this we were approached by a Turk, who wanted to sell us a rug.

'Not at the moment,' I replied. 'We are going to look at the Old Town.'

'I see you on the way back,' he said.

And he did. He was waiting for us and he took up where he

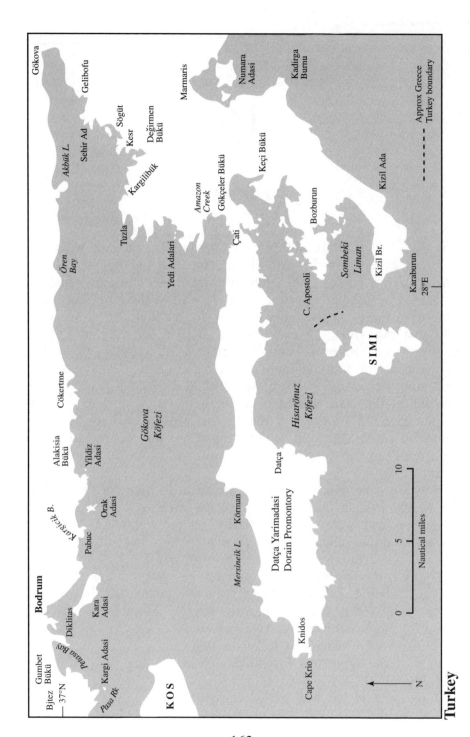

Turkey

162

had left off. The best thing about Turkish salesmen is that they are good humoured and not offended when you say 'No.' Haggling is part of the process. I adopted the procedure of offering a third of what was asked, hoping to get the article for half.

That evening Bob and Angelique and Stephen and Caroline, the young couple from the trimaran next to us, came aboard for drinks and a jolly party. Stephen told us of a two-day coach trip to Ephesus at £37 each and we agreed to go with them.

The next morning the four of us set off in the coach to Pamukkale, an extraordinary waterfall of warm lime water, milky white, tumbling over the rocks to a shallow pool. This was supposed to be good for your health, so I took the opportunity of bathing in it. Next we stopped at a hotel for a swim and lunch, followed by a long drive to Kusadasi, and a pleasant hotel. We all showered and then the four of us explored the town, ending with an extremely good meal in a fish restaurant. We bargained for the fish we wanted, paid for it by weight, and then it was filleted and served at our table.

The next morning we had breakfast on the roof of the hotel and at 0900 left for Ephesus, an ancient Greek town, complete with all its streets lined with the remains of ancient buildings. We were given a guided tour and then, in the free time allotted, the four of us walked up the Street of the Kouretes to the legendary library. From Ephesus we went to the peaceful, wooded valley where Mary's House was built by St John for her last years. In the lane up to the house were cloth and plastic tags tied to the hedgerows, prayers from Muslims to Mary, Mother of the great Mohammedan prophet, Jesus Christ. The peace and quiet were a great contrast to the bustle of tourist crowds at Ephesus.

On our return journey to Bodrum we were impressed by the green, fertile countryside interspersed with areas where up to thirty factories were being built with dormitory towns of up to forty blocks of flats. Signs of growth were everywhere in this vibrant, enchanting country and we returned to the boat after two happy and relaxed days.

On Saturday, after shopping in the excellent meat and vegetable markets, we quickly cleared the port authorities and left Bodrum at 1330. At 1745 we arrived at Cokertme, which consisted of a couple of tavernas, each with its own ramshackle pontoon. We chose Rosemary Taverna. We had a friendly greeting from a neighbouring boat owner, who took our warps and introduced himself.

'My name is Sanar. I am a famous film director and this is my wife, Ayla.'

'How interesting! I am pleased to meet you.' We shook hands.

'And I was clarinettist in a well-known New York Orchestra.'

'Really!'

'And I sang in a New York Opera.'

'We've a right one here,' I murmured to Joan.

Sanar then invited us to join him and his wife, the lovely Ayla, for dinner in the taverna. We were the only foreigners amongst all the Turks. During the meal the Turkish band played 1930s dance music and Sanar invited his wife to dance a foxtrot. Not to be outdone, we joined them. Here we were, one of two couples, dancing a foxtrot to a Turkish band on a sawdust floor in a Turkish taverna, watched by curious Turks. Then Sanar began to sing – in a lovely, trained voice. We learned later that he had produced many Turkish films, which were currently being shown on Turkish television. By inference, he must really have been a member of a New York opera and a New York orchestra. His wife, Ayla, was a bank manager. They both spoke fluent English and were fascinating company.

The next day, Sunday, we sailed to Söğüt and anchored in 55 feet, with a stern warp to a tree. We were to find this an increasingly normal method of mooring and we developed a technique to cope with it. The problem, particularly when the wind was offshore, was that the boat swung on its anchor chain away from land before I could row ashore and fix the warp. I left the boat with the engine on slow astern, pulling towards the land, with Joan in control, while I rowed as quickly as I could to the shore. Once ashore I had control and Joan could put the engine into neutral. Sometimes the stern warp was as long as 150 feet.

We enjoyed a pleasant walk through the woods, but our evening meal in the cockpit was spoiled by wasps. In the morning, after a quiet night, we had another attractive walk, and saw lizards and cicadas and a huge dragonfly.

At 1000 the next day we motored the five miles to Snake and Castle Islands, a playground for Cleopatra where she imported sand from Africa to form a beach, reputedly for Antony's benefit. The evening was very windy, but having dropped two anchors we were

164

relaxed. In the afternoon we went ashore to inspect Antony's Beach and then continued to the ancient theatre, now with trees growing through the terraces. After dark the wind died, the swell subsided and we had a peaceful night.

The next morning we motored seven miles to Değirmen Buku. We were stopped from going to the head of the bay by a police launch. The President of Turkey was in residence there. Instead, we went to an unnamed bay on the east side, where we were well received by the taverna staff, and backed stern-to to their jetty. At 1800 four gulets arrived and moored all round us. We felt like sardines. However, they protected us from the gusty wind. We enjoyed a pleasant walk through the pine and deciduous forest and then a meal in the taverna, with a choice of starters, main course, ice cream and a bottle of wine at a total cost of £8. Our meal was enlivened by conversation with Hillbrant and Hansgeorge from Munich.

The next morning we walked through the beautiful woodland to the Presidential Villa and back round the inlet. I had a swim in the clean water off the jetty and a shower in the open on an adjacent lawn. We hosed the boat down and filled our tanks.

More gulets arrived in the evening. One, driven badly with no fenders down, would have hit us many times and done considerable damage if Joan and I had not fended off with our big fenders. It anchored badly across our bows, with us fending it off, until the skipper put out a second anchor and straightened himself.

Our last meal had been so good and inexpensive that we dined ashore again. This harbour was one of our best: beautiful, with trees, shrubs and flowers; comfortable, with mooring pontoons; cheap, with no cost for the mooring, free toilets, showers and water and very inexpensive meals; good swimming; peaceful at night and quiet during the day when the gulets had departed.

The next morning we left early and motored across the bay to English Harbour, so named after its occupation by English MTBs in the last war. We dropped anchor and moored to a tree. A neighbouring boat swung too close to us, so we re-anchored and moored to another tree, helped by a Swiss couple, Joe and Mona, from *Waltzing Matilda*, who told us how to deal with wasps. You cut a lemonade bottle in half, put beer in the bottom half, invert the top half and insert it into the bottom half with the neck open, and place it some distance away from where you are eating.

On Friday we left English Harbour and motored thirteen miles in a force one wind to Yedi Adalari, the Seven Islands. Here, in the bay behind the islands, we anchored in a narrow creek on the eastern side. Just inside the creek, to the right, is a neck of land that protects you from the sea and from the west wind. We put out two stern warps to rocks ashore. We were in a small, sheltered space and had a quiet day. That evening, during our meal in the cockpit, we were attacked by wasps and put Joe's theory to the test. The results were amazing. The wasps buzzed angrily around the lemonade bottle, but did not come near us. In the morning there must have been twenty dead ones in the bottle.

That night we were glad of our two stern lines. The wind got up to gale force and we could hear it whistling through the tops of our masts. Amazingly, at water level we were quite sheltered and once we got used to the noise and realised that our lines were holding we had a peaceful night.

On Saturday 18th July a period of strong winds and gales was forecast so we decided to make for Bodrum and hole up in the comfortable marina. We had a nice welcome from the marina attendant and the girls in the office, who all recognised us. It was very hot and in the afternoon the wind rose to near gale force. We found that we were next to Sanar's yacht, *Mert.*

On Sunday I tackled the windlass pawl, which was not working. At first I thought that the spring was too slack so I shortened it. Then I discovered that it was the plastic pawl actuator. The cam had collapsed. I inserted a small plastic tube, part of an electric terminal, to strengthen it and this appeared to work. The wind was now so strong that we took down our awning. In the afternoon we visited the castle and the museum.

On Monday with a force eight gale and very rough seas we decided to stay in Bodrum. We enjoyed a stroll through the market streets, lunch at a pizza restaurant and drinks with Sanar, after which Ayla left for Istanbul. We invited him to dine with us that evening.

The wind blew strongly all night, but dropped in the morning, so we decided to leave. We cleared Bodrum at 0800 on Tuesday, motor sailing in a force one wind, but shortly afterwards the wind increased to force three and we were able to sail. At 1000, with the wind force four, we saw a trimaran overtaking us at great speed. It was Stephen and Caroline in *Uhuru.*

We arrived at Knidos at 1200 and moored alongside *Uhuru.*

David, of *Bug's Bunny*, a catamaran we had met in Kalimnos, took our warps. They all came aboard for coffee and then we all had lunch together in the taverna.

After our siesta we went for a long walk round the ancient ruins, joined by David. Knidos had been an ancient and thriving commercial port with a trireme harbour on one side of a narrow neck of land and the commercial harbour on the other. Surrounding the harbour are the ruins of the city, with its temple of Aphrodite, two theatres, one at the water's edge, and a fascinating jumble of fallen masonry and broken artefacts lying higgledy-piggledy everywhere, as yet unsorted and unclassified. The only habitation was a temporary taverna, and the only visitors were yachtsmen and tourists from gulets. After our walk we had drinks in *Bug's Bunny*, a meal aboard *Blue Pearl* and a quiet night.

The next day, with the barometer rising, we decided to leave, at first motor-sailing in a force one wind, and then sailing at 6.5 knots when the wind increased to force five. Later the wind died and we arrived at Datča in a flat calm and moored stern to quay. *Uhuru* followed us in and moored at the shallower end. We invited Stephen and Caroline and Noel and Manella, a couple from a neighbouring gulet, to drinks, and they invited us all to lunch aboard the gulet, giving us an opportunity to inspect one of these attractive boats. Our lunch was in deep shade underneath the large overhang of the upper deck, cooked by the mate and served by the captain. There were several cabins, each comfortably equipped with two bunks, shower and toilet. In the afternoon we swam from the beach and Stephen instructed me in the use of my newly purchased snorkel.

The next day, Thursday 23rd July, we hoped to leave by 0700, but two charter boats had moored astern of us, using our cleats and boxing us in. We had breakfast and waited to give them a chance to move away. At 0800 I decided to wake the skipper of the boat astern of us. He was a German and very surly, but eventually they both moved off. Then I had to clear the anchors that had been laid across ours by two neighbouring yachts. I had to clamber down our anchor chain to do this and received applause from some watching yachtsmen. We finally got away at 0820 and with the winds varying from flat calm to force three we motored or sailed to Keçi Bükü, a beautiful bay with an island, mountains, pines and two attractive restaurants.

167

On Friday we had a make-and-mend, a lazy day. We explored the bay in the dinghy, swam off the boat and had lunch in Kardi's restaurant, which had primitive showers but good toilets.

On Saturday we left for Bozburun, passing *Uhuru* anchored in a bay behind the island, and as we approached the harbour we waved to Paul, last seen in Serifos, who was just moving to another anchorage. We anchored just outside the harbour in 35 feet. We went to Osman's restaurant for our evening meal where we enjoyed our starters, but only one swordfish kebab was brought for our main course. I waited while Joan ate this and mine was not brought until after she had finished, a pity as it was otherwise a good and inexpensive restaurant. We thought afterwards that we should have shared the first meal and also shared the second when it arrived.

Osman recommended his second taverna managed by his uncle in Serče Liman, so we decided to call at this attractive, out-of-the-way anchorage. The narrow entrance opened on to a large narrow bay surrounded by rocky cliffs. Two of Osman's sons greeted us and when we had dropped anchor they took our stern warps and made them fast to the rocks. That evening we had our best-value meal of the cruise, baked aubergines and salad for starters, baked grouper, well cooked and garnished with vegetables, caught locally by the boys and chosen by us from the several fish offered, bread, wine and coffee, all for a total of £11! For good measure a belly dancer entertained after the meal.

On Monday we left harbour at 0700 in a fickle wind. We adjusted the sails over thirty times in the next four hours and arrived at Marmaris at 1130 and took on 150 litres of fuel. We had called up the marina on our approach and received a warm welcome from the two marina attendants, who took our warps and settled us in. Letters from Jill and Peggy were waiting for us in the office.

The next day we explored the town, new buildings erected on the ruins of the old ones destroyed by earthquake in 1958. Like Bodrum, the quay is lined with gulets and open-air restaurants. After our siesta we spent two hours in the swimming pool and in the evening were invited aboard *Solifi*, where Anne and John Wilson entertained us with drinks and talk about the many mutual friends we had met in the Mediterranean. They were from Poole, but their boat was now based in Malaga.

On Wednesday we had Anne and John aboard for drinks and in the evening enjoyed an excellent meal at the marina restaurant,

168

'Pineapple', to celebrate our wedding anniversary. The gales on Thursday kept us in harbour, but on Friday we sailed to Ekinčik in the usual on-and-off winds. On Saturday we attempted to sail to the Gulf of Fethiye, but gave up after a few miles because of the near-gale headwinds and returned to Ekinčik. On Sunday we sailed, in variable wind, to Kapi Creek in the Gulf of Fethiye. We moored stern to a rough quay with a bow line provided by the restaurant. In the evening we dined ashore at the creek-side restaurant, sharing a table with Linda and Jim, dentists from Birmingham, in a flotilla boat.

The next day we motored two and a half miles to Wall Bay, a lovely bay with a good anchorage, stern to trees, and a good restaurant. In the afternoon we walked round the footpath to look over Ruin Bay, also lovely but with many gulets and flotilla boats. On Tuesday morning we motored to Goček for shopping and anchored in Goček Bay. In the afternoon we moved on to Boynuz Buku for the night. On Wednesday we motored to Tomb Bay, but this was too exposed and had too many motor yachts and surfriders, so we continued to Tersane Island and anchored in Tersane Creek with long lines ashore. An Italian boat, wanting to moor next to us, started to remove one of our lines, but I stopped him. The next day we sailed to Fethiye, on Friday to Karacaören Buku, on Saturday to Kalkan and on Sunday to Kas.

On Monday we had a make-and-mend, planning to leave early on Tuesday for Cyprus. This was our departure point from Turkey where we had to hand in our transit log. Police were not available until 0800, but then they quickly stamped our log. Then we proceeded to the harbour master. He insisted that we must pay £15 for a second transit log to leave Turkey. I protested. The harbour master did not speak English so he put me on the telephone to a suave English voice that advised, 'Better pay up, chum, or it will be the worse for you.' It was a crooked racket, but time was running out for us, so I paid him. We next went on to Customs where the officer told us that the second transit log was not necessary. He spoke strongly on the telephone to the harbour master. We both had to return to the harbour master's office as he had not stamped our log, but he did not give us back our money. Then back we went to Customs, who cleared us on our original log and disregarded the second one. After a delightful time in Turkey this left an unpleasant taste. So much for our early start!

17

Cyprus

The night passage to Cyprus was uneventful and we arrived at Paphos on Wednesday 12th August, at 1345. At first we anchored in the middle of the harbour but, seeing a vacant space, we re-anchored stern-to to the mole. The next day customs and the harbour master cleared us quickly and we were charged £8 for one night, with the second night free. We liked the harbour: showers and toilets were good and we found excellent shopping nearby. We enjoyed a good meal at the Pelican restaurant, on the front, but the service was poor. We had to remind the waiter about each course.

We were up early on Friday and motor-sailed, against a light headwind, to Limassol, where we berthed in the marina. The toilets were quite good, but the showers were primitive, open to the sky and wind, with only a rusty grating to stand on.

On Saturday we caught the bus to Limassol with the intention of inspecting the commercial harbour for a possible berth the next year. After a long and weary walk from the bus-stop to the harbour we found everywhere closed, but a friendly policeman took us into his office and gave us chairs and large chunks of ice-cold water melon to eat while we waited for a harbour official, who explained all about anchoring in the harbour. No buses were operating for the return journey so we had to take an expensive taxi.

On Saturday we paid the harbour dues of £16 for two nights in the marina and were then charged an extra £14 by customs just for entering and leaving the harbour, although we had officially entered Cyprus at Paphos. This made a total of £30 for under-par services – another racket. I protested and was then told, just as we were leaving, that we could have used the facilities of the adjacent hotel.

171

We were under way early on Sunday 16th August, and arrived at Larnaca Marina, our journey's end that year, at 1300. We took a temporary berth on a pontoon until we were given an official one, belonging to an owner who was absent for the week. We fell in love with Larnaca straight away: the finger pontoon was good, with water and electricity available; the showers and toilets were good; and the police, customs and marina officials were all helpful.

On Monday we settled in. We booked to haul out on Tuesday 1st September and to fly home on 15th September. In the evening we explored the row of outdoor restaurants along the beach and chose the Dolphin, where we enjoyed a Greek salad, followed by a fish main course and an ice-cream sweet, accompanied by an excellent Cyprus wine, Orlando.

On Tuesday we made the rounds of tourist office, post office, bank and the police station, where, as I had left my driving licence at home, I enquired about a temporary one. They told me to report to the transport department on the edge of the town. We bought food, had lunch aboard and, after a siesta, walked to the excellent market, where we bought fish, cold turkey and fruit. We enjoyed our evening meal in the cockpit.

On Wednesday we walked the two miles to the traffic police who, after giving me a simple eye test, agreed to let me have a temporary driving licence. Then they asked for two passport-size photographs. That meant a walk back to town to the barbers for the photographs, back again to the traffic department and back to the boat, a long, weary, six-mile walk. We gave up after the barbers and returned to our kinder routine of lunch, siesta, showers and dinner in the cockpit, on the melon, cold turkey and salad, pineapple and cream that we had purchased in the market. The next day I collected my temporary driving licence. On Monday we walked miles looking for a car for hire for three days. All car firms except one were either closed or fully booked.

On Monday I went to collect the car, an old banger waiting beside a man who sat at a table nearby to collect my money. As it was an old car I began to test all the controls before driving away, lights, indicator, screenwash, when a hand was thrust through the open window and the ignition key snatched away! I looked round, startled.

'You are not a driver,' the owner shouted. 'You don't know how to start the car.'

172

I have driven about half a million miles, and naturally I protested. He would have none of it and insisted on returning my money. In the end, I saw the funny side of it and the next day described it to Sheila, in *Brimwhym*, the boat next to us.

'I'll take you to Stevens, the car firm that hires a car to us,' she said, and that afternoon she drove us to the out-of-town car hire firm. I booked a new Mazda 323 for Thursday to Saturday at two-thirds of the cost of hiring the old banger. In the afternoon I pumped up the dinghy, washed it thoroughly in fresh water, and then filled it with fresh water to clean our genoa and all the warps and sheets. I hung the sail upside down to dry, took down the main and mizzen and then stowed all the sails and ropes in the fore cabin.

On Thursday we picked up our car and drove eastwards to Aiya Napta; we did not like the crowded beaches or the pervading smell of ice-cream and fish and chips, so we drove on to Fig Tree Bay, a lovely cove with excellent swimming and a shady tree overlooking the bay under which we ate our picnic lunch.

On Friday we drove up to the Troodos Mountains and booked for the night at the Jubilee Hotel. We drove to Mount Olympus and walked one of the nature trails. In the afternoon we drove to Pendoulas to visit the ornate Kykos Monastery and back to the hotel for dinner.

The next day, after a Continental breakfast, we asked for a nature trail leaflet and chose Number 3 – a lovely walk, rather like Scotland, through the forest, along a mountain stream, crossing and re-crossing stepping stones, until we came to the Caledonian Falls. We drove back to the marina well pleased with our two-day excursion away from boats and boating and finished the day with swordfish steaks at the Dionysus restaurant.

On Sunday Joan records in her diary: *Quiet evening. Meal from tins, corned beef; peaches and cream – using up stores!*

On Monday the sailmaker came to measure up for our new cockpit cover and for the extra pieces to our awning. Sheila and Frank came for drinks in the evening and we enjoyed a lovely roast lamb meal in the cockpit. After this we took down the awning and prepared for the next day.

On Tuesday we were up at 0600. We took in our electric cable and singled up on our warps, ready for hauling out. 'Mike the Crane' was an expert. The boat came out without trouble and was soon propped up in its winter position. Mike sent us away while he pressure washed the hull, saving us the laborious task of scraping off the barnacles. We took the opportunity of calling at immigration for our passports.

On Wednesday the man came to measure up for the extension to our stainless steel ladder. We regularly swam from the boat and while I usually dived in, Joan went down the stern ladder. We had had this made with the bottom of the ladder just touching the water. This was a mistake, for it was difficult for me to get a foot on the bottom rung and very difficult for Joan. The extra piece was hinged to the bottom and extended three feet under the water – it could be pulled up out of the water by a lanyard. We were to find this a great boon in our subsequent swims. Another man came to service our faulty refrigerator. Apparently it needed topping up with gas but had no gas valve for doing so. He promised to fit one. We put up our awning with its extension and found it very satisfactory.

On Thursday 3rd September we joined the MV *Atalante* for a cruise to Israel and Egypt. On joining the ship we were singled out from the long queue to have our baggage thoroughly searched. When I asked, 'Why us?' we were told that we were the type to be running drugs – an elderly couple, living abroad beyond their means! The ship was comfortable, our cabin air-conditioned and our table companions very pleasant and agreeable. This was our first-ever cruise together in a big ship and we made the most of it. That evening at the floorshow we won first prize, a bottle of wine, for being the longest-married couple, forty-eight years! That night we sailed to Haifa.

At Haifa a fleet of air-conditioned coaches took us to Bethlehem to see the Church of the Nativity, and then to Jerusalem to see the Old City, the Via Doloroso, the Mount of Olives, the Wailing Wall and the Golden Dome. We had an excellent guide, an Israeli girl called Ruth. She made our long coach journey interesting, explaining what was happening everywhere. The Israelis were reclaiming land along a marshy river and all round us we saw evidence of industry and organisation, newly created farmland, olive groves, factories and houses.

That night the ship took us on to Port Said and a coach trip to Cairo, again with an interesting and informative guide, an elderly Egyptian lady with good English, who was a bundle of energy.

She took us round the Tut an Khamun exhibition in the Cairo Museum at breakneck speed and then on to the Pyramids and the Sphinx. The coach ride took us through similar countryside to that of Israel, reclamation of marshy riverside. What a contrast! Half-finished buildings, rusty machinery, work on drainage begun and long since stopped! Even our coach broke down and we had to wait for half an hour for a replacement and a further three-quarters of an hour for an escort through a no-go area. We were taken to a carpet manufacturer where we were treated to a cold drink and an exhibition of carpets they wished to sell to us. Joan expressed her approval of one rather large carpet and the vendor concentrated on her, trying to sell her the carpet for £1000.

We thoroughly enjoyed our cruise and were to remember it later when we finally sold *Blue Pearl* and wondered what to do with ourselves.

In the following week we thoroughly cleaned inside and outside the boat, polished the stainless steel, dismantled and cleaned the toilet, fitted the new hatch rubber, cleaned out the water tanks, and had the Perkins man winterise our engine. The sailmaker made and fitted our new cockpit cover and supplied us with a small awning, made to my design, to be used while sailing. On Sunday we discovered the Book Swap. Run by a semi-permanent resident boat owner, it opened on Sundays in a room adjacent to the showers. About two hundred paperbacks were on display and all you did was to change one of yours for one on offer. We replaced ten of ours, giving us plenty of reading for our return to the boat the following year.

On Tuesday 15th September we were up at 0220 and caught the 0635 flight to Prague and then to Heathrow.

18

Dartmouth Interlude II

After our Mediterranean idyll we arrived back in England on Tuesday 15th September to a life full of social events, hard work and disasters. Jack and Peggy met us and took us to their home in New Malden. The next day we all visited Richmond Park and enjoyed a lovely walk in Isabella Plantation, a very English garden after the Mediterranean.

On Thursday we took a train to Greenwich to see Julia and her partner, Tom. Tom showed us the boat he was building from scrap materials. Julia drove us all to New Malden for an enjoyable meal with Peggy and Jack.

The next day we took a train to Truro to stay with Jill and Rob at Gwel-an-Porth in Falmouth. Throughout the latter part of our Mediterranean cruise we had received a series of faxes from Jill describing the deteriorating situation of their building firm. They had built a large showroom with several office suites above for a client who had declared himself bankrupt, owing them £100,000. Their contract with the client stated that they owned the building until all debts were settled. Two months after signing their contract the client had taken out a mortgage with a bank. The Public Trustee had decided that the bank had priority over the builders and that the bank would own the building. Jill and Rob were contesting this and, as they could not afford a solicitor or a barrister, were presenting their own case.

At Falmouth Jill was working hard on her case, researching similar cases and producing an affidavit. I immediately set to to help her with this and spent the rest of the day working on it.

On Sunday we finished this work and immediately left for Dartmouth. Our disasters were not over. In the evening Peggy telephoned to tell us that Joan's Aunt Jessie had died. This was sad news for us. Jessie was the widow of Jack Mead, who owned Bullhornstone Farm on Dartmoor. It was here, during the war, that Joan and I had become engaged, and Jessie had a special place in our affections.

On Monday I continued to work on Jill and Rob's case, but on Tuesday we resumed normal Dartmouth life with bridge at the Yacht Club. On Wednesday we went on a museum outing to the Fleet Air Arm Museum at Yeovilton and a visit to the sixteenth-century house and gardens at Montacute. Aunt Jessie's funeral was on the Friday.

I had suffered a recurrence of the back pains that had immobilised me towards the end of my teaching career and was now having daily heat treatment. Work had always been good for this condition and Joan and I put in several hours each day in our garden, cleaning and clearing after our long absence, and planting for the following spring.

On Monday 5th October my niece, Pamela, and her husband, Ian, together with my sister, Maisie, came to visit us. We enjoyed two relaxing days, exploring Dartmoor and the Avon Dam and walking along the coastal path at Dartmouth.

On Thursday George Thompson, the Commodore of our Yacht Club, asked me to run bridge classes for club members. I agreed to this, accepting the large amount of preparatory work it entailed.

On Saturday we left for Falmouth to give support to Jill and Rob, who were now threatened with losing their home. They were by now nearly penniless and Rob was selling his expensive woodworking machinery to help pay the bills. We took the opportunity of visiting Tresawsen, the seven-acre nursery they had bought, on which they had hoped to build their next home. We could stay only for two days as I was due at Torbay Hospital on Monday for a hearing test. This revealed the deterioration in my hearing and the need for a hearing aid.

Our normal activities were now well under way, bridge at the Yacht Club on Tuesdays, Joan's literature class on Wednesdays, a visit to the Captain's house, Royal Naval College on Friday in aid of the Royal Lifeboat Society and the Yacht Club Cruising Supper on Saturday. Throughout this week I continued work on the garden and on a talk I was to give Probus on our Mediterranean cruise.

On Friday 23rd I had an eye check-up at Torbay Hospital and learned that my eyes had also deteriorated.

On Saturday we were back at Gwel-an-Porth and in the afternoon had a long talk with Jill and Rob. Having consulted my financial adviser at Dartmouth, I had prepared a rescue package. However their debts were more than I had anticipated and beyond my help. Joan's diary records that *Freddie, Jill and Rob did not sleep well that night.*

The next day we continued our efforts to solve the financial problems and left after lunch for Dartmouth. On Tuesday Jill telephoned. The solicitors for the bank had been trying to obtain a delay for the hearing on 3rd November. Jill had opposed this. She now told me that she had been successful and asked if we would come to give support on that day.

I spent much of the remainder of the week converting photographs to slides and preparing my talk. On Monday 2nd November we left early for Falmouth and I worked with Jill and Rob on their case until the afternoon. Tina and Tom arrived at 11.00 p.m. The family had gathered to support Jill, who was presenting the case.

On Tuesday 3rd November the case began at 10.30, and from 10.40 until 1.0 p.m. Jill was in the witness box. The barrister tried to question her on the construction of the building, but she told the judge he must wait until she called Rob as an expert witness. She presented her case well and I was proud of her.

Her main contention was that the building contract included a clause that gave them retention and title of ownership until all invoices were paid. This was supported by the Sale of Goods Act 1979, designed to support just such a case. As the invoices had not been paid, the building remained in their possession. The barrister for the bank argued that under the much earlier Land Act any building erected on the land became part of the freehold and the building was therefore owned by the bank.

In the afternoon Jill called Rob, who gave a detailed account of the construction of the timber-frame building. The barrister, who had not asked Jill any questions on the financial side, now questioned him on the invoices. Just as he had tried to catch Jill out on the construction, now he tried to catch Rob out on the finances. Jill objected and this objection was upheld by the judge, who told him he must put these questions to Jill. The judge then adjourned the case. On Wednesday we left for home.

On Tuesday 10th November we had the Bridge Club's annual lunch at Stoke Lodge, a very good lunch followed by Chicago bridge, the proceeds of which were given to a local charity.

On Wednesday I gave my talk on our Mediterranean cruise, with slides, to Probus at Stoke Lodge. On Friday I saw my doctor about the pains in my back and he arranged for an X-ray. In the evening we dressed up for Probus Ladies Night dinner at Stoke Lodge. On Monday we gave a lunch party to some of our friends.

On Monday 16th November Jill telephoned early. They had received their first summons for unpaid bills and had decided to put Tresawsen, their nursery, up for sale.

On Wednesday Joan started a cold and I followed her the next day. We spent the next two days in bed, taking turns to provide meals.

On Sunday we drove to Falmouth and on Monday 23rd were all in court to hear the judge's decision. The judge expressed his sympathy for Jill and Rob, 'a small firm that had done nothing wrong'. However, the Land Act took priority over all other arguments, even the agreement over possession of the building entered into two months before the mortgage. His judgment was therefore in favour of the bank, the owner of the freehold. That evening Jill and Rob had a brief board meeting and decided to put their business into liquidation.

I had worked with Jill and Rob to prepare their case and had sat through the hearing. From a common sense point of view their case was incontrovertible. Based on a legal document, prepared by a solicitor, they owned the building until it was fully paid for. Two months after that agreement, the purchaser offered the building as collateral for a mortgage. In my view the purchaser had no right to offer an asset that he did not own, nor the bank to accept it. The bank should have ascertained the position before offering the money. What was needed was a benchmark judgment that challenged the all-powerful Land Act and acknowledged the rights of the builder under the much later Sale of Goods Act, designed to protect companies such as building firms from non-payment of accounts. If Jill and Rob could have employed a barrister and gone to appeal they might well have achieved this. I think that in this case the law failed to provide justice.

On Tuesday we drove home to Dartmouth and on Wednesday Peggy and Jack joined us for the remainder of the week, leaving

Plaque on a rock at Frikes (Chapter 14)

Delphi amphitheatre (Chapter 14)

Corinth Canal (Chapter 14)

Argonauta Restaurant, Paroikia (Chapter 15)

Agrilithi Bay (Chapter 15)

The ruined Italian headquarters at Kastelano, Agrilithi Bay (Chapter 15)

The small memorial, Kastelano, Agrilithi Bay
(Chapter 15)

The minaret, Bodrum (Chapter 16)

Bodrum harbour
(Chapter 16)

Pamukkale
(Chapter 16)

Ephesus
(Chapter 16)

Mary's House (Chapter 16)

Sanar and Ayla (Chapter 16)

Söğüt (Chapter 16)

The theatre, Castle Island (Chapter 16)

Fallen masonry at Knidos (Chapter 16)

Keči Buku (Chapter 16)

Wall Bay, Fethiye (Chapter 16)

The nature trail,
Troodos Mountains (Chapter 17)

The Golden Dome and Wailing Wall, Jerusalem (Chapter 17)

The Sphinx, Cairo (Chapter 17)

The Red Arrows at Larnaca (Chapter 19)

Warblers join us on the passage to Rhodes (Chapter 19)

alace of the Grand Masters, Rhodes (Chapter 20)

The garden restaurant, Rhodes (Chapter 20)

Our new sailing awning (Chapter 20)

The leper village at Spinalonga (Chapter 20)

The cliff walk at Port Kaio
(Chapter 20)

The lighthouse, Port Longos:
Nikos and Freddie (Chapter 20)

Cartagena: the square leading to the castle (Chapter 22)

A nineteenth-century submarine at Cartagena (Chapter 22)

A Lisbon precinct
(Chapter 23)

Ville Close, Concarneau
(Chapter 24)

The end of the voyage (Chapter 24)

Freddie and Joan on their return to Dartmouth (Chapter 24)

us just time to prepare for a lunch party at Margaret and Ivan's house, where we met sixteen of our friends. It was good to sink ourselves in social events and this helped to take our minds off the trauma at Falmouth.

On our return to Dartmouth I had sent in our renewal notice for *Blue Pearl*'s mooring to the Dart Harbour Authority. On Thursday 3rd December I received a letter from the assistant harbour master saying that as we were late, he had taken us off the list and we were to lose our mooring. This was another big shock. For six years I had paid for the mooring, using it for only one year. I had given the harbour master permission to use the mooring in our absence. Now, when we were thinking of returning to Dartmouth, he was taking it away from us.

We continued with many social activities until Christmas: lunch or drinks parties with Bill and Doreen, Kay and Richard, Mary, and Joan, an old friend; supper and bridge with Kay and Richard, and Tom and Nesta; the Yacht Club Annual Dinner and the Senior Members Lunch; and Probus Christmas Lunch. Joan continued with her literature classes and I with Probus and Exeter Flotilla meetings. I had eye tests and new glasses and started physiotherapy for my back at Dartmouth Hospital. And, of course, we gardened, late preparations for winter, with pruning, weeding and bonfires.

Christmas rushed upon us, bringing Jill and Rob. Our party was a quiet one, enjoying Joan's cooking and my wines, walks with the dogs round town and along the coast, and many discussions. We were not in the mood for merrymaking. They left on the 28th, and 1992 ended on a sombre note, with much sadness and more difficulties ahead. The weather became wet, windy, cold and gloomy, matching our mood. Cyprus seemed a long way away.

1993 started with a bright morning and Joan and I enjoyed a walk along the Embankment, buoyed up by the sunshine. In the afternoon the weather changed and rain and a series of gales set in. When I could I worked in the garden, uprooting old shrubs and clearing unwanted scrub; indoors I cleared the games room and set up a workshop where I could deal with household needs such as making a shoe-rack for my wardrobe, replacing chair seats, inserting a mortice lock in our front door and window locks in our ground floor windows

On 11th January we booked our flight to Cyprus. On the same day the assistant harbour master relented and promised us a mooring for May 1994 and I booked to haul out in October 1993 at Creekside Boatyard, near where we live. Also on this day I had a hearing aid fitted.

Joan's literature classes and my Probus meetings started on 13th January and bridge at the club and at home with friends soon got under way. I continued with my visits to the physiotherapy department at Dartmouth Hospital, had an X-ray at Brixham, which showed no damage to the spine but revealed some arthritis, and started a series of twisting exercises, lying down, sitting and standing, which completely removed the pain. I am still doing them many years later and the pain has not returned.

Jill and Rob arrived on 28th January with their trailer containing twenty-three shrubs from their nursery, conifers, azaleas, hydrangeas, camelias and others, some of them specimen plants. They had been unable to afford Christmas presents and this was their way of compensating. They turned to and helped in the garden, Rob using his rotavator to hoe through the shrubbery and his tackle to pull up unwanted shrubs. We were lucky with a window in the weather and with Jill and Rob's help were able to get on top of the gardening, ready for our departure.

Local parties with our friends had re-commenced in the New Year, George and Margaret, Jeffrey and Marjorie, Ken and Barbara, and we had friends to lunch or dinner. On Saturday 27th we gave our big lunch party to twenty guests and Joan once more rose to the occasion, with steak and kidney pie, chicken and leek pie, salmon quiche, ham and a variety of salads and vegetables, followed by banoffee pie, trifle, peach tart, rhubarb fool or chocolate cake. Jill and Rob arrived to help, Jill with preparation and serving and Rob with pre-lunch drinks and wines.

March fled past, with a silver wedding reception at our nephew's, a week's visit to Peggy and Jack with a return visit from them, and visits to and from our niece, living nearby at Newton Ferrers.

As soon as Peggy and Jack left for home I hired a concrete mixer and laid the foundation for a crazy paving path through our shrubbery. I followed this up with a last tidying up of the garden.

We had two more events, the cruising supper at the Yacht Club and the AGM at the Bridge Club. Then it was time to go.

19

Larnaca

On Sunday 28th March Jill and Rob arrived to take us to Bristol Airport to catch the 1410 Falcon Airways flight to Larnaca Airport. We found *Blue Pearl* as we had left her, in good condition. We found some coffee aboard and Bob, a friendly neighbour from *Brimwiln*, gave us some milk for an evening drink. We had had dinner on the aeroplane and this was all we wanted. By 2200 we were in bed.

On Monday we filled up with water and then made the rounds, to the yard office to sign in, to immigration to exchange our passports for a landing pass, to the market for meat, fish, fruit and vegetables, and to the supermarket for milk and groceries. By lunchtime we felt that we had never left the boat and were ready to resume work.

In the afternoon we sent a fax to Jill and Rob to tell them of our safe arrival and had one in return, the first of many faxes concerning their desperate efforts to survive. They had returned to Dartmouth, where Rob drained our water system and began the difficult repair of our faulty kitchen mixer tap. He needed to obtain spare parts so he left our system drained. My fax to Jill on April 5th records some details of our life at Larnaca:

Dear Jill and Rob,

Thank you for your Fax No. 1. Sorry the tap gave so much trouble, but thanks for looking after it and for watering the garden.

This week has flown past. Temperatures during the day are in the seventies and we have now changed to shorts. Nights are cold – about 50 degrees. Have finished wiring the new mains lighting system and installed a contact breaker. This involved taking down several ceiling panels and for two days we were in a muddle. All is tidy now and the lights are working well. The pulse charger was not working, but a man from a neighbouring boat came and put it right for £5. He also repaired our Mase portable generator for £10. This is a feature of the boatyard. People from other boats are willing to help you, some who are living on a shoestring for a small fee. We use the mains to top up our batteries. The fridge is working at only half capacity and we are waiting for a man to come and top up the gas. I have fitted the anchor brake pawl and that is now working well. I have also tried out our new sailing-awning, bought last September. It is excellent and very necessary in the hot sun.

Shopping is fun. We go to an excellent market for meat, fruit and vegetables. The butcher recognised us from last year and has given us prime cuts, the best we have purchased in the Mediterranean. We bought some grapefruit and tangerines from a market stall and he made it up to 2 grapefruits, 30 tangerines, 2 oranges and 4 lemons – all for 50 cents, about 70p. The grapefruits are the biggest and juiciest we have come across. Greens and tomatoes are excellent and very cheap. We buy for three or four days at a time and I take my haversack for the heavy bulk. We bought a nice bottle of Keo 1988 red wine, like claret, for 83 cents, about £1. For the rest, we still have some left from last year.

Hope all is well. Love to you both from Mummy and Daddy.

On Wednesday 7th we received a disturbing fax from Jill. The building society with whom they had mortgaged their bungalow to support their business had issued a summons at County Court, Truro, claiming repossession. This was in spite of the fact that Jill and Rob had made a fair offer to cover the interest on the existing mortgage. They were given only seven days to reply, although this ran into Easter. The building society solicitor had sent a curt and bullying letter rejecting this offer, although the local branch manager had said that with a small addition to repay some capital he would accept it. Jill and Rob had promising purchasers for Gwel-an-Porth, their bungalow, and an interest shown in their nursery, Tresawsen. It was essential to buy time so that they could effect a deal. The branch manager, with the backing of head office, finally settled for a monthly payment that, with help from us, Jill and Rob could just meet.

A fax from me to Jill, dated 7th April, and Jill's reply, on 8th April, summarise the deal and the urgency of the situation:

Your Fax No. 2 received. Very sorry to hear of developments. We are here for the next two weeks – three weeks if necessary or even longer – so that we can stay in touch and see your problem resolved. The Office here is closed from Friday to Monday. Cannot receive faxes but can send up to 2200. Last fax must be in by 1600 Thursday.

Confirm offer re £500. I left you a letter for the Building Society and one for our Bank re standing order. If necessary, will dictate a letter by fax or telephone.

Assume proposals will be accepted. Probably nothing done now till after Easter. When your proposals are accepted and detailed arrangements are completed send a fax and I will telephone you to complete arrangements.

If the Building Society does not agree you must fight it on the proposals we have suggested. Essential you try another agent and make every effort to sell.

We are now polishing the boat. Leaving anti-fouling till nearer launch.

Love – M and D.

Extract from Jill's fax No. 3, dated 8th April:

The Branch Manager of the Building Society has written his agreement to our proposals and is now on holiday. The Solicitors yesterday morning refused our proposal on the telephone and when told that we had a letter agreeing to it, asked for a copy to be faxed to them immediately. We've heard nothing since! We have assumed that everything now stops because it is Easter and we have now found that we have until 23rd April to get our formal reply into Truro County Court. I think the Solicitor was looking for a fat fee. So although everything is in diabolical limbo, the pressure time wise is not so great.

While all this was happening we got on with the many jobs in the boat: we polished the boat's hull with the help of trestles lent by Tom and Anne from *Alpine Rose*; I overhauled all the winches but one that had seized up; the Perkins man came to remove our injectors.

On Friday 9th April I took the last winch to pieces and overhauled it till it worked properly. The Perkins man came to service our engine and replace the injectors with new ones – he claimed that the old ones he had removed were not Perkins injectors. I had last had the injectors cleaned at Malta. I asked him to let me have the old ones back and he promised to send them to me. In the evening Pat and Ralph, neighbours from Dartmouth, whose boat *Misandre* was a few yards away from ours, arrived in Larnaca and came to dinner with us.

The next day I tackled the changeover valve to the holding tank, which had seized up, and the cooker, in which the oven burners would not light up.

On Sunday we accompanied Ralph and Pat and David Townsend from a 42-foot Rival to the Anglican church where the bishop took the service, followed by a visit to a most interesting arts and crafts exhibition of local work.

On Monday 12th April I began work again, taking the cooker to pieces. I eventually found the fault. The burner bracket was bent and not directing gas into the intake pipe. I corrected the fault by bending the bracket until it matched up with the intake pipe. The cooker then worked perfectly.

The stopcocks in the oily locker that drained the cockpit had seized up solid and nothing I could do would release them. Ralph came to help with his large Stilsen, but the control wheel broke off. I asked the stainless steel engineer if he could help. He tried, but gave up after five minutes. He told us that we would have to grind away the outer skin fitting, and offered his grinder for hire on Thursday.

Jenny and Will, great friends of ours in Dartmouth, had arrived in Cyprus for a walking holiday and in the evening came to visit us and stayed to dinner. We spent a pleasant evening discussing the Troodos Mountains, which they were going to explore.

Earlier in the day we received a fax from Jill, which brought us up to date with her building society saga:

We've had a letter from the Building Society Manager as promised. Extract reads. 'Solicitors have been instructed to

186

withdraw court proceedings on the basis ... as agreed that payment ... is received, commencing this month... Should payments not be received, our solicitors will make a fresh application to Court for a hearing.'

We will pay you back the money you lend us from the sale of Gwel-an-Porth and Tresawsen. Our bank also has an involvement with Gwel-an-Porth and will have to be paid first. Your repayment may have to wait for the sale of Tresawsen. As an 'aid' for future use we suggest you write to us a letter offering to lend us the money for the building society monthly payments to be repaid from the sale of the properties. I will write back to you confirming and accepting on that basis and we can use these letters as and when necessary. How does that seem to you?

Jill also told us about Rob's work on *Tomboy*. In their successful days they had bought an old fishing boat and now that Rob was out of work he was refurbishing it. He had been trained as a shipwright and now was replacing faulty planks, putting on a new deck, building a new cabin top and overhauling the engine. If they came through their ordeal they would use it for pleasure and fishing; if not they would sell it. I sent a fax in reply:

Dear Jill and Rob,

Your fax number 5 received today and am answering it at once by special permission. This weekend is Greek Orthodox Church Easter and things are mostly closed down until Tuesday.

Agree to your proposal and will write a letter offering to lend the money for the Building Society monthly repayments, to be repaid from sale proceeds of your properties. This will be either Gwel-an-Porth or Tresawsen, but as soon as the bank will allow I confirm that you can go ahead with the arrangements as agreed.

Launch delayed by difficult gate valves of cockpit drainage. Had to cut them away with grinderette from the outside and bang them through inward. New skin fittings not available until Tuesday. Replacing gate valves with ball valves. Hope to launch now at the end of next week.

Jenny and Will arrived on Thursday and in the evening came to dinner.

Glad to hear Tomboy is progressing well.
Love, M and D.

Over the next week we continued to work on the boat, installing the new ball valves for the cockpit drains, an unexpectedly difficult job as I had to make room for the handles to turn in a space crowded with pipes and other valves. Because of the overcrowding the valves had to be screwed in from the outside and as I was giving Joan instructions through the hull a digger came alongside to dig a trench and drowned my voice. We had to stop, clean off the mastic and wait for the digger to finish before we could proceed. As we completed the second installation he arrived again and I finished by running up and down ladders to give Joan instructions. We finished the job at 1800.

On Wednesday we booked a car at Stevens Car Hire for Monday 8th May. On Friday morning we went to the Metro supermarket for our big order for the cruise, over £100. We saw the manager and arranged a discount, two free litres of wine and a free delivery to the boat. We collected three trolleys full of stores, saw them loaded in the delivery van and had a free ride in the van back to the boat. We spent the afternoon stowing it all.

On Saturday I worked all day on wiring all our skin valves to our sacrificial anode and refitting the locker floor to accommodate the new valves. Joan shopped and did a large load of washing and ironing. In the evening we had dinner aboard *Misandre*, Ralph and Pat's lovely 41-foot Moody. David and Barbara Townsend from *Pomone* were also guests and in spite of heavy rain we enjoyed a splendid meal and good conversation, mostly nautical. Back at *Blue Pearl* we found that the rain had revealed a serious leak in our fore hatch.

On Monday 26th April we collected our hire car from Stevens and set off across country to Troodos. As we climbed into the hills the road became narrower and less made up until we found ourselves on a dirt track, quite lost. We had seen no signposts for some time. We were unable to position ourselves on our map, which seemed to have little to do with the terrain over which we were driving. We had no compass and there was no sun to give us direction. Eventually we came across a digger team who were working on one of the roads. They pointed the way to a made up road and eventually we reached a navigable highway that led to Troodos.

We looked in at Kekapetria, deep in a valley, and at the attractive village of Platres, but we preferred our Jubilee Hotel in Troodos and booked in there for two nights. We had time for a short walk, half way along the Persephone Trail, enough to renew our acquaintance with the grand 'Alpine' scenery and the quaint notices on the trail itself. That evening we enjoyed dinner in the company of a German couple, Ulla and Gotz Langlan.

On Tuesday we drove to the Kaledonian Falls, visited last autumn, and walked back for some way along the trail until we met Ulla and Gotz coming the other way. In the afternoon we took the Artemis Trail, four miles along a circular route on the north side of Mount Olympus, at 6000 feet, the highest mountain in Cyprus. Snow up to two feet deep covered the route. This was an exhilarating walk, which reminded us of our spring holidays in the Lake District when we used to love walking above the snowline. We returned to our hotel for showers, dinner and a pleasant evening with Ulla and Gotz.

On Wednesday we left after breakfast, called at Paphos for lunch, explored the lovely coastal area of north-west Cyprus, investigated possible anchorages in Coral Bay and Lathi Harbour and arrived back in Larnaca at 1915 for a fish supper at the Cuckoo's Nest.

On Thursday we had two unexpected guests. Herbert and Joan Walker, friends from Dartmouth and members of the Dartmouth Yacht Club, who were holidaying in the south-east corner of Cyprus, called on us for coffee and a chat and then went on to *Misandre* for a sandwich lunch. In the late afternoon we started on the anti-fouling and finished the first side by 1800. We completed the second side early the next morning and I dealt with the charts and bought cord for our lazy jacks. In the evening we went with Pat and Ralph to a violin and piano concert at the Town Hall. Afterwards they came back to *Blue Pearl* for drinks.

On Saturday we took out the plexiglass in the fore hatch, cleaned off the rubber compound and replaced the glass with fresh mastic. Just after lunch we had a superb display by the Red Arrows who come to Cyprus to work up. We had watched them every year at Dartmouth Regatta from our garden, sometimes flying below our level.

On Monday I fitted the new lazy jacks, a rig that caught and folded the mainsail as it was lowered. For this Joan had to winch me to the top of the mainmast with two buckets of tools. I drilled into the crosstrees and pop riveted two brackets, fitted blocks and fed through lines linked to the end of the boom.

On Tuesday 4th May we were at last launched, an easy launch but a tight berth. That evening we dined out at the Cuckoo's Nest.

On Thursday we collected the new fan belt and our old injectors, despatched by the Perkins agent. We shopped for fresh vegetables and fruit for three days and finished some minor outstanding jobs. I reported to the police that we were leaving the following day. We had a 'bon voyage' fax from Jill and I sent her one in return:

Dear Jill and Rob,

Hopefully the long journey home is about to start. Have cleared customs and the police and we leave at 0600 tomorrow morning. First stop Rhodes. Will try to fax you there.

Had Bob, a very helpful single-hander from the boat next to us, to drinks yesterday lunch time and Pat and Ralph to dinner in the evening, a lively, long, chatty evening. The weather looks promising. The glass is up and hopefully the first part of the journey along the Cyprus coast will be in a slight wind. It is always from ahead so we have to motor anyway.

We bent on all the sails on Wednesday and tried out the engine and the lazy jacks. All seems well. We are looking forward to the journey. 300 miles to Rhodes will take us three days and two nights – arriving p.m. Monday. Probably fax you on Tuesday. We will get a nice, long plunge into sailing waters. We are hoping to get quite a bit of rest on the passage – perhaps not sleep, but certainly resting our very tired limbs. The new sailing-awning, made last September, goes underneath the boom and should give us protection from the fierce sun, my own design and very quick and simple to rig

Bye for now. Hope you soon have good news. Love M and D.

The forecast that evening was bad, gales along the south coast of Cyprus. On Saturday morning it was blowing a near gale from the west so we stayed in harbour. I repaired two navigation lights and serviced our outboard engine. After lunch I again tackled the small leak in the toilet. I took the pump to pieces and replaced all the rubbers, valves and screws. I tried it out. Water poured out everywhere. I took it all to pieces again. Some gritty pieces emerged with the water and when I put it together again it worked perfectly. We had a late meal and retired to bed at 2230, very tired.

On Sunday we set the alarm for 0500. The wind was howling so we decided not to leave but perhaps go in the afternoon if the wind abated. The wind did not ease so, like all the other boats waiting to go, we stayed put.

At 0630 the next day, Monday 10th May 1993, we decided to leave and at 0730, helped out of our tight berth by our neighbour, we cast off and began the 3000-mile journey to Dartmouth.

20

Larnaca to Port Longos

The log reveals how quickly we resumed our sailing mode:

Monday 10th May
0740 Left Larnaca. Courses 135°/3, 182°/6, 195°/9, 243°/12
round the headland.
1000 34° 45'N, 033° 34'E. Wind force 4, heading us. Motor-
sailing, main and motor, into an unpleasant, lumpy sea.
1100 Wind increased to force 5. Reefed main.
1200 Log 22.6. Off Cape Kite. Co. 243°.
1600 Log 47.7. Off Cape Gata. Co. 291°.
2000 Log 68.6. 34° 35'N, 032° 07'E. Co. 296°. 214 miles
to Rhodes.
2100 Wind eased. Sea becoming calmer.
2400 Log 92.7. 34° 35'N, 032° 07'E. Co. 296°.
Tuesday 11th May.
0200 Log 105.1. Very cloudy.
0400 Log 117.6. Rhodes 296° 187 miles. Heavy rainstorm.
0730 A small bird (a warbler?) landed on deck. He accepted
some grain and tart crumbs and sipped rainwater. After exploring
the rigging and underneath the dinghy he settled underneath
the spray hood, unperturbed by our movements. Later he was
joined by his mate and the two birds moved freely about the
boat, sometimes flying away and then returning. At one time
they were joined by two other birds – all of this about seventy
miles from the nearest land. Later, when the sun came out, they
flew off and joined a passing merchant ship.

For map, see page 146.

1100 Five dolphins joined us and sported for an hour.

1200 Log 168.5. Barometer steady on 1016. Course to Rhodes 295°, distance 132 miles.

1600 Co. 294°. Rhodes 105 miles.

2000 Rhodes 294°/82.4.

Wednesday 12th May.

0000 Log 239.6. Rhodes 295°/59.4. Barometer 1014. Wind dying and heading us. Commenced tacking 20° either side of course, first to port.

0400 Log 260.1. Rhodes 295°/40.7. Wind increasing. Able to lay the course.

0805 Rhodes 297°/17.7.

1200 Moored in Mandraki Harbour, Rhodes. Distance 315.2 miles. Time 2 days, 4 hours, 20 minutes.

The whole passage was under main or reefed main and engine. The wind headed us round Cyprus and was 25 degrees to port on the passage across to Rhodes. At one time it increased to force five, but was mainly about force one. The sea was lumpy around Cyprus, but generally quiet across to Rhodes. As we approached Rhodes the wind got up to force five and we had a difficult pontoon to back into with the wind coming across us.

Mandraki Harbour is the ancient harbour the entrance of which was reputed to have been straddled by the Statue of Helios the ancient sun god, one of the seven wonders of the world known as the Colossus of Rhodes. This statue was destroyed by an earthquake in 227 BC.

We found that a new pontoon had been erected along the eastern mole, equipped with water and electricity points. This was not mentioned in our up-to-date pilot book, and it was a good omen for our stay in Rhodes.

At Customs we were told that since 1st January 1993, Common Market Day, transit logs were no longer needed. This was to cause us much hassle later, in Crete and in the Peloponnese, where they seemed not to have heard of the change. We had an early meal and retired to bed to catch up on sleep.

The next morning we walked ashore and found the supermarket close to the marina. On the way back we invited Bernard and Valerie from the Olsen 35 next to us, who had helped us to moor the day before, to drinks at 1830. From them we learned that a sirocco, the hot wind that carries sand from Africa, was expected.

The gale blew all night, up to force ten. The boat on the opposite side of the pontoon broke its mooring ring and for a while was adrift, supported by boats on either side. Several of us turned-to to capture it and eventually secure it. We had our stern-line fairlead snapped in two. The next day we found all the boats covered in sand up to the cross trees and we spent most of the day cleaning it off.

The next day, Friday, we shopped in the nearby market, enjoyed a quiet afternoon resting and, after tea, explored the nearby town. I cooked the evening meal, my usual steak, onions, tomatoes, peppers and chips, which Joan pronounced very good.

On Saturday we were out early to enjoy a walk round the Old Town, just ambling past tourist shops, leaving the major interests till Sunday. On Sunday we returned to the Old Town, along the Knights Road, past the Inns of Knights, to the Palace of the Grand Masters. The names are redolent of the mediaeval history of the town. We visited the Museum of Decorative Arts, the Byzantine Museum and the Archaeological Museum, and the Mosque of Suleiman. As it was Sunday morning there were few people about and all the buildings were free. When we were sufficiently steeped in history and mediaeval architecture we had lunch, a mouth watering mousaka and a shandy, in a beautiful garden restaurant, the Socratous. In the afternoon we took a bus ride to the famous Rodini Park, which was disappointing – it was neglected and had no flowers.

On Tuesday we took the bus to Lindos, an attractive, ancient town and harbour about thirty miles south of Rhodes. We climbed the steep, narrow steps, lined with colourful stalls, to the Acropolis, where we admired the Temple of Athena and looked down on the small, safe harbour. On our return to Rhodes we found a large Greek boat endeavouring to disentangle his anchor chain from two others, including ours. I helped him by disengaging our bitter end to be passed underneath his chain.

On Wednesday 19th May we prepared to leave Rhodes, but first I had to move another boat's anchor from across ours. We left at 1100 and motor-sailed in a light wind and brilliant sunshine, with our new sailing awning up, to Alimnia, a deserted island off the western coast of Rhodes. As we entered the almost enclosed cove we were greeted by the boat at anchor, 'Hello, *Blue Pearl*. Would you like to come to supper?'

'We'd be delighted.'

'Can you bring some rice?'

It was David Townsend in *Pomone*, whom we had last seen in Larnaca. We enjoyed the curry and updating each other on our adventures since Larnaca.

After a quiet and restful night we left Alimnia at 0645 for a typical one-day passage to Pigadia in the island of Karpathia. The log sums it up:

> *Distance 51 miles. Time 9 hours 30 minutes. After some light and variable winds under main and engine, at 0910 the wind settled in the west at force 3 and we cut the engine. We sailed the rest of the way under mizzen, main and genoa. The wind gradually increased to force 5 and our speed increased from 4.5 to 6.5 knots. Arrived Picadia at 1615.*

The next morning we were up at 0530 and away by 0615. The wind was fickle, first westerly force five to six, then dying, then increasing. We were greeted by many dolphins as we approached Crete and as we came to Sitia a friendly couple of them sported around us and escorted us as far as the harbour. We tied up alongside the mole at 1745 after a 63-mile passage in 11.5 hours through some of the most dangerous waters of the Second World War. Karpathia, as I well remember, then known as Scarpanto and under Italian rule, was a large Italian air base from which high-level and torpedo bombers were dispatched to attack British ships, and fighters to harass the aircraft from our carriers.

On arrival we were greeted by the port police, who demanded to see our transit log. We explained what had happened in Rhodes and were told to report to the police again in the morning.

The next morning, at 0930, we reported to the police, who sent us to the Customs Officer, who said he would make out a transit log for us. Again we explained what had happened in Rhodes and showed him our Rhodes entry paper. He told us we must wait until 1000 when he would consult with a higher authority. We waited in the office. Eventually an English-speaking voice came on the telephone line and again I explained what had happened in Rhodes. Finally the Customs Officer said, 'No problem', and we were allowed to leave at 1050. We decided to have a make-and-mend, interrupted by a port official who came and charged us 1170 drachmas.

The next day, Sunday 23rd May, we were asked to report to the Port Captain to pay our harbour dues. When I told him we had paid 1170 drachmas the day before, he told us that was for water, which we had not had. He sent for the water man and made him repay the money.

Sitia was a delightful, small harbour, with outdoor tavernas lining the waterfront and some interesting shops in the small town.

The next day we left at 0930 and motor-sailed in light headwinds to Spinalonga Lagoon, where there is a deserted leper island we hoped to visit. By the time we reached Spinalonga strong winds were sweeping across the lagoon, making it untenable for anchoring. We sailed slowly under genoa past the leper village, inspecting it from the sea, and then quietly on to Ayios Nikolaus, arriving at 1600. We were directed to a space just by the corner of the mole. We spent a pleasant hour wandering round the pretty harbour, with its lovely inner lagoon, and turned in at 2130 for an early night. Ten minutes later the police awakened us. We must move a few metres along to make space for a huge incoming ferry.

Our passage the next day followed the usual pattern. We left at 0600, motor-sailed in a force one headwind until 1110 when a good wind piped up and we sailed the rest of the way, under main and genoa, at 6 knots, arriving in Iraklion at 1320.

We motored into the Venetian, or inner, harbour, as directed by our pilot book, but found no vacant moorings in the marina or along the moles, so we anchored between two yachts in the middle of the harbour. At the port police we had the usual problem, 'No transit log?' and had to wait until they contacted Athens before being released. Nellie and Romul Roman, from the yacht *Yeema* on passage to Sydney, came aboard for drinks and to look at our charts of the Aegean and Eastern Mediterranean.

Fishing boats in Iraklion leave in threes, a large one towing a smaller one towing the smallest. At 0600 we were awakened by a loud bang and found that the smallest of the returning boats had been released badly and had given us a glancing blow. There was no serious damage. When Romul left at 0630 we moved into his much safer position and enjoyed a peaceful anchorage.

That morning, Tuesday 25th May, we took the bus and a picnic to Knossus, to see the ancient Minoan city. The palace and many buildings, built in 1700 BC, were restored by Sir Arthur Evans in 1900, and, in spite of the rebuilding, gave a good impression of

197

the ancient city with its bull worship. We were especially interested in the palace with its labyrinthine multitude of small rooms and frescoes of bull worship, which gave us an insight into the legend of Theseus and the minotaur. Then we returned to the Archaeological Museum in Traklion to see the display of statues and pottery recovered from Knossus.

The next day we motor-sailed to Rethimon in a light wind and slight sea and tied up alongside the mole. We saw *Yeema* in the inner harbour. At 0600 the next morning we were awakened by a large ferry tying up to our bollard. We left at 0945 and motor-sailed to Soudha Bay.

I had particularly wished to visit Soudha, an anchorage used by HMS *Eagle*, the aircraft carrier on which I served in 1940. Our pilot book warned us that this was a naval base and some yachts had been turned away. In fact the port police were the most – indeed the only – helpful police throughout Crete. We moored alongside the quay, where gypsies were staying with their vans.

After a peaceful night we left at 0700 the next morning and motor-sailed to Kissamos. From the log:

> *Anchored in the new harbour, but we were asked to move and go alongside an unfinished, unlit place on the quay behind a coaster that would he leaving.*
>
> *Argument with the Port Police, first about 'no transit log', then because they wanted to charge us 2 days for a 4 hour stay. I simply refused. A shouting match. I shouted louder and they reduced the charge from 1274 drachmas to 474 drachmas. The Port Captain tried to ease the situation and seemed to be on our side. Of course, neither of us could understand the other.*

We left Kissamos at 0630 the next morning, glad to be leaving Crete, where the officials generally had been less than helpful. By 0700 the wind was from the west, force three, and we were sailing north west under main and genoa. Off Anti Kithera the wind began to die and head us, and a current set us towards Pori Island, where one of Nelson's ships was supposed to be wrecked and the survivors died on the island. Their ghosts are said to be heard in this area. We had to alter 25 degrees to port to compensate. Navigation was visual.

At 1530 we arrived in Kithera. We first anchored in the harbour in a strong wind and were then invited to tie up alongside a charter boat, a Gibsea 40, in the lee of the mole. Antony, the skipper, came aboard for a drink. The Port Captain wanted our transit log and as we hadn't one he allowed us to stay for one night only. This was a pity as this was a charming small port with a chora overlooking the harbour.

The next day, Sunday, we motor-sailed to Port Kaio in a light wind and anchored in six metres at the south end of the cove. Soon afterwards Romul and Nellie arrived in *Kyeema* and we caught up on news. A strong wind got up and we dragged, so we re-anchored with two anchors. In the evening the wind dropped and we had a quiet night.

The next day we had a make-and-mend and enjoyed our first swim of the cruise. We had a meal ashore that was so expensive that we only had the starters. In the afternoon we had a lovely walk round the cove along a hill covered in spring flowers.

On Tuesday 1st June we left Port Kaio and had an easy motor-sail in a calm sea, ending with an hour's sailing. We arrived at Kalamata at 1600 and spent an hour and a half motoring round this large harbour before we found a berth against a derelict wall. No one helped. Three times we approached a vacant part of a quay and were waved away. As soon as we moored a harbour official, noticeably absent when we were searching for a berth, came to check our papers and arrange for payment of dues: 'No transit log?' The same old routine! Then, suddenly, everyone was charming. They arranged for the fuel man to come in one hour to fill our fuel tank. We took on 200 litres, but he charged us for 263 litres plus his time. Later we met yachtsmen who told us to beware the fuel man, who cheated.

Miraculously, very late in the evening, we found a large supermarket, butchers and greengrocers, all open, and bought all the stores we needed for three or four days. We decided to leave at 0700 the next morning.

On Wednesday we paid our harbour-dues. They insisted on two days although we had moored at 1730 the night before. I paid without argument so that we could clear Greece and get away from all the hassle and fraud.

After an interesting passage through the islands, using visual, radar, echo sounder and log, we arrived at Port Longos in Sapientza Island. The Pilot Book describes it as follows:

On the SE end of Sapientza Island there is the deserted bay of Port Longos. Anchor in the southern part of the bay in 5–6 metres on a sandy bottom. Good shelter although strong easterlies send a swell in. The lighthouse can be reached by a track from the bay.

This seemed an ideal harbour before tackling the 310-mile passage to Syracuse. We were tired of the hassle and cheating we had met in Greece and here we could relax, shrug it off and prepare for our journey.

When we arrived at Port Longos we found a newly created fish farm across the entrance. We anchored in the southern area of the bay as directed by our Pilot. Our relief at clearing all official ports was shattered when a customs launch arrived and tied on to us. The Customs Officer demanded to see our transit log. I told him I hadn't got one.

'What! No transit log?' he thundered.

The usual hassle followed. He radioed Kalamata for instructions. I expected arrest, confiscation of boat, or at the least being towed back to Kalamata. An hour later, the official appeared in the cockpit,

'No problems, Captain!'

We were free! We both enjoyed a swim. Later in the morning a figure appeared on shore, calling out to us, 'Captain, I have fish.' He must want to sell us fish from the fish farm, but we couldn't face more roguery. I told him we did not want any. We next saw him swimming out to us, using a plank as a float and wearing one flipper.

'Captain, I have fish. I am Lighthouse Keeper.'

He looked cold and exhausted and his voice was plaintive. I took pity on him, invited him aboard and gave him a whisky. He told us he was Lieutenant Nikos Sabakis of the Royal Hellenic Navy and was Keeper of the Lighthouse. He had come to invite us as guests to a fish lunch at the lighthouse. I gave him a pair of shoes to climb the path and we took him back to shore in our dinghy, to climb the steep winding path, through trees and shrubs, to the lighthouse. There he showed us all over the lighthouse, powered by solar panels and huge batteries. Then he laid the tablecloth, sheets of an old newspaper. He served us each with three fried fish and salad.

'What about you, Nikos?'

200

'I cook more.'

The fish were very fresh and among the best we have tasted. We ate the second lot Nikos brought us. We were full. Nikos returned with six more fish and started to serve them to us.

'No, Nikos,' I said, laughing. 'We are full. You eat.'

He gave us each an apple to eat while he ate his fish.

We spent a pleasant two hours talking about our homes and families. Nikos's English was good. He showed us photographs of his family and we took photographs of Nikos and the lighthouse. When it was time to leave he gave us a traditional parting gift, a beautiful conch shell. He wanted us to come back for soup at 2100, but we were conscious of the long sail ahead of us and the early start, so we declined.

We had seen some of the worst of Greece and now we were seeing the very best – Greek hospitality, Greek warmth and Greek friendliness. This was the lasting impression we were left with.

21

Port Longos to Mahon

On Friday 4th June the weather forecast was wind west north west force three to four, cloudy, thunder, sea slight. Our barometer was 1011 and rising. We decided to leave for the 310-mile passage, across the Ionian Sea to Syracuse in Sicily.

We left at 0650 and waved to Nikos Sabakis as we passed the lighthouse. The wind was west south west force one, the sea lumpy, and we were motor-sailing under main and genoa on a course of 275°.

At 1445 the wind increased and we were able to sail for a short while, but by 1600 we were back to motor-sailing. From the log:

> *1700 Wind southerly, force 3. Engine off. Main and genoa. Speed 5 knots.*
>
> *1730 This maddening wind! Veered to southwest force 1, leaving a 2–4 foot swell and short, choppy seas heading us. Very uncomfortable. Back to motor-sailing. Wind heading us. Took in a reef for the night, handed genoa and continued motor-sailing at 5 knots.*

The night passed quietly enough, with no incidents. Joan and I soon fell into our routine of one hour on and one off, with one hour social chat. The off-watch person stretched out on the lee berth cushion, head under the cockpit hood, and always slept soundly. Every twenty minutes the watch keeper swept the horizon carefully with binoculars and every hour on the hour I went below and recorded the time and ship's GPS position and made a radar

For map, see page 88.

sweep. The radar was on the twenty-mile range and would easily pick up a ship at that distance. Every two hours I marked the positions on the chart. A series of crosses recorded our progress. It was easy to see if we were deviating from our course, already marked out on the chart.

The first incident occurred on Saturday morning, when we turned to starboard to avoid a container ship on a collision course. At 1150 the wind veered to the north west, force three, and we killed the engine and sailed under main and genoa at 5 knots. At 1200 the wind died and we were in heavy rain, motor-sailing again. At 1230 the wind veered further to the north, force five. Again we killed the engine, set the genoa and sailed at 6 knots. At 1400 we had rain, a thunderstorm and lightning overhead. We were in a squall, force seven. We shortened the genoa and took in a reef in the mainsail. At 1500 the wind was north force four and we were sailing at 5.5 knots in a lumpy sea under reefed main and genoa. At 1530 the wind dropped to force one and we handed the genoa and switched on the engine. At 1600 the log recalls:

Log 178.2. Syracuse 273°, 121 miles. Sea extremely unpleasant. Waves 3–5 feet, coming from ahead, but a slop in all directions. Difficult to move in boat and do anything Both hands needed to hold on.

That night we had a full, bright moon and our passage continued uneventfully, following our night routine. At 0815 on Sunday morning the wind was once more north north west, force three, and again we switched off the engine. This was pleasant sailing. The seas had eased and we were on a fine reach, sailing at 4.5 knots.

At 0900, with Joan on watch, I was lying on the cockpit cushion relaxing after a tiring night, when I heard voices. It was like hearing a group of about a dozen people, men and women, all talking at once in another room. I could not quite follow what was being said, but the language was English. I looked at Joan, but she appeared not to be troubled, so I kept the experience to myself.

At 1010 we sighted land and at 1315 we arrived at Syracuse, 310 miles in 2 days 7 hours. Willing hands helped us to moor as we backed into the town quay. The berth was lovely, stern to a tree-lined promenade. Within ten minutes the port police had arrived and cleared us. What a difference from Greece!

204

Alan, on *Avengore* next to us, had the water on and lent us his hose. We were able to fill our empty water tanks. That evening we sat and watched the families parading along the quay. Alan came aboard for a drink and gave us pointers for southern Sicily, and Alf from another nearby boat, had wintered many times in Larnaca and knew Ralph and Pat and Bob. We enjoyed a quiet and relaxed night.

The next day, Monday 7th June, we collected Italian money from the bank and went on to the market where we bought a roasting joint of pork, vegetables and excellent fruit. In the afternoon I worked on the log. After tea we were sitting in the cockpit when we saw four small boys, nine or ten years old, stealing the safety light from the stern of a neighbouring boat. I leaped ashore and gave chase, but they were too quick for me. In the evening we enjoyed a super meal in the cockpit, melon, roast pork, roast potatoes, broccoli and courgettes, jam tart and cream. Life was good.

The next day I spent all morning servicing the engine. In the afternoon Mike and Eric from *Dionysus*, based at Malta, came aboard for tea and after our evening meal we went aboard *Dionysus* for wine.

On Wednesday we left our mooring at 1100, set the main and genoa, killed the engine and sailed out of harbour, one of our best performances. At 1200 the wind died and I turned on the engine. It faltered and died. We turned round and ghosted back to Syracuse in the light wind. Back in harbour I rounded up, head to wind, in our old mooring. Joan dropped the anchor and the wind blew us back into our mooring, where Mike and Eric took our warps and made us fast. They came aboard and worked for three hours to find the fault in the engine. The water separator release screw has a brass nut on a plastic screw. When I had serviced the engine I had cross-threaded this screw so that air was getting into the system. I ran the engine for an hour to make sure all was well.

We stayed in harbour overnight and left at 0940 the next day, again under main and genoa. At 1000 the wind died to less than force one, and we were motor-sailing. At 1215 the wind increased to force three; we switched off the engine and sailed at 5 knots. At 1230 the wind died again. We handed the genoa and motor-sailed, under main and engine, to Porto Palo and anchored just off the beach in the north east of the harbour at 1515.

Porto Palo was where I had called for the night on my lone

passage from Catania to Malta. Now, with Joan's company, on a sunny afternoon, it no longer looked sinister and threatening. Four other yachts were there, in the special anchorage for yachts some distance from where I had previously anchored. In the dark the previous year, with no other yachts at anchor, I had missed this anchorage.

The next day we left at 0645 and motor-sailed in a gentle headwind to Licata, 70 miles in 11.5 hours. The next day, Saturday 12th June, we left Licata at 0600 and again motor-sailed in a light head wind. At 1300 the wind began to increase; at 1400 it was force five and at 1500 force six and we were tacking, hard on the wind. I would have liked a reef in the main, but the sea was rough and Sciacca was close. We entered the harbour and lowered the mainsail inside, no finesse about neatness or tiers. We were glad to have the lazy jack, which furled the sail neatly along the boom and held it there. We moored alongside a floating pontoon. It was difficult to pull *Blue Pearl* alongside in the force seven wind, blowing off, until a Sicilian motor-boat owner helped us. This was a good, quiet berth, although the strong wind continued well into the night.

We had only 10–15 gallons of fuel in our tank and the next day we walked a long, weary way round the harbour to look for fuel, without success. On the way we passed a large number of fishing boats, which we thought were derelict. By 1100 the wind, which had died, was up to force five and in the afternoon reached force seven. A waterman told us it was the meltemi. It reached force eight before dying in the early hours of Monday. We had a noisy night with about a hundred boats leaving. In the morning we saw that the 'derelict' boats had gone. They were the fishing fleet.

The wind quietened during the morning. Another long walk round the now deserted harbour led to our being directed to the 'boat factory', a Johnson's agent. There a waterman took us in his car to a garage at the top of the town where I negotiated a delivery of fuel in drums at £3 per gallon, three times the normal price in the Mediterranean. Water would also be delivered in a tanker, 200 litres costing £10. Water and fuel facilities were available in the harbour at normal prices, but not for yachtsmen.

On Tuesday we left Sciacca at 0630, motor-sailed to Cape Granitola through a fishing fleet, and then sailed at 5 knots, under reefed main and half genoa, in a rising wind and growing sea. We arrived at Marsala at 1430. The sea outside the harbour was very rough so we sailed into the harbour and lowered our sails inside. We tied stern to the pontoon. We found an excellent supermarket where we stocked up for three days, including several bottles of marsala, of which there were about twenty varieties in the supermarket.

We left Marsala at 0615 the next morning, Wednesday 16th June, under main and motor in almost a flat calm and biggish, rolling seas. It was not unpleasant. At 0805 we reefed the main so that we could harden it more and achieved a speed of 5.5 knots. At midnight the log recalls that we passed two fishing boats to starboard and a large ferry, blazing with lights. At dawn we passed two more fishing boats, and another ferry overtook us and crossed our bows. Otherwise little happened until 0545 when a thick mist developed and visibility dropped to half a mile.

At 0700 on Thursday the wind backed to the west, force two to three, and we were able to set a full main and genoa and switch off the engine. Our speed was 4.5 knots. From the log:

At 0800 again heard voices, very similar to the ones heard before. This time I asked Joan if she could hear them and she replied, 'Yes.' The radio wasn't on and the voices did not seem to be mast or rigging noises. They lasted about a quarter-of-an hour.

At 1200 we arrived at Cavioli Island, Sardinia, and explored Carbonera Bay. The wind, force four, was blowing straight in and the entrance was full of rocks. We decided to go on to Cagliari. The wind was now south west force three rising to force five and we were hard on the wind, with a speed of 5–6 knots. This was good sailing. Altogether, we covered 181 miles in 34 hours, 4 minutes. The inner yacht quay was filled with fishing boats. The marina looked full and was unwelcoming. We tied up on the outer quay, but were told that we must move at 0800 the next day.

The next morning, at 0800, we moved to an adjacent wall. We met pleasant people in the neighbouring boats, including three Frenchmen whom we had met in Sciacca. This was a difficult wall, with a heavy chain that wanted to rub against our side. The wind, fortunately, changed to the south east and held us off.

At 0700 on Saturday an officer called and told us that we must move from the wall, to which he had directed us the day before, because a naval vessel was coming in. We decided to go to the new marina for fuel, forget about Cagliari and shopping, and make for a secluded bay, Malfatano, 30 miles away.

We left at 0845 and sailed under main and genoa until 1130 when the wind backed to the north east and decreased. We continued under boomed-out genoa and goose-winged main. At 1400 the wind increased to force seven, then eight. We took a reef in the main and furled the genoa, spilling the wind and sailing at 6.5 knots. The sea became rough. We entered Port Malfatano with huge, breaking seas. The harbour was untenable, so we lowered the mainsail and motored out comfortably to Port Teulada, arriving at 1600.

In Teulada there was no room on the wall and no anchorage. A fishing boat invited us to tie alongside and the two lads on the boat helped us to moor and then winched me to the crosstrees to release the main halyard, trapped in the boisterous sea at Port Malfetano. They told us that the wind was the gregale, that they would not be going out and we would be all right for the night. We invited them aboard for a drink. At 2000 the boss returned and shouted to us to get away. He nearly released us bows first with a very strong headwind and had to be restrained by his partner. He was very angry. We tied up alongside in the now empty space astern of him and hoped for the best.

The next day, Sunday, a fisherman told us that the gregale would continue so we stayed in harbour, with the big seas pounding the other side of the wall. We worked on boat jobs. At 1700 a big catamaran we had seen at Cagliari arrived and then a large ketch tied up alongside us. They had had a rough ride from Carloforte. As we were leaving early we changed places.

We left Porto Teulada at 0545 the next morning in a force six north-easterly wind, with a reefed main and two-thirds genoa. At 0850 the wind died and a thunderstorm approached. At 0925, with full main and genoa and the wind north east force three, the thunderstorm was overhead. At 1005 the wind died and we began motoring. At 1045 the wind picked up again so we set the genoa, turned off the engine and sailed to Carloforte at 5 knots, arriving at 1205. We tied up stern to the north quay.

There were several British boats in this attractive harbour, among them Richard and Sue in *Ifwe* on one side of us, and Henry on the other. Flowering trees lined the town quay, but there weren't many restaurants. We had an expensive lunch in a restaurant facing the quay and tea in the cockpit, watching the families, parents, boys and girls, parading along the quay. After tea the wind veered to the south east and got up to gale force eight, blowing directly on to our quay. I was worried about dragging onto a submerged ledge along the quay so, with the help of Richard and Henry, we put out a second anchor.

At midnight a French boat near us left for Sicily, but returned at 0200 and partly cut Richard's warp. Richard spent the rest of the night physically holding his boat off the quay. One boat that had no engine lost its anchor and spent the night sailing back and forth across the harbour under storm jib. Two boats motored round the harbour all night, and four other boats left our quay to shelter against the east mole on the other side of the harbour.

On Tuesday afternoon Joan went shopping while I stayed to keep an eye on our boat. When she returned she found Richard and Sue, Henry and me drinking tea aboard the French boat. In the evening the French boat again left, dragged his anchor onto ours and picked up both our anchor lines. After he had freed himself we had to re-anchor, on a longer chain.

At 0700 on Wednesday *Ifwe* and a small French boat left for Tunisia. A big brown cat, *Courtney's Luck*, began to take up their anchor, but found that their anchor chain had wrapped itself round a large concrete block on the bottom. Henry and Carlo, from the trawler *Corach*, dived and freed the chain, so they brought the cat onto the wall, next to us. Margo and Silas from the cat came aboard for drinks and brought a load of books to swap. Henry came next for a cup of tea. Joan shopped for four days.

The gale had brought its problems, but it also brought the skippers and crews together. We became very friendly and in the strange way that life offers we enjoyed the difficult times.

On Thursday 24th we left our mooring at 0530, spent some time in the harbour clearing our log, which had seized up with weed and barnacles, and left Carloforte at 0600, bound for Mahon in Menorca, 200 miles away.

As Joan says in her diary: *Very horrible sea all day – hardly any wind – what there was was on the nose – tried sailing, but no use – motor-sailed at 6 knots plus – knocking off the mileage – 195 miles to go.* And later: *Uncomfortable even lying down because of crossing seas. Small moon for a while. Lots of stars.*

From the log:

Friday 25th June
1230 Wind force 3 from NW. Full main and genoa. Engine off Speed 3.5 knots. Sea kind for a change. Best sailing this year. For the third time we heard the voices – for about half-an-hour. Joan thought they were singing.
1345 Wind dying. Speed down to 3 knots. Engine on.
1545 Arrived Mahon. Moored at Club Maritimo. Distance 200 miles. Time 36 hours, 15 minutes. A most unpleasant passage with large, lumpy seas, and little wind, heading us. Seas came from three different directions, NE, NW and SE, from three previous gales.

A fitful wind near the end gave us a breather – nearly a beam wind in a gentle sea – but it lasted only an hour. At dawn we were worried by the masthead light of a gigantic yacht overtaking us. It turned out to be the morning star. We were greeted off Menorca by dolphins and swimming turtles. I was amazed to see that turtles use a form of breast-stroke.

We booked for three nights at the Club Maritimo and met Dorothy and Brian from *Ramrod*, last seen in Larnaca and Rhodes. Faxes from Jill and our granddaughter Julia, and a letter from Joan's sister, Peggy, were waiting for us at the club. Jill and Rob had been given two months' grace by the building society to sell their house. Julia proposed to join us in Alicante for part of our cruise.

On Sunday we had a make-and-mend and enjoyed a good dinner in an outdoor restaurant along the quay. Our three days in Mahon had been restful and necessary after the hard going from Larnaca to Mahon, 1621 miles in seven weeks. It was time to be on the move again.

22

Mahon to Gibraltar

On Monday 28th June 1993 we motored round the Isla del Lazareto, at the harbour entrance, to Cala Teulera, where we knew from our previous visit we would find a quiet and restful anchorage with shelter from the rising wind.

The next day we left at 1115, aiming for Cala Covas. As with Sicily and Sardinia we were returning along the southern side of the Balearics, the side we had not seen on our way out to Cyprus. By the time we reached Cala Covas the wind was force five and increasing, blowing straight into the cala. The big seas and breaking waves across the entrance made entry impossible. We looked in three other calas, all impossible for the same reason, and reluctantly returned to Cala Teulera, after sailing 31 miles.

The wind had died by the time we left Teulera on Wednesday, but the seas were still breaking and Cala Covas and neighbouring calas were still not tenable. We continued on to Cala Santa Galdana, a large bay with a fine beach surrounded by hotels and restaurants. The area of the beach was crowded with surfboarders and pedaloes, so we dropped our anchor on the southern edge of the harbour. We enjoyed our customary swim and later walked through the holiday complex to shop in the supermarket. A bad swell developed during the night and we had a disturbed and restless sleep.

At 0930 the next morning we left for Cala Son Saura, five miles away. We had tried and found three other calas all unsuitable in the lumpy swell. Son Saura, surrounded by pine trees and scrub, with sandy beaches, was more attractive to us than the overcrowded Santa Galdana. The water was clean and we could easily see our anchor and chain stretching away from us. It was also warm and we enjoyed our swim. Shortly after this a squall came and we put out a second anchor. A French boat arrived and a young man plunged overboard and swam out to us.

'You are a long way from Totnes,' he called.

We did not recognise him and, as Joan writes in her diary, *We could not invite him aboard as he was not wearing swimming-trunks!* He swam away without saying who he was. We enjoyed a very quiet night.

In view of the difficult anchorages, large swells and breaking seas we decided to head for Majorca. We left Son Saura at 0720 on Friday 2nd July and arrived at Porto Cristo at 1330, 35 miles in 6 hours 10 minutes. There were large swells and troubled seas at the entrance so we followed our newly adopted practice of sailing into the harbour and taking down our sails in the limited space inside. We berthed bows on to the pontoon and picked up a stern line.

We liked the harbour. We were on a good pontoon with power points and water, and good showers and toilets in the marina. The small town was a longish walk round the harbour and across a bridge, but the shops were good and we found a bank and a laundry. Several faxes from Jill were waiting for us and we exchanged faxes with her and Julia. The upshot was that Julia could not join us on the date we had set for arrival in Alicante and would now join us in Gibraltar.

On Saturday night we had a gale, the tramontana, north east force eight, all through the night, with large waves sweeping over the protecting mole into the inner harbour. The gale lasted throughout Sunday and we decided to stay a further night, in spite of the high cost. I used the opportunity to take down a panel in the stern cabin and replace the fairlead, broken in the gale in Rhodes.

On Monday we took on fuel, left at 1230 and sailed to Porto Colom, twelve miles away, a large bay with a narrow entrance that gave perfect protection We had our usual swim, followed by a lovely meal in the cockpit, with the evening light bringing out the yellows and whites of the ancient town and breaking up the colours on the water. We enjoyed a quiet night and an early morning swim.

The next morning we left harbour at 1145 and sailed quietly in a light wind and moderate sea to Porto Petro, six and a half miles away. There are three arms of the harbour for anchoring. Our first choice was occupied by the noisy Club Méditerranée, so we anchored in the main arm with, eventually, twelve other yachts. That day we enjoyed three swims and intended to stay another day and night, but after a restless night caused by a heavy swell, although no wind, we decided on a night passage to Espalmador. That evening I swam round the boat and washed her sides.

At 1850 on Wednesday July 7th we left in a light south-west wind, moderate sea and poor, murky visibility, under reefed main and motor. At 2400 we were able to set the genoa and sail for a spell, but the wind soon died and we furled the genoa again and resumed motor-sailing. We arrived at Espalmador at 1230 and anchored off the beach, 100 miles in 17 hours 40 minutes. It had been a fairly dull night passage, with little wind and a moderate sea. We passed five fishing boats off Isla de Cabrera and used the radar to slip through. One boat with no lights we didn't see at 400 yards. We saw a well-lit ferry and, in the morning, two other yachts.

Espalmador was where, two years before, we had recovered a floating oak plank, which I had adapted for use as a gangplank in marinas or harbours. We had used it many times, when moored either stern to or bows on to the pontoon. Now we spent a pleasant day at anchor. The wind was off the beach so the sea was calm. Swimming was good and we had an opportunity to do odd jobs in the boat.

Santa Cruz, a Portuguese boat from Vilamoura which we had met in Porto Cristo, anchored next to us and we exchanged news, and Tony, from *Samsara*, a single-hander we had first met in Syracuse, swam over for a chat.

In the evening the barometer began to fall, the weather became dull and cloudy and many boats left. During the night the wind changed to south west force five, blowing straight onto the beach. Waves began to break and we were in them. By 0630 most boats had left what was now an uncomfortable anchorage, open to the wind. We decided to leave for Puerto de Sabina on Formentera. At 0730 we motored round to Sabina.

Puerto de Sabina was expensive – £20 per night, showers and water extra. During Saturday night the barometer, which had fallen several points began to rise. The wind, after a lull, changed to north east force six. It was still at force five in the morning, but up to gale force eight on Sunday night.

On Monday 12th July we left Puerto de Sabina at 1040. The wind was north east force five and we sailed with goose-winged main and preventer and genoa poled out. Our speed was 4.5 knots. At 1250 we had a sudden change of wind to south east force one to two. We took off the preventer and sailed on a broad reach, but our speed was little more than 2 knots, so we switched on the engine. We had big unpleasant following seas from the gale. At 1415 the wind increased to force three, so we killed the engine and sailed at 4 knots. At 1500 the wind decreased and we switched the engine on again. At 2400 we passed a yacht with top lights and pulpit lights all on. This was most misleading and we failed to recognise it as a yacht until it was close to. At 1000 we looked in at Cabo de Palos, our destination, a small harbour we had liked on our way out, but a strong wind was blowing into the harbour and waves were breaking against the inner wall where we would have moored, making it untenable. We were now under sail again and continued to Cartagena, where we arrived at 1330 and moored alongside the wall near the yacht club. Distance 145 miles. Time 28 hours, 50 minutes. Although the wind was not strong, the seas built up by the gale had been unpleasant and difficult.

There was a beautiful square next to us, leading to the cathedral, with a lovely shopping precinct beyond. Just to the right was a submarine built in the nineteenth century. The clubhouse near us provided a warm welcome and showers and toilets at no cost. There was no charge for our mooring. We would like to have stayed longer but we now had a deadline to keep.

The next day, Wednesday, we left Cartagena at 0730, under main and motor, in a force one wind from north north west. The seas were still big and unpleasant. At 0830 the wind increased to force three, so we killed the engine and set the genoa. At 1100 the wind dropped to force one and we were motoring again. At 1300 it veered to the south east, force three, and again we killed the engine and sailed, at 4.5 knots. At 1405 the wind died so we handed the genoa, turned on the engine and motor-sailed to Garrucha, arriving at 1600, 46 miles in 8.5 hours. It had been a frustrating sail, with the engine on and off, and big unpleasant seas.

All was changed at Garrucha since our Pilot was printed. Now a small marina was available. We were given a berth for £10.50 and when we had moored were told that showers and toilets were not working. We had showers in the cockpit from the hose. We were both very tired.

The next day, Thursday, Joan shopped in the excellent vegetable market while I watered the boat. An English boat, *Dame Blanche* from Dartmouth, berthed alongside us on the way to Turkey. At 1015 we left Garrucha in a force one headwind and motor-sailed to San Jose, 29 miles in 5 hours 15 minutes. The officials there were helpful, but there were no toilets or showers.

The next day, Friday, we left harbour and motor-sailed to Almerimar in a force one wind and slight sea. 38 miles in 6 hours 30 minutes. Almerimar is a new marina complex – soulless, but with showers working. The supermarket was closed. *Thankful*, a Bermuda 39, came in next to us. We invited single-hander Laton Frewer aboard for drinks, and he gave us a list of good harbours and anchorages in Portugal. Later, we went aboard *Thankful* and gave Laton a list of places on the way to Majorca. That night we watched a fiesta with a boat procession and fireworks.

The next day we left Almerimar in a force one wind and motor-sailed to Motril, 36 miles in 6 hours 25 minutes. We took up a club berth and were then given a good position on an end berth. We met John and Sue and their two children in a boat from Bristol. They used to have a holiday home in Kingswear and kept their boat on the Dart. Later, we had an excellent meal with them in a restaurant they recommended.

On Sunday we left Motril in a thick mist and little wind. Using radar, we passed two boats quite close, but did not see them. Later, as we passed Malaga, we ran into an industrial haze, which again reduced visibility to one mile. At 1540 we arrived at Benalmadena, 48 miles in 8 hours 25 minutes. We found that Benalmadena had deteriorated since we were last there: there were no 'sailors' to help us alongside; the men's showers were not fitted up; the women's showers were flooded and too dirty to use.

We left harbour the next day, Monday 1st July, at 0700, again in a force one headwind. From the log:

0910 Thick fog. Visibility 100 yards. Navigating by radar and GPS.

1000 A large fishing-boat passed us 200 yards away on our port side but we did not see him. Tracked him on radar. Saw him astern of us at 400 yards (visibility better that way). He was very large.

1005 Log 17.1. Europa Point 241/32.8.

1100 Fog lifted.

1130 Fog again.

1200 Fog lifted.

1230 Sea becoming very confused. Swell 6–7 feet. Tacked 20 degrees to find a steadying wind. Hardly any.

1500 Log 43.6. Wind W force 6, against the current. Huge seas. Very difficult to make headway. Half genoa.

1600 Tacking hard on the wind to make headway.

1730 Arrived Gibraltar, 52 miles in 10.5 hours.

A very difficult journey, first fog, then headwinds and heavy seas. Rounding Europa Point was exciting. We were hard on the wind on the port tack with our leeway taking us on to the rocks. I was tempted to tack away, but I held my course, making two knots over the ground. We passed five yards away from the rocks on our lee side. A tense moment and then we were past, with the wind free as we turned towards Gibraltar.

Greeted by friendly police and Customs. Quickly cleared. A good reception at Marina Bay Marina. Letters waiting, plus a fax from Jill. Julia to join us here. Felt relaxed and pleased to be in Gib. on schedule.

We enjoyed a walk around Gibraltar and did some shopping, but our main task was to prepare for the long journey up the Portuguese and Spanish coasts. On Tuesday I dismantled the toilet and thoroughly cleaned the pump and hose. On Wednesday I serviced the engine. Julia arrived in the middle of this and, at my request, immediately turned to to help me. She had been travelling for 36 hours, but made no complaint. On Thursday I worked on the charts and on the navigation and then we did the major shopping. On Friday we collected new Gaz bottles. *Samsara* arrived in a berth near us and Tony, now an old friend, came aboard for coffee. In the evening we celebrated our forty-ninth wedding anniversary with dinner at Bianca's, our favourite restaurant. On Saturday Julia helped Tony to move his boat to Sheppard's Marina. We watered *Blue Pearl*, took on 199 litres of fuel, and were ready to leave.

23

Gibraltar to La Rochelle

Our first port of call on the long haul up the Spanish and Portuguese coasts was Barbate, a little-known harbour, little used by yachts. We left Gibraltar at 1130 on Sunday 25th July in a light headwind, and motor-sailed all the way, arriving at 1815. The most noticeable event was seeing the tuna nets stretching in a broad curve from the harbour entrance as far as the eye could see out to the south.

Barbate was an interesting and accommodating little harbour. It catered mainly for the fishing fleet, but recently a small marina had been added and we found a comfortable berth with toilets and showers available. The town, though small, had some good food shops and we stocked up with last-minute stores.

The next day, with a passage of over two hundred miles ahead of us, we intended to leave early, but there was a thick fog with no visibility in the darkness. By 1130, although the sun was unable to penetrate the fog, visibility was up to 100 yards and I decided to leave. We knew we had to navigate past the tuna nets before we could turn westwards, but with Joan and her keen eyesight on the bows, Julia on the helm and me at the radar, I thought we could manage. The tuna net was held in place by small trawlers, anchored every four hundred yards. With our radar set on the largest scale I intended to go from trawler to trawler, turning on to each new course when we sighted it.

As we moved to the harbour entrance we met the fishing fleet returning and each skipper as we passed shouted and waved us back. I knew from reading up about the area that the fog was likely to be coastal and might hang around for a long time. I decided to continue. Our system worked well. I gave Julia the course to the first trawler, which she steered until Joan called out that the trawler was fifty yards ahead. Using the radar, I gave Julia the next course that took us to the next trawler until Joan gave a sighting report. We continued with this until we cleared the trawler net, over four miles long. We had worked well as a team and this augured well for the cruise. As we came to the end of the line we ran out of fog. The way to the north was now open to us.

The passage was an easy one. We were in three watches, one hour on, one hour on standby and one hour off. The standby could sleep on the cockpit cushion on the lee side. This meant two hours of sleep followed by one on watch, luxury by our standards. Little happened during the passage. At 1600 a fishing trawler speeded up and passed close astern of us. The sea was easy until night time when it became lumpy. Sunrise was spectacular, with a glaring, red sea. The light wind now headed us and we were motor-sailing again. At 0945 on the second day we were buzzed by a light aircraft. The most spectacular event occurred as we rounded Cape Saint Vincent. A line of about a hundred dolphins in echelon formation crossed our path ahead of us. We saw the loom of Lisbon at 0400 on the third day, eight hours before our arrival. Now we passed numerous fishing boats, some so small they did not show on our radar. At 1200 we arrived at Lisbon, a distance of 260 miles in a little over two days.

As you pass the imposing statue of Henry the Navigator on the north bank of the Tagus, there is a succession of docks. We entered the second, Doca de Bon Sucesso, where we filled our fuel tank. Here they told us to go to the third dock, Doca de Belem, where they gave us a berth in the fourth dock, Doca de Santa Amaro, close to the enormous bridge that crosses the Tagus. In Santa Amaro we could not identify our berth and as no officials appeared we took an empty berth. Immediately an official arrived to tell us that we must move to the berth allocated, which he pointed out. It turned out to be too narrow for us. Back we went to the first berth to search for the official. He told us to move 'hopefully' to a third berth nearby. This was satisfactory and we reserved it for four nights at a very reasonable cost of £30 – but what a performance, especially after a long and tiring passage!

Lisbon is a lovely city. The town centre was a bus ride away, but there was an excellent supermarket nearby. We were particularly impressed with the overhead walkways and moving pavements, which made shopping easy.

On Thursday we spent the morning shopping, settling harbour dues and purchasing a transit log, and rested in the afternoon. In the evening Carlos, a friendly man who had helped us to berth, came aboard for a coffee. He brought a map of Lisbon and pointed out places to visit.

We spent all day Friday exploring the city, the cathedral, the castle, Castella Santa Jorge with its cool gardens and splendid views, the lanes in the old city and the grand squares, precincts and shops. We had a pleasant lunch in a patisserie and returned to the boat, leaving Julia to explore further.

On Saturday 31st July we watered and cleaned the boat and set off at 1415 for an easy sail under full rig down the Tagus to Cascais, where we anchored in Cascais Bay. The wind had freshened to force six so we laid a second anchor. During the night the wind increased to a force eight gale and we were glad of our two anchors.

On Sunday the glass had risen slightly and we left at 0815 under main and motor in a northerly force one wind, heading into an unpleasant lumpy sea left over from the gale. We arrived at Peniche at 1705, distance 43.8 miles.

The anchorage described in the Pilot was now all occupied by large mooring buoys, mainly taken up by fishing boats. We tied on next to a British boat. Police visited us straight away and asked for our transit log, which fortunately we had obtained in Lisbon. At midnight we were awakened and entertained by a fireworks fiesta.

The next day, with little wind, we continued under main and motor in a very rough sea, with waves up to two metres. Throughout the passage the sky was overcast, cloudy and dull. At 1600 we were able to set the genoa and sail, hard on the wind. At 1800, after a most uncomfortable and unpleasant passage, we arrived at Figuera da Foz, distance 56 miles. We had passed very many fishing flags but only four boats. We wore safety harnesses most of the way. In harbour it was easy to moor to buoys fore and aft.

The next day, Tuesday, we again left in a northerly force one wind. There was a big swell, but the sea was not lumpy. We ran into belts of mist and half way we started tacking, using wind shifts for the best tack. We arrived at Leixoes at 1830, distance 65 miles. That evening Julia cooked our meal, a Spanish omelette and cauliflower cheese.

The next day we left harbour at 0730 in a thick mist with

visibility 200 yards. The wind was less than force one from the north. The mist soon cleared as we got out to sea. It was cold most of the way and a lumpy sea headed us, reducing our speed to 4 knots. The drizzle forced us to wear oilies for most of the twelve-hour passage, although the rain cleared for the last hour, giving us a pleasant sail in warm sunshine. We arrived at Bayona at 1930.

Unlike our previous visit on the way out, the reception at Bayona was cold and hostile. We first called at the fuelling pontoon to ask for a berth, but were unable to get alongside. We went round to a neighbouring berth and were waved away by an irate official. We went to the other side of the bay and found an empty berth on a broken-down pontoon with no electricity or water. In the morning I radioed for the marina dinghy to take us to the clubhouse and was told we could move to one of the main pontoons. We checked at the *lavanderia*, but found that clothes had to be left for a full day, so Joan spent the afternoon washing while Julia and I oiled and greased the engine and watered the boat. After tea we played cards and in the evening had a meal in the clubhouse, which was poor and expensive.

On Thursday we showered in the clubhouse, then shopped for three days. I telephoned Jill and discovered that their house was still not sold. We took on 150 litres of fuel at the fuelling berth and left Bayona, in fog with visibility down to 500 yards. The wind, at last, was favourable, west force two to three, and, using GPS, radar and dead reckoning, we sailed from waypoint to waypoint until we arrived at Islas Cies, where we anchored in 21 feet in Playa Area das Rodas. It had been a short but interesting sail. We were restricted by shallows and we tacked until radar gave us the required distance off shore and the echo sounder the relevant depth. Visibility was never more than 600 yards.

The next morning, Saturday 7th August, after a quiet and comfortable night, we left our anchorage at 1015 and motor-sailed until 1200, when the wind got up to force three. We killed the engine and sailed comfortably through the islands into Ria d'Arosa. After lunch the wind decreased and we were down to 2 knots until 1400 when it picked up again. With Julia on the helm we had a tacking race with a Spanish boat, which we gradually overhauled. We arrived at Caraminal at 1545.

The anchorage mentioned in the Pilot was no longer available, but we were welcomed by the Club Nautico officials and given a free berth for one night. There was no clubhouse, but the harbour was surrounded by parks and gardens and the town was attractive.

The next morning we sailed to the Ria de Muros in a rising headwind, reaching force six from the north east as we approached Muros. There was some shelter in the bay, but the seas were quite rough where we had to anchor. As we prepared to drop the anchor between two yachts another British boat that had been taking its sails down suddenly tore in in front of us and dropped his anchor just as we were about to do so. I had to go hard astern to avoid a collision. We eventually anchored in 25 feet and I put out a second anchor. It was too rough to go ashore in the dinghy. We had strong winds all night and breaking seas.

The next day we stowed the dinghy on the foredeck and at 0930 left Muros under main and genoa, with the wind north north east force three increasing. When it reached force six I took in a reef in the main and three rolls in the genoa. Our speed was 6 knots. At 1330 we rounded Cape Finisterre and entered the Bay of Biscay. There was some mist round Finisterre, but the seas were not too bad. After Finisterre the wind increased and the seas built up. We made short tacks for the remainder of the passage along the coast to Camarinas where there were two small pontoons in the harbour. The leeward sides were full and I did not like to back into the windward side in the strong wind, so we anchored in a sheltered position by the beach, using two anchors, and enjoyed a comfortable night.

On Tuesday we went ashore in the dinghy, shopped and had lunch at a pavement café. A strong wind got up and we had a wet ride back to *Blue Pearl*. Again we enjoyed a quiet night.

The next day, Wednesday 11th August, we left at 0800 and motor-sailed in a light headwind and choppy sea until 1330 when we were able to set the genoa and sail at 6 knots to La Coruna, where we arrived at 1815.

We liked La Coruna from the moment we entered it. We found an easy and pleasant anchorage, were welcomed by the club, which had good facilities, and enjoyed our walk round the town, particularly the lanes and the main square.

It was time for Julia to leave and we booked her a train through to London via Paris, leaving at 2005 on Saturday, arriving in London on Monday. We would miss her. She had fitted in well as crew, always ready to take her turn on watch, ever eager to helm the boat, particularly in bad weather, cooking the occasional meal, making a third at bridge and teaching us a new form of whist that she called 'Sergeant Major'. The passage up the Portuguese coast had been hard and unrelenting. We had aimed to reach La Coruna in time for Julia's departure, so we had pressed on with long daylight passages and single night stops. Most of the way we had experienced headwinds and lumpy seas. Frequently, with light winds, we had been forced to motor-sail in heavy seas, not the most comfortable mode of sailing, but Julia had endured this with us without complaint, even revelling in the worst conditions. Sailing seemed to bring out the best in her and we had enjoyed her company. That evening seemed strangely quiet.

The next morning we up-anchored at 0900, to find that our log was not working. I removed it and cleaned it of the barnacles that clogged it. The poor sailing conditions continued, a force one wind from the north east and big seas from the previous gale heading us, and once again we were motor-sailing. At 1430 we arrived at Cedeira and joined four other yachts at anchor, in a lovely setting of hills and trees.

The next morning we left under main and motor at 0830 in a flat calm and poor visibility. By 1400 the wind had increased to force two, still heading us. At 1430 it veered to east force one and I set the genoa. We arrived at Ribadeo at 1845, 58 miles in 10 hours 15 minutes, a not unpleasant passage with little wind and a calm sea.

We anchored in Ensenada de Arnao in an unpleasant swell. A fisherman told us we would be better inside the high bridge so we moved to the small harbour at Punta Mirasol and moored alongside the quay.

The next morning we left Ribadeo in a mist and little wind and motored to Luarca, where we arrived at 1315. The inner harbour was fully occupied by fishing boats so we moored in the outer harbour, stern on to the harbour wall with a trip line to a buoy forward. This was a good mooring, though subject to some swell.

We went ashore to shop in the afternoon, but found all the shops were closed so we decided to stay another day. We had now decided to cut out further exploration of the northern coast of Spain and sail direct to La Rochelle, a distance of 264 miles. I spent part of the evening working out the navigation. I checked our fuel and found that the tank appeared to be empty. The next morning I bought a can of 10 litres and used this to motor to the diesel jetty in the inner harbour, where I took on 230 litres for £95. We visited the bank and shops and returned to the outer harbour. The wind and swell had increased and mooring was now more difficult.

The next morning, Thursday 19th August, we went ashore early to buy fresh meat and vegetables. We were unable to contact Julia by telephone, but Jill was able to tell us that she had arrived safely. Back aboard we deflated and stowed the dinghy, cleaned the log, and left Luarka at 1030 on a course of 059° for La Rochelle. The wind was negligible so we motor-sailed under full main in a large swell and lumpy sea. From the log:

1200 Wind E force 2–3. Sea worse.

1605 Wind dropped and backed. Unable to hold course so altered to 051°.

1700 Log 30.5. Boat slamming into rough seas. Eased course to 044° to steady her.

1800 Log 35. Altered course to 040°.

2100 Log 49.4. La Rochelle 064°/214 miles.

Fri. 20th August.

0000 Log 62.6. La Rochelle 065°/202. Co. 040°. Starboard tack. Very bumpy sea.

0700 Log 92.3. La Rochelle 071°/175. A/c to 115° Port tack. Motor-sailing, using wind changes for her best tack.

This has been an intensely dark night. No moon. The boat has moved and jerked violently in the wild sea. Difficult to move up and down from cabin to cockpit. Our world has shrunk to these two places. I down to the chart table every hour to do the navigation, read the log and write up the GPS position, bearing and distance to La Rochelle. Joan down to the galley. I found it difficult to mark the cross and enter the time on the chart; the safety line I constructed for Joan has kept her safely in position. I don't know how she has done it, but meals have come regularly: cereal for breakfast; sandwiches and fruit for lunch; a hot evening meal; coffee regularly.

1100 Log 113.1. Co. 110°.

1400 Log 129.7. La Rochelle 060°/151. Co. 115°. Not making the headway we would like because of the heavy seas.

1500 Log 135. La Rochelle 058°/148. A/c to 045°. Starboard tack.

1830 Decided it was impossible, with present headwinds, to reach La Rochelle tomorrow before the tide falls too low. Therefore we need a third night, so why slam into heavy seas? Turned off engine and sailed under main and genoa. Wind so light that our speed was reduced to 2.5 knots.

2000 Log 158.5. La Rochelle 064°/126. Reefed main, expecting stronger winds in the night. Engine on in low revs. Speed 4.5 knots. A/c to starboard tack.

2300 A/c to 080°.

Saturday 21st August.

0430 Wind freshening.

0500 Log 193.4. La Rochelle 057°/90.5. A/c to 060°.

0530 Thunderstorm five miles astern. During the night we kept one-hour watches. Off watch you slept on the lee cockpit seat on a long cushion, covered by a waterproof sheet to keep out the cold and damp. The hood made it seem cosy and like home. On watch you could catnap, but must take a careful look round every ten minutes or so and look at the radar regularly. We saw nothing for almost the whole journey across the Bay.

0645 Under furled genoa and main. Engine off. Speed 4.5 knots.

0800 Wind dying. Let out full genoa.

1000 Log 212.8. La Rochelle 060°/72. Co. 041°. Wind east force 3. Full main and genoa. Speed 5.5 knots. Good sailing at last.

1300 Log 227. A/c to 033°, following the wind.

1400 Log 231.4. Tacked.

1800 Log 247.2. La Rochelle 063°/41. A/c to 068° degrees.

1900 Weather forecast: 'Low over South Biscay. Wind force 6–7 from south west, increasing to gale force'. Decided to run into La Rochelle under genoa, which I could control from the cockpit. Handed main and put a hammock lashing on it. (Once before with a following gale the tiers had broken loose.) The slower speed suited our need to arrive in La Rochelle after dawn.

2000 With the boat snug and our evening meal finished, Joan said, 'You can't go into La Rochelle looking like that.

I'm going to cut your hair.' And, with night closing down and a gale approaching, this she did, in the cockpit. I was struck by the priorities of a woman and by Joan's insouciance about the imminent gale.

Sunday 22nd August.

0300 Log 279.5. La Rochelle 078°/10. Could feel the tide pulling across us. From here navigation was visual, using lights, GPS and radar. Our speed was down to 3.5 knots. Had to lay 50° off course to compensate for the strong tide. Arrived off La Rochelle as dawn broke.

0730 Arrived in La Rochelle, tied up at the accueil/fuel jetty in Port Minimus and allocated a berth in the new marina.

24

La Rochelle to Dartmouth

We were very tired after our crossing and were glad to put into the new marina, Les Minimes, where we were given a good, comfortable berth, four nights for the price of three, which suited our needs. Nearby we found a *laverie*, where Joan was glad to do two loads of washing, and a *cave*, where I was glad to buy wine from the barrel at seventy-five pence a litre.

We followed up with diesel and water, but were unable to receive electricity from the pontoon. A friendly French neighbour tested our wiring and quickly discovered a loose connection. At first we thought we would catch one of the frequent water-buses to the town quay to explore the old city. The weather, however, was discouraging, overcast with some showers and a strong, cold wind, so we decided on a restful day in the marina. Fortunately, the marina boasted a pleasant restaurant, *Le Dolphin*, where we had salad for starters, an enormous steak for me and veal for Joan with plenty of vegetables, finishing with ice-cream and coffee, all for £20, including wine.

We spent most of the day reading, with Joan doing some light laundry and tidying up and I writing up the log and doing some navigation. We sent a fax to Jill and then retired to bed early for a long and exhausted sleep.

The next day we made our trip to the city centre and learned that we could have enjoyed a berth in the inner harbour, in the centre of La Rochelle. The marina we were in was huge and soulless and we would have enjoyed the atmosphere and surroundings of the inner harbour. We loved the ancient, narrow lanes of La Rochelle, and the market, where we found a wine vendor. I asked the price of some bottles on display, but when I told him I wanted three cases of Bordeaux he told me not to bother with the cheap wines on display. He would deliver three cases to the boat that I would like very much. And he did. They were little more expensive than the wines on the stall, but when we drank them later in England we found that they were very good indeed.

Five years later, when we were calling in at La Rochelle in a cruise ship, Joan and I sought out the wine seller, still in the same position on the corner stall. I told him how much we had enjoyed his wine, bought five years before. He called his wife over and we had a pleasant conversation in French.

Our best buy in the market was a bag of melons – 'fill your plastic bag for fifteen francs,' about £1.50. We spent a pleasant hour sitting on the quay, entertained by a young couple of mime artistes. Their technique was to creep up unheard behind a couple of strollers and exactly mime the gestures of the people in front, who seemed to have no idea they were being followed.

By Thursday 26th August it was time to depart. We were feeling refreshed by our three-day break. Faxes from Jill were encouraging. She and Rob were endeavouring to sell their house, their nursery and much of their equipment to be able to purchase several acres of farmland with a house, barns and outbuilding, get planning permission to convert them to holiday homes and set up a holiday complex with swimming pool, tennis courts, restaurant and other facilities. Jill's faxes were forward looking with lots of ideas for the new complex.

On Thursday 26th August we left La Rochelle at 0900 under reefed main and two-thirds genoa in a north-easterly wind, force four to five. Long tacks brought us to St Martin, Ile de Ré, at 1230, a distance of 12.3 miles. Just outside the harbour we stowed the sails and motored straight into the inner harbour through the open lock gates. The harbour was crowded, with clusters of several boats rafted to each other. Manoeuvring was tricky, especially when after we had settled into our place a large boat came in, moored on the outside of us and then, as the skipper and crew were going to be absent from their boat for several days, he wished to be on the inside. All the boats in the raft had to move in very little space, but with patience and good humour the tricky manoeuvring was accomplished without hitch.

The next day we shopped in the morning, and in the afternoon walked along the sea wall to the Citadel. On Friday we were able to leave at half-tide at 1230 under main and genoa, with the wind north east force three, and make long tacks to Sables d'Olonne, where we arrived at 1800, 28 miles in 5.5 hours.

We berthed in the marina and after a restful night left next day at 1030 and motor-sailed in a force one headwind to Port Joinville, Ile de Yeu, arriving at 1600. The marina was very small and there were only two berths left. Fortunately I had called them up on the radio while on passage and booked a berth. By 1700 the harbour was packed.

By 0730 the next day, enough boats had moved and we were able to leave. The wind was again force one from the north east and we motor-sailed in a calm sea to Le Palais, Belle Ile, 50 miles in 8 hours 40 minutes.

Le Palais is a pleasant, small town, with good shops. We moored in the outer harbour between two buoys, and found that more and more boats arrived and tied up to the same buoys as others until the small harbour was crowded. Large ferries enter and leave at speed, causing us much bumping with their wash. The cost, however, was only £6 per night.

The next day we were up at 0715 ready to leave, but there were no signs of other boats leaving. At 0830 I asked the boat next to us if they would take off their warps to the forward buoy and let us out, and we were soon on our way under main and genoa to Lomener, a small harbour opposite Ile de Groix, where we arrived at 1330. We anchored in 27 feet in the bay outside the harbour. We had some swell during the night but it was not uncomfortable.

We left at 0815 the next day with the wind force three to four and enjoyed a good sail under main and genoa to Concarneau, 26 miles in 5 hours 15 minutes, our average cruising speed.

We were now on familiar cruising ground and intended to spend three nights in this delightful port. There was plenty of room in the large marina and three nights would cost only 285 francs, under £10 per night. We followed our old routine on arrival – tidied up, put up the awning for the first time since the Mediterranean, reported to the Capitainerie, then walked into town to look for a supermarket and launderette, and then back to the marina for showers and a pleasant evening dining in the cockpit and watching the other boats arrive.

The next day, Thursday 2nd September, we went to the launderette early, visited the bank and shopped in the closed market. We sent a fax to Jill, telling her we hoped to be in Dartmouth on the following Thursday or Friday. In the afternoon we rested and after tea walked round the Ville Close, taking photographs of the picturesque lanes and buildings. In the evening we again dined in the cockpit, on fresh lemon sole, a leisurely meal followed by a quiet night.

Friday was a busy day. In the morning we shopped in the open market, the closed market and the supermarket, filled up at the fuel jetty, paid our berth fees, watered the boat and scrubbed the decks. After lunch I wrote up the log and Joan cleaned and polished the stainless steel. In the evening we enjoyed a good meal in a *thon*, or tuna restaurant – salad, tuna and French fries, ice cream and half a litre of house wine, all for £18, very good value.

At 0750 the next day we left Concarneau in a flat calm under main and motor. A leak had occurred in the hot water system, which I soon cleared by tightening a jubilee clip. There was some mist.

By 1110 the wind had increased to force three from the east so I set the genoa and turned off the engine. The mist had cleared and, using visual navigation, we had a pleasant sail to Audierne, where we arrived at 1440. Unfortunately the wind had gone round to the south east and the harbour is exposed in southerly winds. We had intended to anchor outside the moorings, as we had done when we last visited Audierne, but instead moved closer in and picked up an empty buoy. The buoys were too close together but, although by evening all the buoys were full, all was well. It was a bumpy, rolling evening. Joan baked a cake for our night passage and we had dinner of roast lamb in the cockpit. By the time we retired to bed the swell had subsided and we had a quiet night.

We left Audierne at 1140, planning to catch the north-going tide of the Raz de Sein at 1230. In the Raz we were sailing at 4 knots and the tide was making 6 knots, so our speed over the ground was 10 knots, enough to give any sailor great satisfaction. It was not to last, however. As we rounded the Pointe du Raz the wind died and we were forced to motor the rest of the way to Camaret, where we arrived at 1610.

We berthed in the outer harbour on a pontoon that had electricity and water. The harbour was almost empty, with only two other boats on the pontoons. We had visited Camaret three times before and had found a good *cave* where we had been able to buy some of our favourite wines, including St Emilion, Sancerre and Vouvray,

230

at ridiculously low prices. This was our main reason for calling here on our way home. I intended to stock up with several cases to add to our collection. It was too cold to dine in the cockpit and the wind was quite strong, force five, blowing into the harbour. However, we had a quiet night and slept comfortably.

The next day we walked into town, first to the *cave* to order our wines. Alas! The *cave* was closed. The girl in the Tourist Information Office next door telephoned the proprietress for us. She came along and opened up, but had to inform us that, under the new European rules, no duty-free had been allowed since last June, neither wines and spirits, nor cigarettes. What she had to offer was very expensive so we went on to the supermarket and bought a few bottles that were 'under offer'.

That evening we were invited to drinks by the young crew from a French sailing-school boat. We invited them back aboard *Blue Pearl*, showed them around and told them something of our voyage. After this we telephoned Jill and told her of the gale warnings all round us.

Tuesday brought another disappointment. Gales continued to be forecast and we had a strong wind of force seven in the harbour. On Wednesday the gales continued, up to force eight, so we lowered the boom to make less windage and put out extra warps. A nicely hand-painted card was delivered from the sailing school inviting us to 'drinks at 2000' on their 'grand yacht', the large yacht accompanying the small boats. We accepted and after our meal went along to find ourselves honoured guests. All eighteen young French trainees were there and took it in turn in twos and threes to come and talk to us about our adventures.

Thursday morning gave us another forecast of gales, especially that night. However, there was a slight rise in barometric pressure and several boats left, including our sailing-school friends, for the short trip to Brest. We shopped and intended to go for a walk, but heavy showers sent us scurrying back to the boat. At the Capitainerie we were told that they had received a telephone call from Jill, asking if we were still in Camaret. The evening shipping forecast gave slightly better weather and the harbour master invited us to see the television weather forecast at 1900. This gave strong winds again that night and again on Sunday, with a lull in between. We decided to make use of this window and I telephoned Jill to say that we were leaving in the morning. From the log:

0800 Friday 10th September. Left Camaret. Wind westerly force 1. Reefed-main, genoa and engine. A squall, force 6, hit us as we approached the Chanel du Four, with heavy rain. Visibility reduced to 1 mile. Navigating by GPS and radar. Courses through the Chanel – 330/2.1, 359/0.8, 071/1.8, 343/8.5. We no longer find this tricky passage frightening and we sped through with the strong northerly tide pushing us.

1200 Log 21. Through the Chanel du Four. Skerries Buoy 032/112. Course 032°.

1530 Altered course to let a large ferry through.

1600 Log 42.1 Back to 031°. Wind increased to force 2. Main, genoa, and engine at half speed. Making 5.5–6 knots.

1700 Altered course to 021° to cross the shipping lane.

1800 Back to 031°.

2000 Log 63. Skerries 031/65.7. Course 031°.

2200 Wind died. Speed down to 5 knots.

Saturday 11th September 0200. Log 93. Skerries 030/31. Course 030°. A black night. Very heavy rain. The latest shipping forecast gave gales approaching from the west. Sole to Channel Islands to Northern France.

Joan woke me at 0200 with the information that there were lights all round us. We were in the middle of a fishing fleet, five miles across. It took two hours of careful navigation to pass through.

0400 Log 102.8. Skerries 026/19.4. Off Salcombe. Another fishing fleet, which I tried to avoid. However, one fishing boat overtook us from about half-a-mile astern. It was side trawling both sides and appeared like a gigantic white ray, about to devour us. At one hundred yards I turned violently away under full throttle, before he sheered off.

0600 Skerries 011/8.9. A threatening, black cloud several miles to the west astern of us. Now on visual navigation and GPS, approaching Dartmouth.

0800 Arrived Dartmouth, to be met by Jill and Rob at the town steps where we unloaded essential stores before tying up at the pontoon.

25

Dartmouth Interlude III

We were back in Dartmouth and it was time to reflect, with a mixture of relief, a sense of achievement, some regret and a need to determine our next voyage.

From Larnaca to Dartmouth we had sailed 3888 miles in four months. Altogether, our Mediterranean cruise had covered 8842 miles and we had visited 225 different places. We had endured some severe weather, run aground, dragged our anchor, faced up to Joan's mugging. Now in our mid-seventies, we were both remarkably fit. If it were possible, our adventures, particularly the night watches, had brought us even closer together. We knew each other's weaknesses and had come to rely on each other's strengths. We had had lots of fun and made many friends.

We had planned a fourth year in the Mediterranean, and we had some regrets that we would not be catching a plane next spring for Malta, our intended stopover. But dark clouds had been gathering on the horizon for Jill and Rob and for Julia, and we both felt that we wanted to be on hand in England.

What next? Two ventures attracted us: the first was to sail across the North Sea and explore either the Baltic or the coast of Norway, or perhaps both; the second was a shorter cruise to Ireland, to explore the south-west coast. We thought we would leave it till later to make a final decision. In the meantime we had the pleasure of settling into our routine in Dartmouth.

Jill and Rob gave us a great welcome. We picked them up at the town pontoon and Rob helped to moor the boat on our own mooring, not used for three years and now needing some attention. I inflated the dinghy to take us ashore, but the outboard would not start, so Rob rowed us ashore against the strong current. At 1800 we returned to *Blue Pearl* and took her to the town quay to unload all our wines, food and most of our clothes into Rob's van to take home. In the meantime Jill had prepared a chicken casserole for supper. Life was good. It was even better when we listened to the drenching rain and gales that blew all night, and realised that we were safely at home tucked up in bed.

The gales and heavy rain persisted all the next day and there was damage all round the south west. How glad we were that we had taken the opportunity to sail home! Jill and Rob took us to Manor Farm, in a village in Devon, to see the house and barns they wanted to convert into a holiday complex. We were impressed with the potential and with the business plan drawn up by Jill. What they needed was financial backing.

On Tuesday 14th September Jill and Rob left for Cornwall and we resumed bridge at the Yacht Club. We were back in the routine of life in Dartmouth: off to the boat to collect all the movables; into the garden to dig, mow the lawn, weed and remove the old bedding plants and plant wallflowers; buy bulbs and pansies in the market on Friday and set up our planters; and prepare bedrooms for Julia and two political refugee friends. They arrived on Saturday and on Sunday set off to Oakhampton Castle to sell a game, invented by a friend. The game, after the style of monopoly, concerning castles, knights and dungeons, was played out using the castle itself as the board for the game.

The next week we played military whist on Monday, bridge on Tuesday, I went to Probus on Wednesday and we had a bridge evening at Tom and Nesta's on Friday. On Saturday Margaret, Joan's niece, and her husband, Richard, came for the day and we enjoyed a sail in *Blue Pearl* to the Skerries and up to Galmpton and home for one of Joan's special meals in the evening.

In between times we worked hard in the garden, clearing and planting and preparing for winter. On Sunday we went to the boat, took off the mainsail, genoa and mizzen and brought the sails home to be delivered next day to Don Campbell for cleaning.

On Wednesday Probus had organised a trip to Hound Tor and Haytor, with lunch at the Moorland Hotel. The weather was good, the food excellent and the walk interesting, with a chance to soak up the marvellous English countryside. On Thursday we motored *Blue Pearl* round to Mill Creek, where she was hauled out for her winter lay up. On Friday we attended a bridge tournament in aid of Cancer Research and on Saturday we enjoyed the Cruising Supper at the Yacht Club.

With these events, working on the boat, gardening, doing some household repairs and the household chores, cooking and ironing, writing letters, life was very full for us, and the week sped by. Jill sent us a copy of the presentation she was making to the prospective financial backers and we were most impressed. Not so the backers – the project was too small for them and they turned it down.

The next week Joan resumed her literature class and on Thursday Peggy and Jack arrived for a week with us. On Saturday Jack went with me to the boat to check the electrics. In the afternoon Jill and Rob arrived and we had a very happy family party, with Joan enjoying her favourite activity, cooking. On Sunday we all drove to Newton Ferrers, where Margaret and Richard had invited us to lunch at the Old Ship Inn.

The next week, on Monday, 11th October, Peggy and Jack left for home and on Tuesday my sister, Maisie, with her daughter, Pam, and Pam's husband, Ian, from Canada, arrived to spend four days with us. Jill and Rob came to meet Jill's cousins and once again Joan was cooking for a party of seven. Jill brought sad news. The farmer who was selling the house and barns had had another offer, which he had accepted. Their deal was off.

We spent a pleasant time showing Dartmouth to Maisie and her family, visiting Haytor, walking up to the quarry and the stone railway lines, and walking along our favourite coastal path in Dartmouth past the coastguard cottages towards Start Point. They left on Friday and Joan and I finished the week with gardening, Joan washing and ironing and I making and fixing a shelf.

With Joan's help I spent much of the next fortnight first laying a concrete base for a crazy paving path through the shrubbery and then laying the concrete base for a large brick cold frame. I found this work very satisfying. Building, creating, gives an aesthetic satisfaction and sense of achievement. The hard work was suitable for cool October days and helped to maintain the fitness developed in our long cruise.

At the beginning of November I began a new project. The Commodore of the Yacht Club had asked me to teach bridge to members of the club. I had fourteen students, all in their sixties or seventies. All had played some bridge but were unfamiliar with modern conventions. I have always enjoyed teaching and I spent several hours a week preparing hands and writing out lecture notes to be duplicated and given to my students at the Monday sessions. Joan joined me at these sessions, helping the students with their hands, and the bridge evenings became popular and well attended.

November sped past. Club events included the Bridge Club annual lunch and bridge at the Stoke Lodge Hotel, Probus Ladies Night Dinner, a Cancer Research tea dance at the Yacht Club, the Yacht Club's Christmas Variety Show, the Yacht Club's Annual Dinner, Probus Christmas Lunch and the Yacht Club's Senior Members Lunch. Parties at friends' houses began: lunch with Joan Chambers, tea with the Whittakers, dinner with Jenny and Will, lunch with the Batterlees, lunch with the de Blaby's, members of my bridge class, and with the Coxes, also members of my bridge class, a curry supper at the Wakelins and drinks and nibbles with the Ellwoods. I had my weekly bridge class on Mondays; we had our bridge club on Tuesday afternoons and both attended a series of weekly lectures on Meteorology at the Yacht Club on Tuesday evenings; on Wednesdays Joan had her weekly literature class and I my fortnightly Probus meeting; on Saturdays we exchanged weekly bridge supper evenings alternately with the Westlakes and the Ellwoods.

On Tuesday 2nd December Jill and Rob came for a flying visit and brought bad news. Their building society had issued them with a summons for repossession of their lovely home. Julia also had problems with her bank over her overdraft.

Peggy and Jack came for three days on Monday 20th December and Jill, Rob and Julia joined us for Christmas. We all went to Margaret and Richard for Boxing Day. In between all these social engagements I laid the crazy paving path with large, flat stones that I dug up in the garden, built the brick coldframe and re-surfaced the garden path with six tons of sand and stones.

1993 had been an eventful year. It had started with Joan's recovery from her mugging, seen the completion of a major part of our cruise, and finished with our daughter and granddaughter in financial difficulty.

1994 began with me preparing a talk with slides on our Mediterranean cruise to be given in the Yacht Club. Joan's diary records several days spent working on the talk. We also worked on the log of *Blue Pearl*'s cruise, which we were hoping to submit to the Yacht Club as an entry for the Tolman trophy, awarded for the most interesting log. I combined the ship's log with Joan's diary in my rather untidy handwriting. Joan copied this out in her neat handwriting and inserted photographs taken on our voyage. I gave the talk in the Yacht Club on Friday 14th January to an audience of about fifty people. It was well received.

On Sunday 16th our social calendar began with a lunch party at the Cresswells, followed by Richard Westlake's eightieth birthday lunch on the 18th, drinks and nibbles at the Crawford-Pooles on the 22nd, drinks and nibbles at the Tonks on February 7th, a buffet supper at the Tomlinsons on the 19th and dinner at the Thompsons on the 24th. We gave a dinner party for six on February 27th, a lunch party for sixteen on March 13th and another lunch party, for eighteen, on the 27th.

We continued with our usual activities, my bridge classes, our weekly bridge club, Joan's literature class, monthly Exeter Flotilla meetings at the Royal Marines Officers' Mess in Lympstone, monthly talks at the Yacht Club and our weekly interchange of bridge evenings with the Ellwoods and Westlakes. On Friday 18th March we attended the Yacht Club fitting out supper and were presented with the Tolman Cup for the best log and the plaque for the most adventurous cruise.

Gardening was minimal and it was too early to start working on the boat. I decided to use my spare time in writing a novel. Jill and Rob were fighting off creditors who wanted to repossess their home and their nursery; their bank had approached me to meet the guarantee I had given years earlier in support of Jill and Rob's business. Julia's bank was pressing for repayment of an overdraft. We needed money to support them. I had written a novel in 1945 while waiting to go up to Cambridge. It was 90,000 words, written in pencil, and I had not attempted to publish it. Now, when I read it, I thought it had potential and I decided to work on it and prepare it for publication. I worked for up to four hours at a time, rewriting much of the novel and giving it more form and coherence. I wrote it in longhand and sent two or three chapters at a time to Jill who typed them up for me.

Set in the Indian Ocean in 1944, the novel told the story of a single action, lasting three days, between a British carrier force and a Japanese one. As I read my earlier words I realised how authentic was the atmosphere I had created. It took me back to my own life aboard a carrier and the period I had spent in the Indian Ocean in 1944. The theme was of ordinary men caught up in an extraordinary situation and how they reacted to it.

By the end of April I had finished the book and I showed it to Richard Webb, a well-known publisher of non-fiction, who lived in Dartmouth. His reaction was upbeat. 'This novel is marketable,' he said, 'but you should approach fiction publishers.' He urged me to take the characters back to the beginning of the war and write a series of novels about them. I began the long and dreary business of trying to find a publisher.

In the meantime the building society was taking Jill and Rob to Court to obtain repossession of their home. Since May 1993 Jill and Rob had paid the building society a monthly sum which included all the interest and a small repayment of capital. They were trying to sell their house to repay the loan. This wasn't enough for the building society and the court hearing took place on Thursday 24th February. The case was thrown out.

The pressures on our family had eased. It was time to think of sailing. However our worries, though diminishing, were not over, and Joan and I decided on the shorter cruise to Ireland. If further trouble developed we could quickly sail home and be on hand. We would leave Norway till the following year. I began finding charts and books and planning a route. On Monday 11th April I went to Mill Creek to see what had to be done to the boat. The hinge of the cockpit hatch was stiff, and broke as I opened the hatch. Joan came with me to the boat on Wednesday and while I worked on the hatches and cleaned the deck she cleaned all the deckhead linings. We were back to boat business. I had the hatch repaired, and David Heale serviced our engine. We followed the usual routines, cleaning and polishing the boat inside and out, servicing the winches and toilet, and anti-fouling. We took out our mooring chains to the trot and on Monday 23rd May we launched the boat and took it out to its mooring.

26

Ireland

Eighteen days after the launch in May 1994 we were ready to leave. The routine was familiar: last-minute work on the boat – David Heale had sent our alternator to Lucas for repair and this needed to be replaced; taking stores to the boat; bending on the sails; checking the echo sounder and log; a last-minute service to our Decca; any spare time to be used on the garden to leave it in good shape for our holiday. By Wednesday 8th June we were ready, but the strong wind blowing directly on to our mooring made it impossible to get away. Thursday was the same. Friday brought a respite. We were up at 0520 and, with little wind, got away easily from the mooring and tied up alongside the floating pontoon. I went back in the dinghy and took up our mooring chains. I then took *Blue Pearl* out to the oil barge and refuelled. Back at the pontoon we stowed the dinghy on deck and I did some quick chart work. At 1245 we were ready, and left in a north-west wind, force three to five, for a sparkling sail to Salcombe.

We soon realised that this voyage, at least in the first half, would be very different from our Mediterranean cruise. We had done it before. We were familiar with all the harbours we would use up to the Scilly Islands. This made the voyage very relaxing. It was a pleasure to find our way into the Bag at Salcombe, tie up at the visitors' pontoon and enjoy a lovely evening meal in the cockpit, followed by a quiet night.

In the morning we had a lie-in, were up at 0745, had breakfast at 0800 in a sunny cockpit and very little wind. The friendly harbour master's boatman advised us to wait until the afternoon when there would be more wind and the tide with us. We were in no hurry. We explored the neighbouring creeks in the dinghy and relaxed in the sunshine. At 1530 we were off. The wind was less than the day before, but we made good headway in a calm sea to Newton Ferrers, where we tied up at the floating pontoon at 1815. We took the dinghy up the creek to Noss Mayo, where Richard and Margaret met us and took us home to a lovely meal in their flat overlooking the creek. We returned to the boat at 2215.

The next day, Margaret and Richard came to us for a restful morning, watching the boats around us coming and going, with lunch in the cockpit. When they left we gossiped with our neighbours, most of whom were on their way eastwards. The next day we left at 1115 in a light wind and motor-sailed with full sails for most of the way to Falmouth, where we arrived at 1845. We telephoned Jill and she and Rob came down for a drink. The next day they came to lunch. Our fridge-freezer was not working and Jill searched for and found an electrician who could come the next day. After lunch Jill drove me to a large chandlers to buy a new fender. We had dinner with Jill and Rob in their lovely home overlooking Falmouth harbour and met some of their friends who came in for drinks.

The next day while Joan shopped I stayed aboard to meet the electrician, Ian Bowden, who told me there was no gas in the fridge. He filled the fridge with gas and all was well.

Jill and Rob came at 1330 for lunch and then we motored up to Smugglers Cottage, where we dropped anchor and had tea. On the way back we passed *Solan's Call*, with Will and Jennie, two of our Dartmouth friends. We circled round them and Jennie took a photograph of us. Back at the pontoon Joan cooked a meal for the four of us and after dinner we were joined by the skipper of a neighbouring boat with his wife and daughter.

We were up at 0500 the next morning, and Jill and Rob came at 0530 in time to cast off and wave goodbye. The wind was west force two and we motor-sailed for most of the way with full sails, to St Mary's, Isles of Scilly, where we arrived at 1800 and anchored in St Mary's Pool for dinner in the cockpit and a quiet night. We had passed a basking shark on the way and several boats going in the opposite direction.

We went ashore next day and joined Vic's Tours in a minibus for a tour of the island. We were impressed with the flowers everywhere. We wandered round Hugh Town for an hour, recapturing the pleasure we had had several years before when we had explored the Scilly Islands in the chartered Centaur. We had lunch on board in the cockpit and then motored through St Mary's Sound round to St Agnes where we anchored in the bay to the south east. After tea we wandered up the dusty road to Middle Town and posted cards, and in the evening sat in the cockpit and watched the tide come tumbling in over the sandbar until the bay became a sound with exits at both ends.

We left St Agnes at 0800 the next day in a force five wind and when we rounded St Martin's set a course of 320° for Kinsale, in southern Ireland, 145 miles distant. I set the main, mizzen and genoa and we made good progress at 6 knots in a lumpy sea. At 1700 the wind had increased to force six and I took down the mizzen and began to put a reef in the mainsail. Before I could reduce sail a very strong gust hit us and the sail began to split. I immediately let the mainsheet go and turned into wind to take the sail down and hoist the mizzen again. All of this took nearly an hour and at 1819 I resumed our old course, under mizzen and half genoa. The wind had increased to force seven, with stronger gusts, but we sailed comfortably at 5.5 knots under the reduced sail. As it so often does in these waters, the sea became very bumpy. I was thrown off the navigator's seat and hurt my wrist. Joan fell against the cockpit steps and hurt her chest. Neither of us felt like eating. It was going to be a long night.

At 2300 the lights of a vessel showed astern, slowly overhauling us. I turned up the radio and heard, 'I am a fishing vessel. Please come in, yacht ahead.' I answered, but got no reply. I turned to port and the boat passed us and gradually drew away.

Morning came, still with a strong wind, and revealed an unpleasant sea. We were relieved to sight Kinsale Head and find the easy approach and entrance to Kinsale Harbour. We were welcomed at the marina by the manager and tied up alongside a big Dutch ketch. We slept all afternoon, had a meal and slept again.

The next day we took down the mainsail and gave it to the marina manager, who arranged to have it repaired. The whale pump for the holding tank was not working. I stripped it, but could find nothing wrong. It must be the diaphragm. I purchased a new one from the chandlers. It still did not work so I ordered a new pump.

The Dutch yacht next to us was called *Complex* and we invited Hans and Inneka, the owners, to drinks after dinner. The next day the weather was cold and drizzly and we went about our business wearing our light oilies – to the marina to find our mainsail still waiting to be collected, to the chandlers to find that our new pump had not arrived, to the launderette and to the shops. The appearance of the town took me back to my boyhood. There were no supermarkets. Shops were old-fashioned, a dairy, an ironmongers, grocers, fruit and vegetable with the wares displayed outside under awnings. We even saw a horse-drawn dray delivering barrels of beer. Gales were forecast all round the coast, force seven possibly eight, and heavy rain.

On Wednesday we went ashore again for more shopping and to collect our laundry and when we returned two Canadians from a neighbouring boat told us that the French boat ahead of us had backed into us and gouged our boat. They had called the boat back and made the skipper give his name and address. Hans took me in his dinghy to look at the damage and we discovered deep scores from the stemhead to the waterline. Hans was most helpful. He had the necessary materials and he cleaned the scratches and filled them with an epoxy filler. The marina manager said that had he been aware he would have impounded the French boat until they paid for the repair. The sail had been repaired at the modest cost of £32. We exchanged further visits with Hans and Inneka, who later became great friends, visiting us at Dartmouth and inviting us to join them for part of their voyage across the Atlantic.

On Thursday there was a steady drizzle and a thick fog out to sea. We decided not to move. After lunch we nosed our way in thick fog to the fuel quay and filled our tanks and returned to the empty place astern of *Complex*. The mist and drizzle continued all day long. It was so cold during our spell at Kinsale that I wore pyjamas as long johns and two sweaters.

On Friday the forecast was wind south east two, changing to north west two, with heavy mist. We left at 0830, put up the sails in harbour and sailed quietly round Galley Head to Glendore, in a thick mist and a lumpy sea. We entered Glendore harbour at 1330 and anchored in ten feet, opposite the bluff. Only one other boat was there, an Englishman in *Tricky Lion*, but at 2000, after our meal, we looked out and found *Complex* astern of us. We exchanged visits with Hans and Inneka and next morning at 1000 *Complex* left for Baltimore. We went ashore for a pleasant walk to Unionhall, about two miles away, a small village with two shops and five pubs. I spent the afternoon repairing leaking hatches. Joan recorded in her diary that at last we had spent a day without rain.

The next day there was a thick mist with heavy rain all day. We decided to wait till 1000 and then 1200. At 1400 we gave up and went to bed. After tea the weather cleared and we watched a harbour race between five Dragons. The wind got up at high water, but we had a quiet night

On Monday we again had a thick mist. The forecast was better. Wind south west force four to five, moderate sea, fog patches. We decided against moving. At 1130 *Artemis of Heyn*, which had arrived the previous evening, moved off and her skipper said he would call us on Channel 16 and report on conditions at sea. This he did. Visibility was 400 yards, wind 5 knots, sea calm. We decided to go and left at 1215 for Crookhaven. The wind increased and we were able to sail all the way under main and genoa. We passed the Fastnet Rock 400 yards away – we could hear it, but did not see it in the heavy mist. Visibility at the entrance to Crookhaven was almost nil and we relied on our radar to see us through. We anchored in 17 feet at 1800.

The next day the forecast was wind south east four to five, visibility moderate. At 1200 we took up our anchor and motored out. At the entrance the sea was rough, but we were able to hoist the main and set the genoa and sail at 4 knots, though in the sudden squalls our speed shot up to over 6 knots. By the time we reached Bantry Bay the fog had again descended on us and we navigated by GPS, radar and echo sounder. We entered Bantry in thick fog and dropped an anchor. Fortunately there were no other visitors and the next day, when we were able to see, we found we were fifty yards off the quay, opposite Bantry House.

On Wednesday conditions were so rough in harbour that we were unable to go ashore, so we decided to leave Bantry and seek shelter on the other side of Bantry Bay, in Glengariff. The passage was tricky and devious, through shallows and narrows, marked by countless buoys. We passed a small island with basking seals. At length we came to a lovely anchorage opposite the big Eccles Hotel. Our luck changed. After lunch we went ashore in warm sunshine, wandering through the village and gardens. In the evening we had an excellent meal in Eccles Hotel for a total of £15. *Afaron*, a thirty-foot ketch, came in in the evening.

After a quiet night we went ashore to find the tourist office. We had hoped to join a coach tour of the Ring of Kerry, but there was no link-up to Glengariff. We also thought of visiting the renowned garden on Garinth Island. The entry fee was £2, but there was a £5 ferry fee even though we had our own transport. We thought this was a con and decided against a visit. Instead, we took a path through the woods and walked to a waterfall.

The next day we caught the 1225 bus to Killarney. This followed a beautiful, scenic route, through narrow, winding roads and deep valleys over moorland and mountains with hairpin bends, through tunnels, alongside ravines. At Killarney we mingled with the crowds, took a jaunting car to the lake and admired its calm beauty. In the evening we returned along a different, less spectacular but pleasant, country route.

On Saturday it rained all day. At 1100 we went ashore in oilies to fill our water containers from the pier hose and to post cards. After lunch the weather was still foul and I used the time to repair three lights, a fuse, a faulty switch and a loose connection. Four more yachts came in during the afternoon, making seven in all. We had intended to dine ashore but the rain decided us against it.

The next day, Sunday 3rd July, we were up at 0545 and away at 0745 for a lovely sail to Baltimore. We arrived at 1600 and anchored near the harbour behind *Swedish Rhapsody*, from the Royal Dart Yacht Club. *Mist of Malin*, also from RDYC was two away. We went ashore and telephoned Jill. Julia needed £300 deposit for a flat; they would send £100. Could we help?

On Monday I posted a cheque for £200 to Julia and spent the afternoon fitting up our horn and Aldis lamp and a small replacement lamp on our chart table. We deflated the dinghy and stowed it. All the other boats had left.

On Tuesday we listened to the early shipping forecast: Lundy, Fastnet, Sole – wind south west force four to five. We left immediately under reefed main, mizzen and genoa, on a course of 127 degrees for the Scilly Islands. At first the wind was force three and we were sailing comfortably. After lunch the wind increased to force five and I handed the mizzen. At 0100 on Wednesday morning the batteries failed: the Autohelm, GPS and log all gave up. I changed over to the engine battery and started the engine, but failed to remember that I must first switch off the GPS. I blew a fuse, which I had to replace. We were now sailing with the engine ticking over to charge our batteries. At 0200 the wind increased suddenly to force seven, with much stronger gusts, typical Fastnet weather. The waves were now steep-to and the boat was pitching violently. I furled the genoa and then linked my safety harness to the jackstay and inched my way forward to the mast to take in a second reef. With one arm round the mast I tried to pull the reef cringle down to the hook. Ten times I tried, but each time the wind took charge and forced the cringle upwards. My arm was tiring. I was running out of strength and I needed to use two hands. I released myself from the jackstay and took my safety strap round the mast and back to my harness so that I was on a short strop, waited for a wave to pass, and then made to pull the sail down with both hands. A violent gust, a heavy pitch, and I was thrown.

Joan cried out. 'Freddie! Come back to the cockpit!'

'Be quiet, woman,' I muttered. We were out of control. The luff of the mainsail was loose. I had to pull the cringle down. Fortunately, because of the short strop I had not been thrown far, and I quickly recovered my position. Once more I waited my opportunity, grasped the sail in both hands and pulled downwards. The cringle was on the hook and I had a firm handhold. The sail was now double-reefed. I crawled back to the cockpit, pulled the mainsheet tight and turned off on the starboard tack. The wind was now force eight and we were sailing comfortably at 5 knots under double-reefed main only.

We arrived at St Agnes at 1200 to be joined immediately by a customs launch and asked where we came from and where we were going to. We had lunch and then slept for three hours.

On Thursday the forecast was good, but the wind had changed from the south west to the east and the anchorage became uncomfortable. I put down a second anchor. All the other boats had gone, but seven more arrived in the evening, one anchoring right in front of us.

On Friday we were up at 0530, listening to the shipping forecast, wind south west force five to six. I put two reefs in the main and with three-quarters genoa, we sailed comfortably to Falmouth. Jill met us on the jetty at 1805 and took us home for showers and supper. Rob drove us back to the boat at midnight. On Saturday we stopped in Falmouth. Jill joined us for lunch and she and Rob came down at 1930 for drinks and dinner.

On Sunday Jill and Rob came at 1030 and we sailed to the Helford River and anchored right up, past the moorings. We made lunch our main meal at 1400 and sailed back to Falmouth, where we arrived at 1800. Jill, particularly, enjoyed the dolphins that sported round us on our way. We had a light meal of soup and cheese roll and Jill and Rob left at 2230 after a pleasant day.

On Monday 11th July Jill and Rob saw us off at 0740 and we motor-sailed, with very little wind, to Newton Ferrers, arriving at 1530. Again, on Tuesday, there was little wind and we left at 0630 for an easy passage to Dartmouth.

Our Irish cruise had been a hard one – in Ireland suffering from frequent rain and fog and on the longer passages from severe winds. The problem I had with the mainsail on our return passage to the Scilly Islands started a nagging doubt in my mind. Joan and I were both seventy-five years old. Although mentally we could cope with whatever came our way, physically I had been unable to reef the mainsail one-handed. Would we have to take on a regular crew? Neither of us wanted that. Could we cope with the long haul to Norway next year? I left that decision in abeyance.

27

The End of the Story

We spent the last two weeks of July and the first two of August 1994 in intense activities, catching up in the garden, servicing the boat, club activities and many social engagements with friends. I had meetings with Richard Webb, who advised me to rewrite the first three chapters of my novel so that the reader got into the action more quickly, and to obtain a supporting letter from an admiral. He also suggested that I should prepare a synopsis of the novel.

Friday 29th July was our golden wedding anniversary. On the Saturday thirty-six members of our two families joined us for a party on our lawn. Julia arrived with Freya and we saw our great-granddaughter for the first time. It was a lovely day. The sun shone, there was a gentle breeze blowing off the sea and the temperature was just right. Rob had supplied us with three trestle tables, which we set up on the lawn and he and Jill helped to serve and entertain our guests. Joan had done all the cooking. Guests enjoyed their pre-lunch drinks on the lawn, while people arrived and relations met and chatted to each other. We were used to giving big parties and were able to set out the tables with our own cutlery and table napkins and deck them with flowers from the garden. Together with all our garden furniture and furniture from indoors, we even had enough chairs. The wine came from our Mediterranean cruise.

After lunch our guests had an opportunity to wander round our garden, along our seventeenth-century wall, and admire the splendid views of the sea and harbour, the woods across the river at Kingswear, the rolling hills to the south west, and the magnificent view of the Naval College to the north. Several guests were staying for the night, Peggy's family at Margaret's, Martin and his family on *Blue Pearl,* and others finding beds in the study and guest rooms. At 1900 we started up again with a barbecue provided by Jill and Rob. This was alfresco, sitting round the terrace, with Rob managing the barbecue and Jill serving. As night settled everyone enjoyed the quiet discussions and peaceful ending to what had been a memorable day.

The following Saturday we repeated the performance for our friends, twenty-nine in all including us. Again Joan cooked her three main dishes and several sweets. Again we held it in the garden in lovely sunny weather, and again our guests stayed on, until teatime, leaving at 1700.

One incident in this period cast a shadow. On Friday 15th July at a hospital check-up I was told that my eyes had deteriorated. Pressure in both of them was at a dangerous level and I was put on to new drops.

On Saturday 20th August we set out on a night passage to Guernsey. We arrived at St Peter Port at 1130 the next day and were put on a waiting pontoon. We had visited Guernsey several times and were well aware of the crowded conditions in the harbour. Unfortunately several later boats were rafted outside us on our waiting pontoon and we were one of the last to be admitted into the harbour. There were few spaces left and we were put outside a 28-foot boat in a berth that was uncomfortable for us. The owners of the small boat inside us were absent, but when they returned next day we were able to swap places with them and this made it better for both of us.

On Monday there was a thick mist, and heavy rain and gales were forecast. We decided to cut out our intended visit to Jersey and make straight for Cherbourg. We left on Wednesday with the wind behind us and, with goose-winged main and poled-out genoa and a 3-knot tide pushing us, we had a splendid, easy sail.

We were looking for rest and relaxation and, as we were in a comfortable new marina, with the weather uncertain, we decided to take advantage of an offer of seven nights for the price of five. We enjoyed an excellent week. We made friends with our neighbours in *Lilistock* and exchanged visits for drinks and bridge with Terry and Nicola, the owners.

A main purpose of our visit to Cherbourg was to stock up with wines to replace those used at our golden wedding anniversary party. We found the best value was at the large hypermarket, about a quarter of a mile away. Here we found half cases of our favourite reds, St Emilion, Chateauneuf du Pape and Nuits St George, and whites, Chablis, Sancerre and Vouvray, from good vineyards at ridiculously low prices. I bought six half cases, loaded them on to a trolley and walked the trolley round the harbour to our boat in the marina. At one point, where the pavement slopes towards the harbour, the trolley veered towards the harbour edge so I stationed Joan on the opposite side to give a compensating pull to port. At another point I came to a steep kerb and a polite Frenchman jumped forward to lend a hand. When we had unloaded at the boat we were able to leave the trolley at a nearby stack to be collected by the hypermarket. The system was so easy that we made a repeat performance and bought six more half cases.

We enjoyed our week in Cherbourg. We shopped, entertained our neighbours and made friends, explored the town, walked up to the museum and gardens at the top of the hill on Cherbourg Fort, and became thoroughly rested. On Tuesday 30th August, at 0415, we sailed to Dartmouth, a calm and peaceful day passage, arriving home at 1800.

We did not know it, but this was to be our last sail in *Blue Pearl*.

Throughout September we worked – on the boat, getting it ready to be hauled out at Totnes; on the garden, getting it ready for winter; and on my novel, getting it ready for publication. Many of our friends, wanting to return our hospitality, sent us invitations to their parties.

A serious development was taking place in the affairs of Jill and Rob. Shortly after the building society was dealt with, their bank manager began to make demands. To provide them with working capital, we had offered a £30,000 guarantee, which would only become operable when the balance of their debt rose above a certain amount. The bank now called in this amount from us, even though the state of Jill and Rob's finances had not been established. I reminded them of our agreement. The bank said they had no knowledge of the agreement and sent a threatening letter. The branch manager stated that he had no recollection of such an agreement and he had no papers referring to it. I produced a copy of a letter sent to my solicitor by the bank manager, agreeing my terms. A long fight now developed between the bank and Jill and Rob, and between the bank and me. For Jill and Rob their nursery was at stake, and for us there was the question of the £30,000. Jill and Rob also had the ongoing problem with the building society over their house.

On Monday 12th September *Blue Pearl* was hauled out at Totnes, and we spent several days clearing the boat and tidying up. On Wednesday 21st we drove to Norwich to see Julia and give some support. On the way home we spent three days with my sister, in Rayleigh. I had been invited as guest of honour at the first reunion of the selective school that had been my first headship. I was its second and last head, for I had closed the school and amalgamated it with two others to form the Sixth Form College. I met some of my old staff and many of my old pupils, who gave Joan and me a great welcome.

The next day we had a reunion at Martin's of all my sister's family, with lovely meals, exchange of photographs and lots of happy reminiscences. The next day I made the long drive back to Dartmouth in seven hours.

Decision time had come. Our family was beset by pressing problems. Almost certainly we would need capital to help with them. My eyes were deteriorating and creating difficulties for me. The episode during our return from Ireland had left me with deep reservations about my ability to cope at sea in storm conditions. How long could we go on sailing? Joan and I came to a decision. We would put *Blue Pearl* up for sale. If she fetched what we hoped, we would sell. If not, we would sail back across the Bay of Biscay to a warmer climate and complete our cruise along the coast of northern Spain. In a strange way we felt relieved at the decision.

We did not spend time on regrets, but threw ourselves into the process of preparing *Blue Pearl* for sale, and this occupied much of our time for the next two or three months. We put the boat into the hands of Leslie, who ran the yacht brokers at Totnes Marine. Before she could get it on the market an event occurred that made me feel happier about selling *Blue Pearl*. On 12th December I would be seventy-five years of age. The DVLA required me to take a Fields eye test before they would renew my driving licence. My eyes had deteriorated too much – I failed the test and the DVLA cancelled my licence. This was a major blow as Joan did not drive, the bus service to Totnes was very poor and I was more or less cut off from the boat. Selling *Blue Pearl* was now urgent.

250

Totnes Marine were experts on hull maintenance and I asked them to eliminate all the scratches. As always they did a good job and restored *Blue Pearl*'s pristine appearance. Lesley inspected the boat, had me write out some details of her 'blue water' history and advertised her in a yacht magazine. An offer was made, which we accepted. She received a good report from the surveyor and the sale went through, on 8th February 1995, to an American who wished to sail her home across the Atlantic.

That was the last we saw of *Blue Pearl*. Hans and Inneka, whom we met again when they called in at Dartmouth on their way south, wrote to us from Portugal that they had met *Blue Pearl* in Portugal on her way to the Azores. Later we read in an Oyster magazine that she had joined an Oyster rally, and arrived safely in the West Indies.

Epilogue

The story of *Blue Pearl* has finished, but this is not the end of our story.

At a second court hearing Jill and Rob lost their home to the building society. This judgment, in my view, like the previous judgment on the ownership of the showrooms, defied common sense and made a mockery of the legal system. Our fight with the bank continued for several months and met a better fate. In a reasonable compromise I paid off half the bank debt, and was given ownership of the nursery.

Jill and Rob have restored their lives. They now own a building firm that builds and sells timber-frame houses. They specialise in high-quality properties, sometimes on difficult sites and they live in the high-tech, four-bedroom house they have built in their nursery. Their future now seems secure.

When Joan and I sold *Blue Pearl* we thought of buying a small motor-boat for local and cross-Channel sailing. We even looked at one, but our heart was not in it. We found a new interest in cruising in large cruise ships. We had first experienced this in a short cruise from Cyprus to Egypt and Israel in 1992, and we now remembered the pleasure that had given us. In June 1995 we were fortunate to book on the *Monterey* for a Mediterranean cruise, two for the price of one, and became hooked on cruise holidays. By shopping around we found enormous discounts and were able to afford two, or even three, cruises per year. In the last seven years we have been several times to the Mediterranean, revisiting old haunts and finding new ones, up the Norwegian coast to the Arctic, close to where my ship was sunk on a Murmansk convoy, to the Baltic capitals, to the Canaries and Madeira, to the Rhine, twice to the Nile, and twice across the Atlantic to the Caribbean and Mexico.

During these years I attempted unsuccessfully to sell my novel, and wrote three more. Two of them followed Richard Webb's suggestion and took the characters of my first novel back to the beginning of the war in the Mediterranean. I gathered from correspondence with publishers and their agents that I had missed the boat with these war stories – they were no longer popular. My fourth novel was the story of three generations across the last fifty years of the twentieth century. I may have lost heart, for I do not think I have pushed this enough to publishers.

I very much enjoyed writing and worked for several hours a day at each of my novels. As always, Joan helped, reading the first draft from the computer, correcting it and suggesting improvements. In the course of this work I bought a computer and became computer literate.

My eyes deteriorated further to the point where for several months I was virtually blind. I had to rely on Joan to read my mail and guide me when I visited town. Two operations restored my sight, but only partially. I was able to read large-print books and compose on the computer using 16-point lettering, reducing it to 12-point when I printed it. At the Bridge Club my friends were kind to me when I mistook spades for clubs and hearts for diamonds.

In the last year Joan has suffered two serious operations. She has come through them, as the surgeon said, as the result of her resilience and determination, virtues I had become well aware of in our sailing days.

We are now living quietly, occasionally visited by friends, still playing, and winning, at bridge. Joan has resumed her literature class and I still attend Probus meetings. I have continued writing and have produced three short stories. We are not sure about another cruise. We think we shall now stay in England, spending a week here and there at some of our favourite towns, London, Brighton, Cambridge, York, Bath, Stratford. The period since I retired has been one of the most exciting, demanding and satisfying ones of our lives. We have now come to the end of that period.

Postscript – January 2007

It is now two years since I finished writing the first draft of this book. Since then I have published two novels.

Joan's health deteriorated and she developed a third cancer. A few days before she died, she said to me, 'Freddie, I've had a wonderful life. Let me go now.' She faced up to death with the same fortitude and resolution she had shown when sailing. At six o'clock on the day she died my daughter Jill and I were with her in Dartmouth Hospital. She was full of life, telling us about the children crabbing and the boats on the river she had seen from her bedside window.

At ten o'clock, after we had returned home, we had an urgent call from the hospital, 'Come quickly.' It took us only ten minutes to get to the hospital, but Joan was already dead. The nurse told us that she had been summoned by Joan, who had apologised for calling her. Her colleague had gone for a commode, while she held Joan's hand and asked her if she were in pain. 'Not at all,' Joan replied – and died, from a massive haemorrhage. When we arrived there was a gentle smile on her lips.

When I first began to write this book I thought the heroine was *Blue Pearl*. Now I know that it was, in fact, Joan – and so I dedicate the book to her.

Appendix 1

Mediterranean Passages

1991	Passage	Miles
May		
11–16	Dartmouth to Bayona	580
18	Bayona to Leixoes	67
19–20	Leixoes to Cascais	166
21–22	Cascais to Vilamoura	164
24–25	Vilamoura to Gibraltar	165
June		
1	Gibraltar to Estepona	25
	South East Spain	
2	Estepona to Benalmadena	34
3	Benalmadena to del Este	40
4	del Este to Adra	35
6	Adra to Aquadulce	30
8	Aquadulce to San Jose	30
10	San Jose to Aguillas	48
12	Aguillas to Cabo de Palos	49
13	Cabo de Palos to Torrevieja	21
15	Torrevieja to Villajoyosa	53
16	Villajoyosa to Morayra	22
18	Morayra to San Antonio	61
	Balearics	
20	San Antonio to Ibiza	48
27	Ibiza to Espalmador	14
29	Espalmador to Puerto de Sabina	16
July		
1	Puerto de Sabina to Cala Llonga	20
2	Cala Llonga to Santa Eulalia	6
4	Santa Eulalia to Cala Portinatx	32
6	Cala Portinatx to Andraitx	13

7	Andraitx to Porto de Sol	8
8	Porto de Sol to Cala Portals	5
10	Cala Portals to Andraitx	13
11	Andraitx to Cala Llado	8
	Cala Llado to San Telmo	3
12	San Telmo to Soller	24
14	Soller to Formentor	35
15	Formentor to Puerto de Pollensa	5
17	P. de Pollensa to Calo es Calo	18
18	Cala es Calo to Porto Cristo	26
20	Porto Cristo to Ciudadela	38
21	Ciudadela to Fontanelles	14
22	Fontanelles to Fornells	16
24	Fornells to Mahon	23
26	Mahon to Cala Teulera	3
29–30	Teulera to Toulon	200
August		
3	Toulon to Hyeres Bay	16
4	Hyeres to Alicastre (Porquerolles)	5
5	Alicastre Bay to Plage d'Argent	5
6	L'Argent to Langoustiere	5
	Riviera	
7	Langoustiere to Porquerolles	3
8	Porquerolles to Hyeres	6
9	Hyeres to St Tropez	37
10	Tropez to Anse de L'Argent Faux	29
11	L'Argent Faux to Menton	23
13–14	Menton to Revellata	91
	Corsica	
15–16	Revellata – Calvi Revellata	12
17	Revellata to Ile de Rousse	12

257

18	Ile de Rousse to Anse d'Orlando	8	**1992**	**Passage**		**Miles**
19	Orlando to Revellata	18	**May**			
20	Revellata to Girolata	25		**Sicily**		
21	Girolata to Ajaccio	37	12	Valetta to Porto Palo		58
24	Ajaccio to Castagne	12	13	Porto Palo to Syracuse		29
25	Castagne to Campo Moro	22	14	Syracuse to Salina Jonice		58
27	Campo Moro to Figari	25				
27	Figari to Bonifacio	9		**Italy**		
29	Bonifacio to Paragnano	2	15	S. Jonice to Rocella Ionica		50
30	Paragnano to Bonifacio	5	16	Rocella Ionica to Crotone		66
31	Bonifacio to Cala Francese	21	18	Crotone to Leuca		70
			19	Leuca to Orthoni		49

September

Sardinia

2	Cala Francese to Villamarina	3	20	Orthoni to Corfu		41
2	Villamarina to Porto Palma	4	23	Corfu to Lakka		27
3	Porto Palma to Maddalena	5	24	Lakka to Mongonisi		7
5	Maddalena to Porto Cervo	10	25	Mongonisi to Levkas		34
7	Porto Cervo to di Volpe	7	26	Levkas to Nidri		11
8	Volpe to Isla Porri	20	28	Nidri to Vlikho Bay		2
9	Isla Porri to Olbia	6	29	Vlikho Bay to Port Vathi		11
10	Olbia to della Taverna	12	30	Port Vathi to Abalike Bay		3
11	Taverna to Coda Cavallo	5	31	Abalike Bay to Sivota Bay		9
12	Coda Cavallo to La Caletta	17				
14	La Caletta to Gonone	27	**June**			
15	Gonone to Arbatax	22	1	Sivota Bay to Frikes		11
16–17	Arbatax to Ustica	173	2	Frikes to Port Vathi		12
			3	Port Vathi to Oxia		24

Sicily

				Oxia to Port Vathi		24
19	Ustica to Palermo	35	4	Port Vathi to Missolonghi		32
22	Palermo to Cefalu	32				
23	Cefalu to Cap d'Orlando	40		**Gulf of Corinth**		
24	Cap d'Orlando to Porto Rosa	21	5	Missolonghi to Trissonia Island		40
25	Porto Rosa to Messina	45	6	Trissonia Island to Galaxidhi		23
26	Messina to Reggio Calabria	6	8	Galaxidhi to Corinth Canal		52
27	Calabria to Riposto	40	9	Corinth Canal to Zea Marina		32
28	Riposto to Catania	20				

October

				Aegean		
			13	Zea (Piraeus) to Kea		26
3	Catania to Porto Palo	53	15	Kea to Kithnos (Leutra)		23
4	Porto Palo to Valetta	57	16	Kithnos to Livadhi (Serifos)		23
			19	Livadhi return		5
	Total for 1991: 3350 miles		20	Livadhi to Port Vathi (Sifnos)		16
			21	Port Vathi to Faros		7
			23	Faros to Paroikia (N. Faros)		9
			26	Paroikia to Naxos		16
				Naxos to Aghios Georgis (Iraklia)		16
			27	Aghios Georgis to Mirsini		3
			30	Mirsini to Astipalia (Stampalia)		52

258

July

1	Skala (Astipalia) to Maltezana	5
2	Maltezana to Agrilithi Bay	4
4	Agrilithi Bay to Kalimnos	38
6	Kalimnos to Kos	17
7	Kos to Bodrum	10

Turkey

11	Bodrum to Cokertme	20
12	Cokertme to Söğüt	21
13	Söğüt to Snake and Castle Island	4
14	Snake and Castle Island to Değirmen Buku	7
16	Değirmen Buku to English Harbour	2
17	English Harbour to Yedi Adalari	13
18	Yedi Adalari to Bodrum	31
21	Bodrum to Knidos	22
22	Knidos to Datča	21
23	Datča to Keçi Bükü	23
25	Keçi Bükü to Bozborun	19
26	Bozborun to Serče Liman	18
27	Serče Liman to Marmaris	25
31	Marmaris to Ekinčik	20

August

1	Ekinčik and return	6
2	Ekinčik to Kapi Creek	26
3	Kapi Creek to Wall Bay	3
4	Wall Bay to Goček	14
	Goček to Boynuz Buku	5
5	Boynuz Buku to Tersane	6
6	Tersane to Fethiye	12
7	Fethiye to Karacaören Buku	15
8	Karacaören Buku to Kalkan	23
9	Kalkan to Kas	15
11–12	Kas to Paphos (Cyprus)	162

Cyprus

14	Paphos to Limasol	49
16	Limasol to Larnaca	33

Total for 1992: 1674 miles

1993	Passage	Miles
May		
10–12	Larnaca to Rhodes	315
19	Rhodes to Alimnia	32
20	Alimnia to Pigadia	51
21	Pigadia to (Karpathos) to Sitia	56

Crete

23	Sitia to Ayios Nikolaus	33
24	Ayios Nikolaus to Iraklion	43
26	Iraklion to Rethimon	40
27	Rethimon to Soudha	24
28	Soudha to Kissamos	54
29	Kissamos to Kithera	52

Peloponnese

30	Kithera to Port Kaio	34

June

1	Port Kaio to Kalamata	50
2	Kalamata to Port Longos	32
4–6	Port Longos to Syracuse	310

Sicily

9	Syracuse and return	6
10	Syracuse to Porto Palo	28
11	Porto Palo to Licata	70
12	Licata to Sciacca	56
15	Sciacca to Marsala	41
16–17	Marsala to Cagliari	181

Sardinia

19	Cagliari to Porto Teulada	39
21	Porto Teulada to Carloforte	35
24–25	Carloforte to Mahon	200

Balearics

28	Mahon to Cala Teulera	2
30	Cala Teulera to Santa Galdana	24

July

1	Santa Galdana to Santa Saura	5
2	Santa Saura to Porto Cristo	35
5	Porto Cristo to Porto Colomb	12
6	Porto Colomb to Porto Petro	6
7–8	Porto Petro to Espalmador	100
10	Espalmador to Porto Sabina	3
12–13	Porto Sabina to Cartagena	145

259

South East Spain
July

14	Cartagena to Garrucha	46
15	Garrucha to San Jose	29
16	San Jose to Almerimar	38
17	Almerimar to Motril	36
18	Motril to Benalmadena	48
19	Benalmadena to Gibraltar	52
25	Gibraltar to Barbate	37
26–28	Barbate to Lisbon	260

Portugal

31	Lisbon to Cascais	17

August

1	Cascais to Peniche	44
2	Peniche to Figuera da Foz	56
3	Figuera da Foz to Leixoes	65
4	Leixoes to Bayona	66

North Spain

6	Bayona to Islas Cies	10
7	Islas Cies to Puebla del Caraminal	28
8	Puebla del Caraminal to Muros	35
9	Muros to Camarinas	45

11	Camarinas to La Coruna	53
15	La Coruna to Cedeira	28
16	Cedeira to Ribadeo	58
17	Ribadeo to Luarka	23
19–22	Luarka to La Rochelle	310

France

26	La Rochelle to Ile de Ré	12
28	Ile de Ré to Sables d'Olonne	28
29	Sables d'Olonne to Joinville	30
30	Joinville to Belle Ile	50
31	Belle Ile to Lomener	24

September

1	Lomener to Concarneau	26
4	Concarneau to Audierne	35
5	Audierne to Camaret	25
10–11	Camaret to Dartmouth	121

Total for 1993: 3859 miles

Year	Places	Miles
1991	93	3350
1992	68	1674
1993	64	3859
Totals	**225**	**8883**

Appendix II

Glossary

Autohelm 600	an electronic device that links the steering with the compass
beat	sail to windward
Beaufort Scale	a scale of wind velocities ranging from 1 to 12
berth bin	vertical locker with a top opening
bitter end	the last link in the anchor chain
boom	the long spar to which the foot of the mainsail is attached
cleat	a metal or wooden bracket to which mooring lines are attached
coaming	a raised frame round the deck or cockpit to keep out water
daymark	a construction in a prominent position on the coast used for navigation
Decca	a terrestrial navigation aid using waypoints
deckhead	ceiling
dogwatch	a duty period of two hours, either 1600–1800 or 1800–2000
echo sounder	an electronic device for measuring depth
fairlead	a fitting through which a line is passed to prevent chafing
fiddle	a small railing round a table or cooker to prevent objects falling off in bad weather
floors	joists that support the deck

forestay	a line or wire from the top of the mast to the stemhead as a support
galley	kitchen
gel coat	the final (glossy) coat in the glass-fibre process
genoa	a large foresail
genoa track	a metal construction on either side of the boat that allows the genoa sheet pulley to be fixed in the most suitable position
George	the automatic steering
gimbals	a device that allows the cooker, or compass to remain on an even keel
GPS	a system of navigating by satellite
gybe	turn through the wind downwind
halyard	a line for hoisting or lowering a sail
hatch	an opening in the deck of a boat to provide access
heads	lavatory
holding tank	a tank specially designed to hold sewage until it can be pumped out
jack strap	a line along the deck to which one's safety line can be attached
jib	small foresail
jubilee clip	an adjustable metal ring used to secure a plastic pipe to a metal one
kicking strap	a line from the boom to the deck to stop it lifting
king post	a sturdy post on the foredeck on which to fasten warps
knee	a bracket underneath the deck to strengthen certain deck fittings
lay up	have the boat ashore for a period
lazy jacks	lines from the spreaders to the boom to secure the mainsail as it is lowered
lee cloth	a canvas cloth arranged to secure a sleeper in rough weather
leeward	upwind
log	an instrument for measuring speed and distance
lubber line	a line on the hull to mark the water level when the boat is laden

luff	the leading edge of a sail; to bring the boat's head into the wind
luff tape	a tape attached to the leading edge of a sail to strengthen it
mainsheet	the rope used for hauling in or letting out the mainsail
mainsheet traveller	a device that allows the mainsheet pulley to move along a slide astern of the cockpit
mizzen	the after sail in a ketch-rigged ship
osmosis	air bubbles in a glass-fibre hull caused by imperfect laying up
plug	the wooden plate used to close a vertical locker
port	left
preventer	a line used to hold the mainsail and prevent it from gybing
pulpit	a guard rail round the foredeck
pushpit	a guard rail round the stern
Q flag	the flag hoisted for customs clearance
reef	the part gathered in when sail area is reduced
sheet	rope used for hauling in a sail
ship's log	the book in which the record of the ship's voyage is recorded
sole	floor
Spanish windlass	a stick used as a device for twisting and tightening a rope
spinnaker pole	used to pole out the large balloon-like headsail
stanchion	a vertical support for guard rails
starboard	right
stemhead	the very forward end of a boat
stemhead roller	a built-in pulley in the stem
tac rag	an impregnated duster that removes dust
tack	a course with the wind coming from forward of the beam
to tack	to change direction so that the wind comes from the opposite side
tier	rope or ribbon used to tie up furled sails
warp	a rope used for making fast or towing a boat
waypoint	a point to which the boat is being directed by Decca or GPS

Appendix III

OYSTER- MARINER 35

Designed by Holman & Pye in association with Oyster Marine

DIMENSIONS

L.O.A.	35'0"	10.67m
L.W.L.	29'0"	8.84m
Beam	12'0"	3.66m
Draft	5'3"	1.60m
Displacement	1600lbs	7258kg

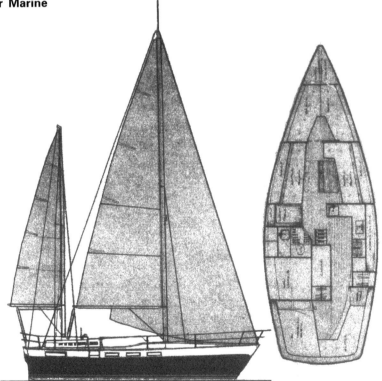

Blue Pearl: The original design before my modifiations